Oh My Goddess!

あぁっ女神さまっ

28

STORY AND ART BY
Kosuke Fujishima

TRANSLATION BY
Dana Lewis AND
Christopher Lewis

LETTERING AND TOUCH-UP BY
Susie Lee AND Betty Dong
WITH Tom2K

DARK HORSE MANGA™

CHAPTER 177

Little Voice, Great Sorrow

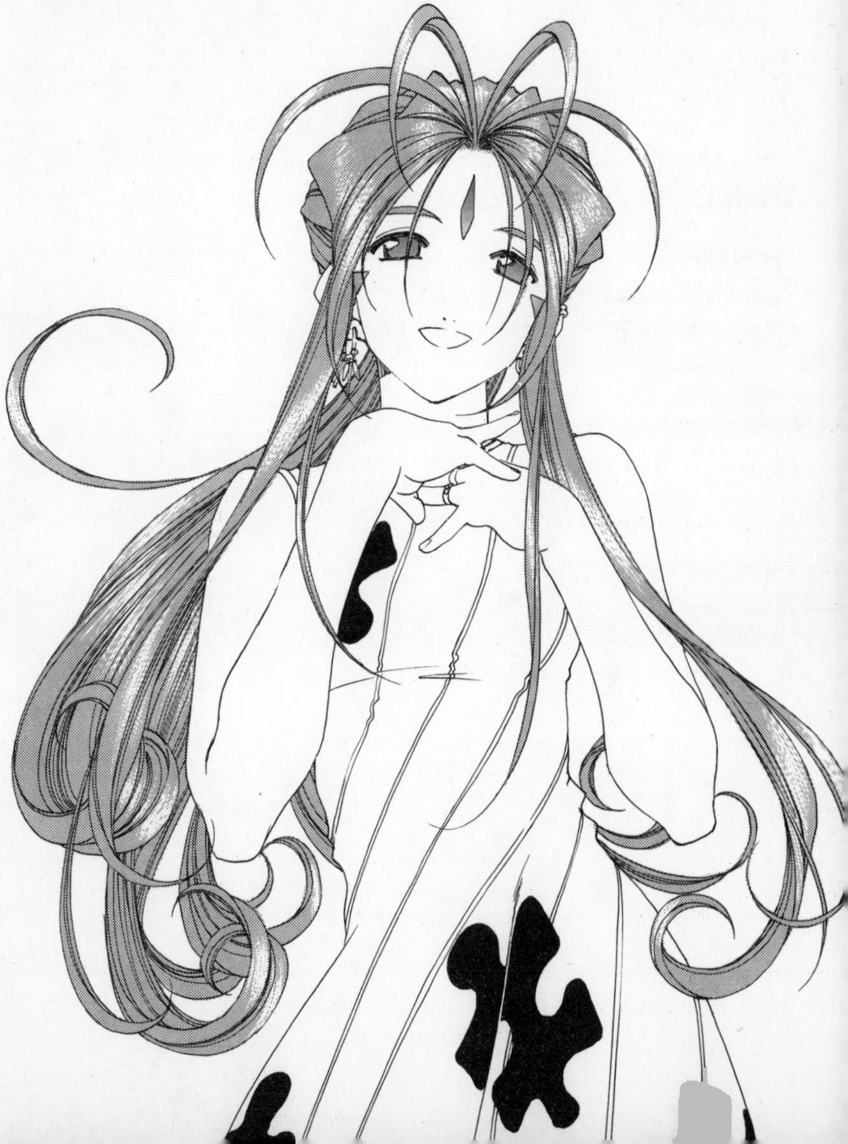

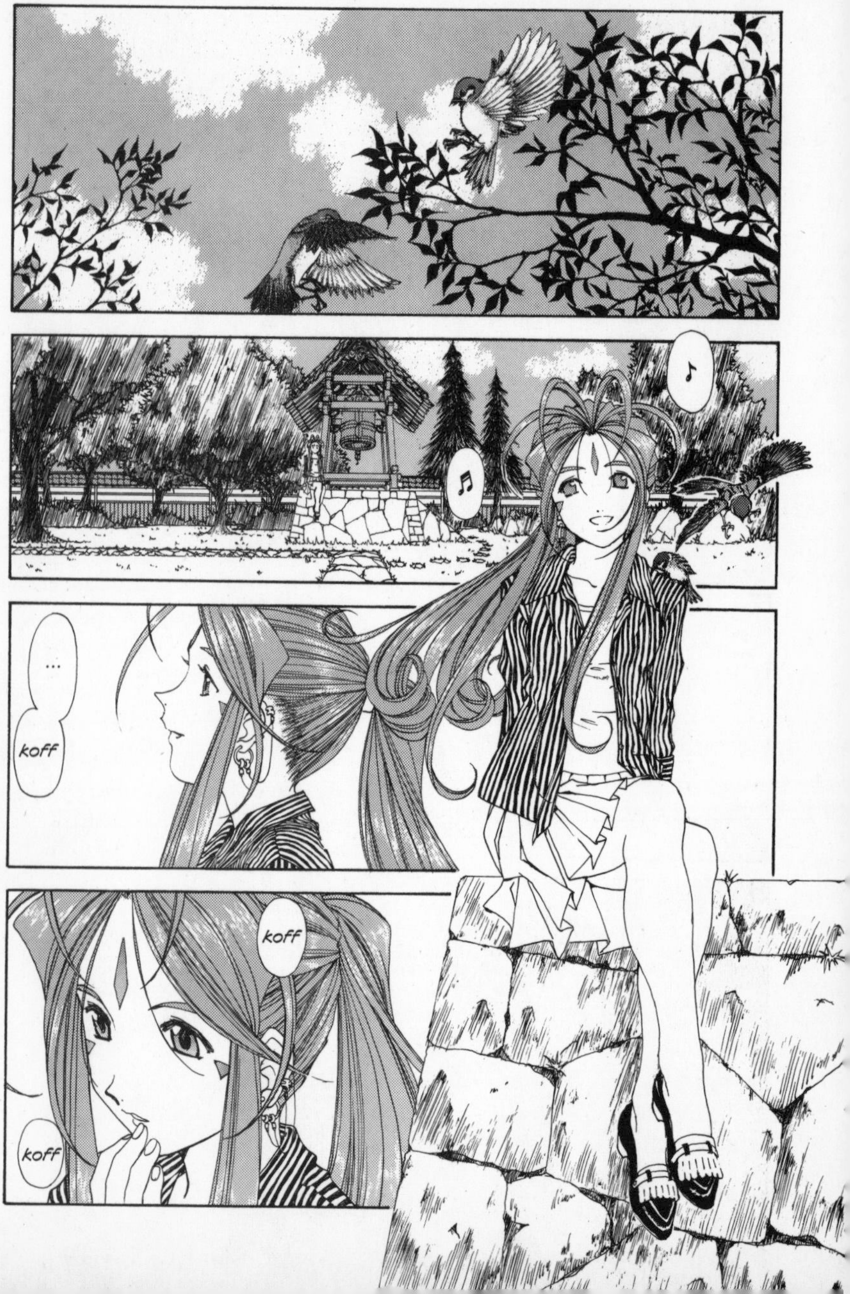
♪
♫
...
koff
koff
koff

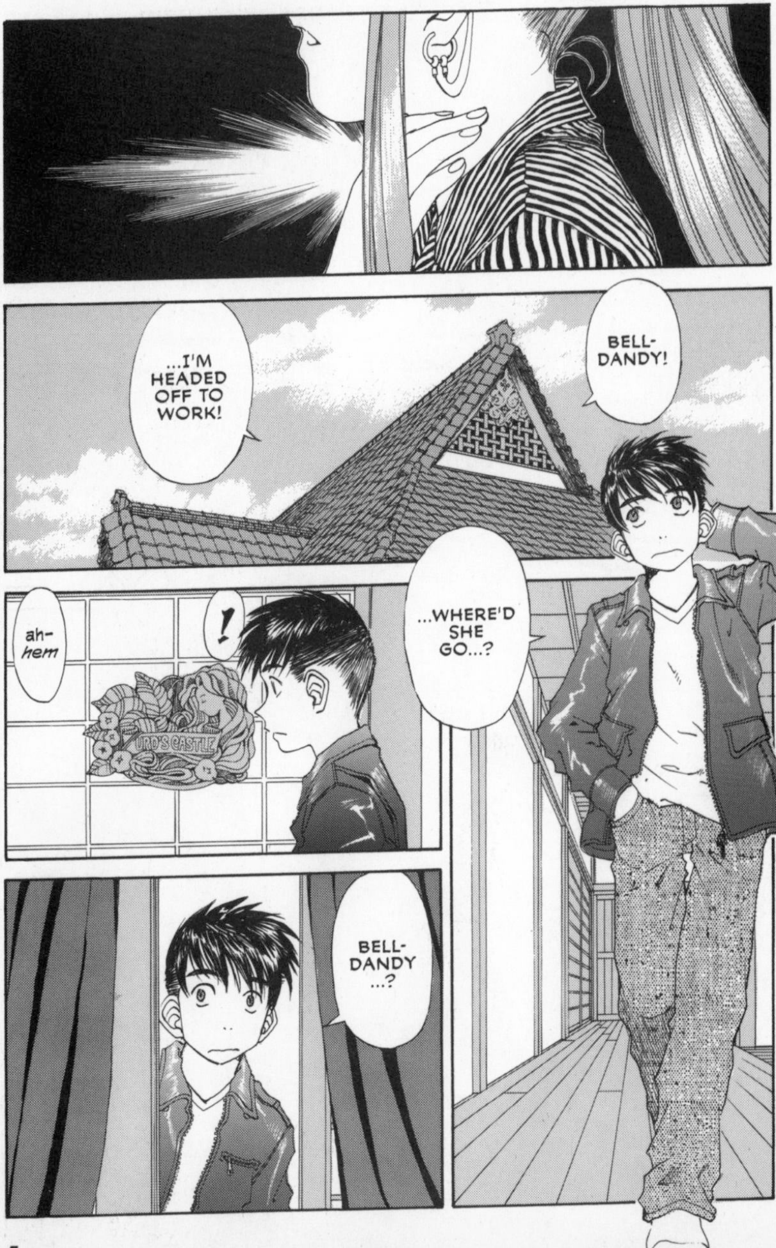

BELL-DANDY!
...I'M HEADED OFF TO WORK!
...WHERE'D SHE GO...?
!
ah-*hem*
URD'S CASTLE
BELL-DANDY ...?

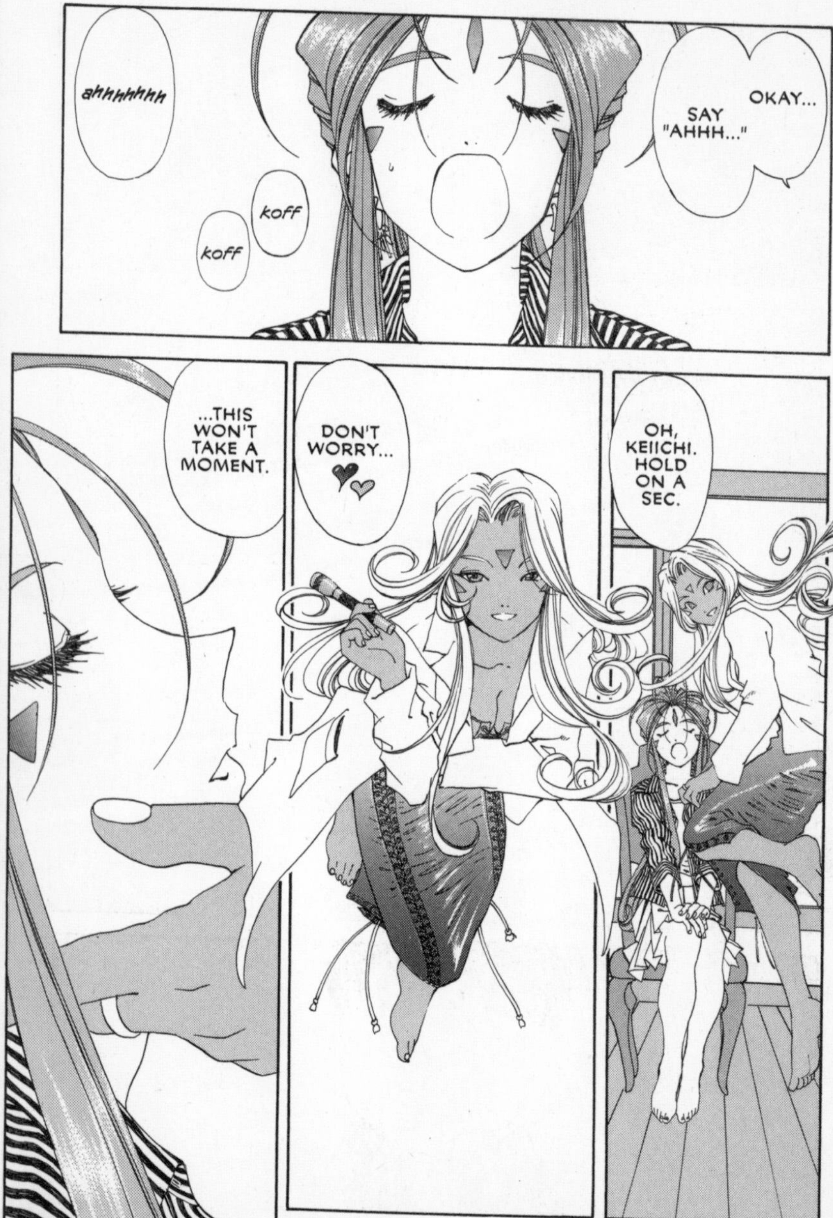
OKAY... SAY "AHHH..."
ahhhhhhn
koff
koff
OH, KEIICHI. HOLD ON A SEC.
DON'T WORRY...
...THIS WON'T TAKE A MOMENT.

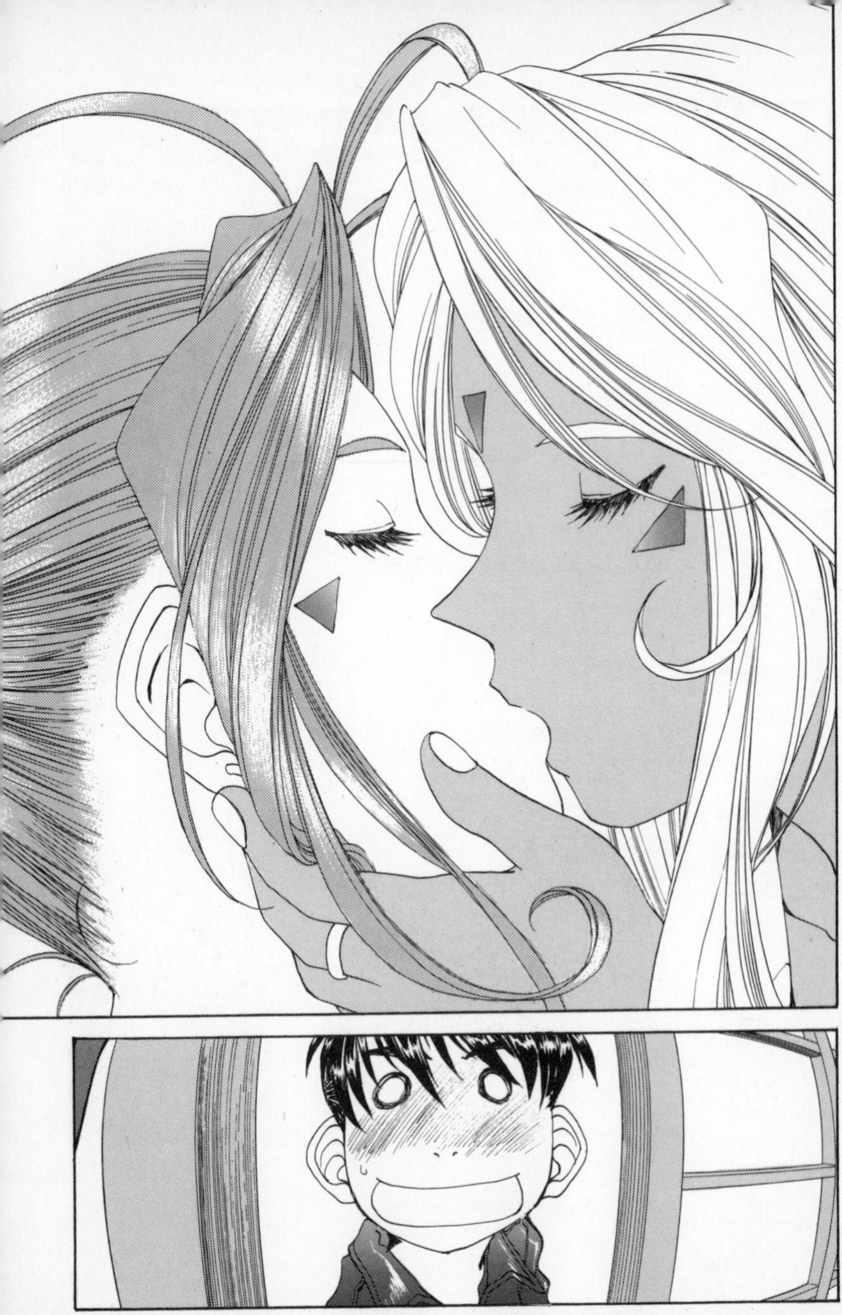

HMPH... I *KNEW* IT WAS AN "AHEM BUG."

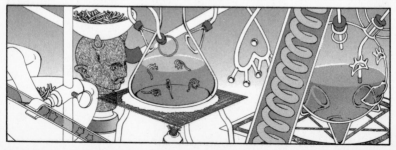

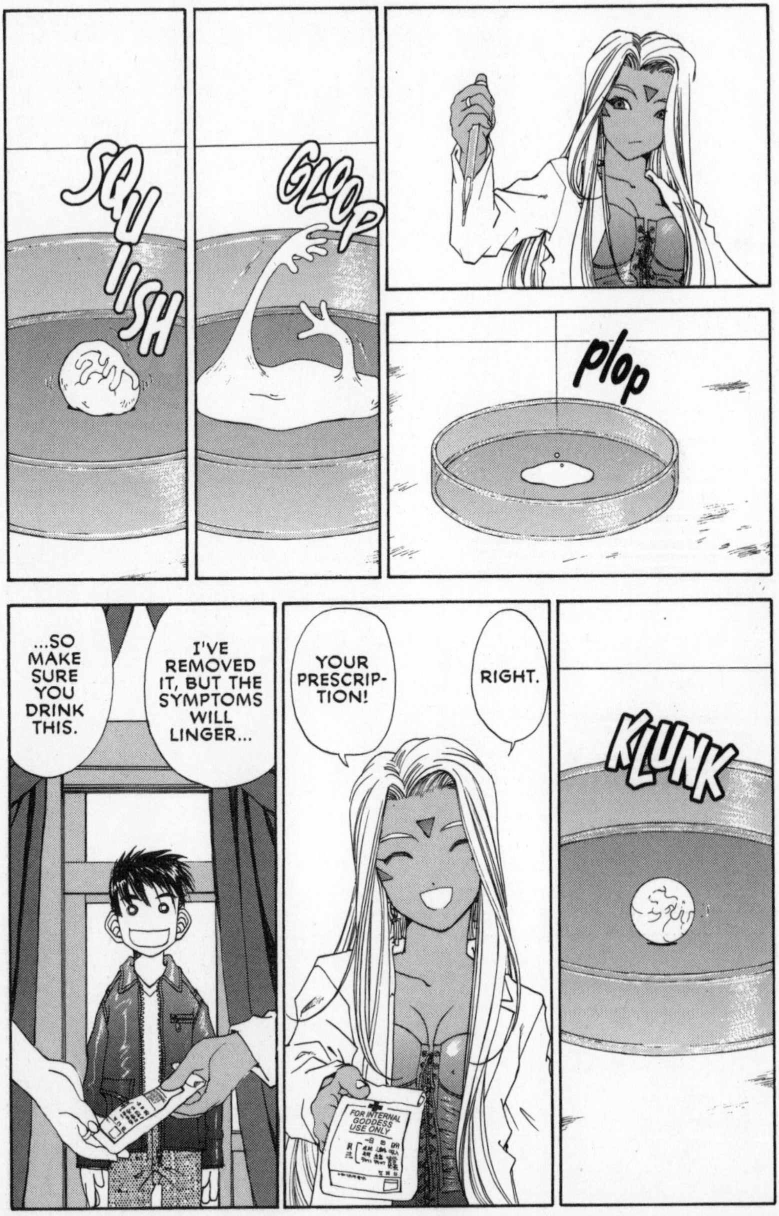
plop
GLOOP
SQUISH
KLUNK
RIGHT.
YOUR PRESCRIPTION!
FOR INTERNAL GODDESS USE ONLY
I'VE REMOVED IT, BUT THE SYMPTOMS WILL LINGER...
...SO MAKE SURE YOU DRINK THIS.

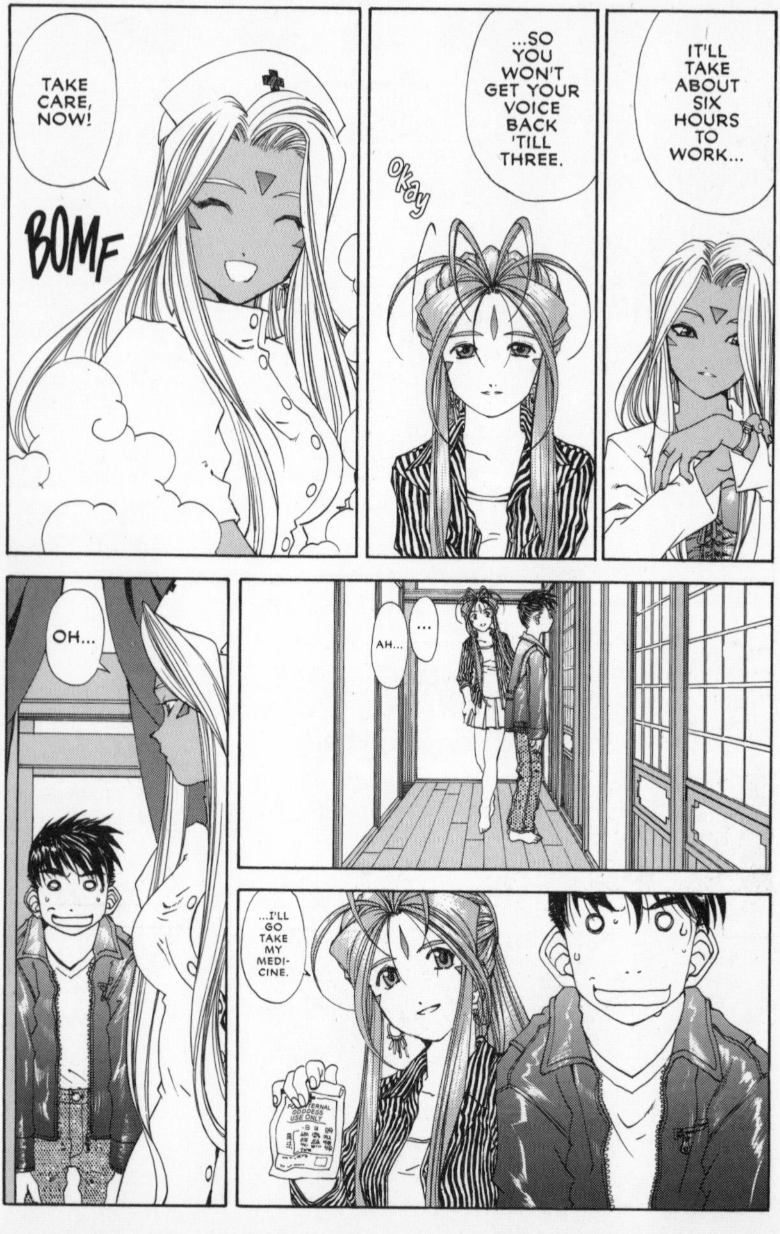
IT'LL TAKE ABOUT SIX HOURS TO WORK...
...SO YOU WON'T GET YOUR VOICE BACK 'TILL THREE.
OKAY
TAKE CARE, NOW!
BOMF
...
AH...
...I'LL GO TAKE MY MEDICINE.
GODDESS USE ONLY
OH...

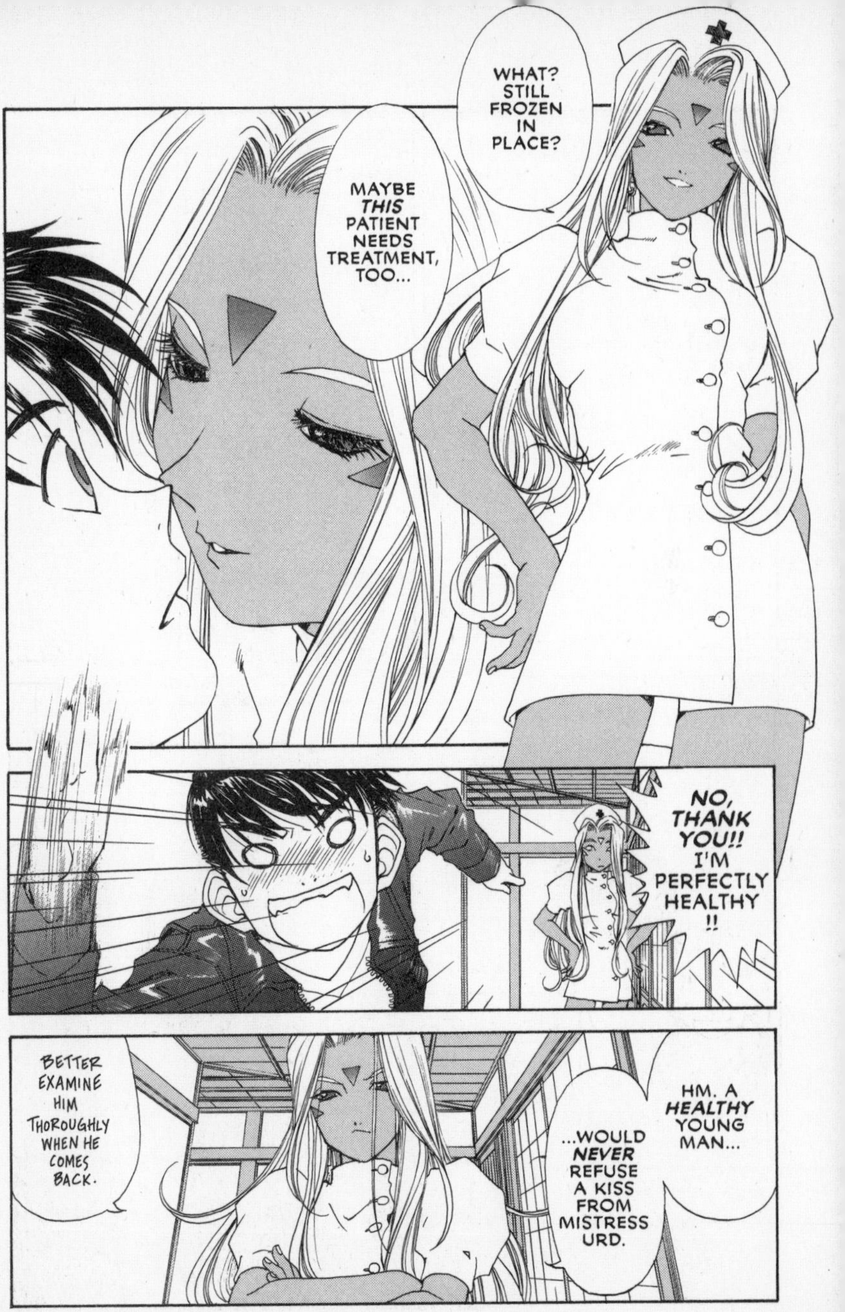
WHAT? STILL FROZEN IN PLACE?
MAYBE *THIS* PATIENT NEEDS TREATMENT, TOO...
NO, THANK YOU!! I'M PERFECTLY HEALTHY !!
HM. A *HEALTHY* YOUNG MAN...
...WOULD *NEVER* REFUSE A KISS FROM MISTRESS URD.
BETTER EXAMINE HIM THOROUGHLY WHEN HE COMES BACK.

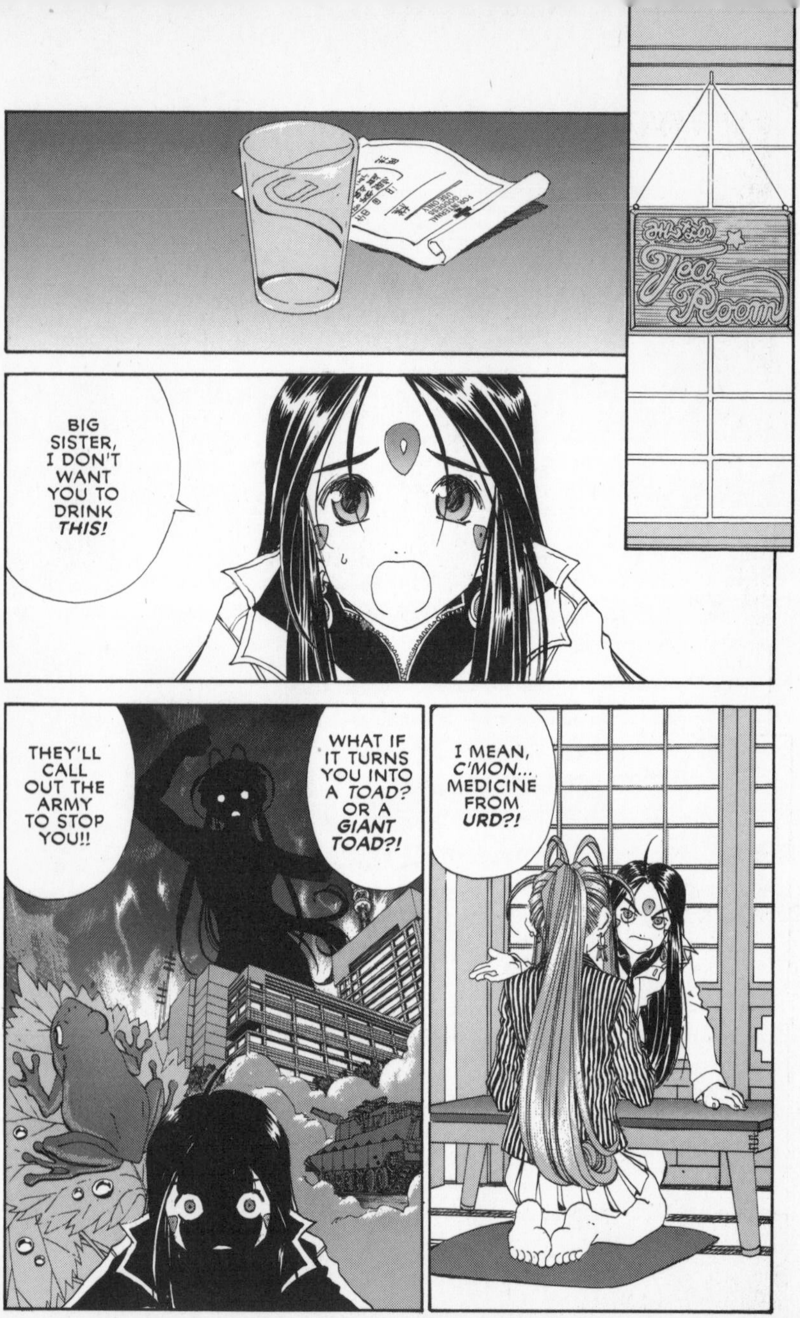
Tea Room
BIG SISTER, I DON'T WANT YOU TO DRINK *THIS!*
I MEAN, *C'MON...* MEDICINE FROM *URD?!*
WHAT IF IT TURNS YOU INTO A *TOAD?* OR A *GIANT TOAD?!*
THEY'LL CALL OUT THE ARMY TO STOP YOU!!

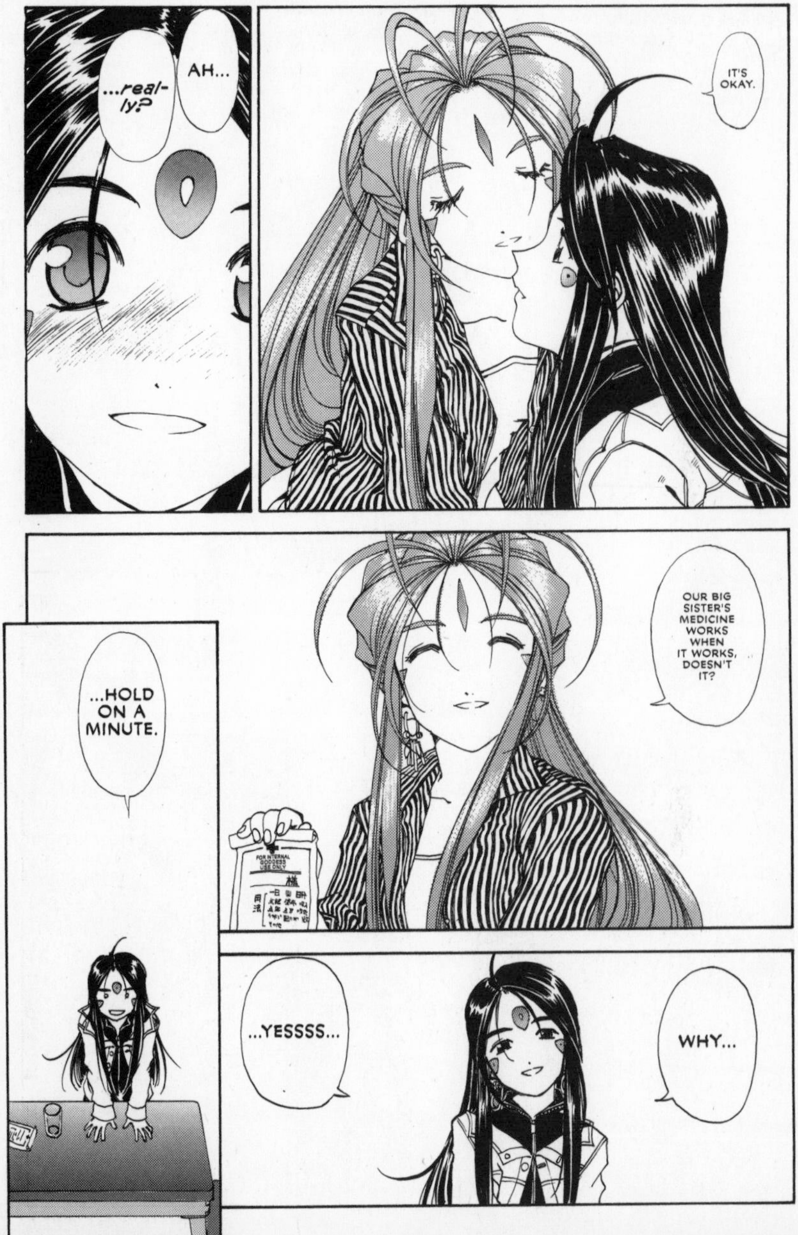
IT'S OKAY.
AH...
...real-ly?
OUR BIG SISTER'S MEDICINE WORKS WHEN IT WORKS, DOESN'T IT?
FOR INTERNAL GODDESS USE ONLY
WHY...
...YESSSS...
...HOLD ON A MINUTE.

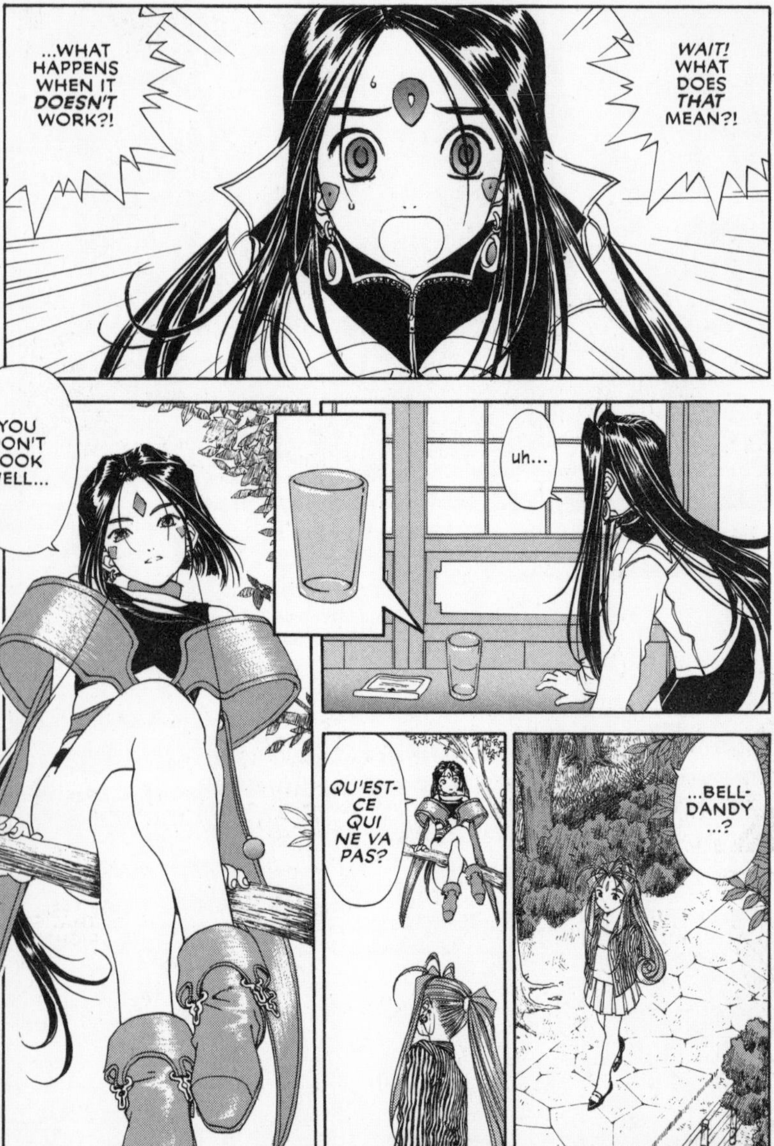
WAIT! WHAT DOES THAT MEAN?!
...WHAT HAPPENS WHEN IT DOESN'T WORK?!
uh...
...BELL-DANDY ...?
QU'EST-CE QUI NE VA PAS?
YOU DON'T LOOK WELL...

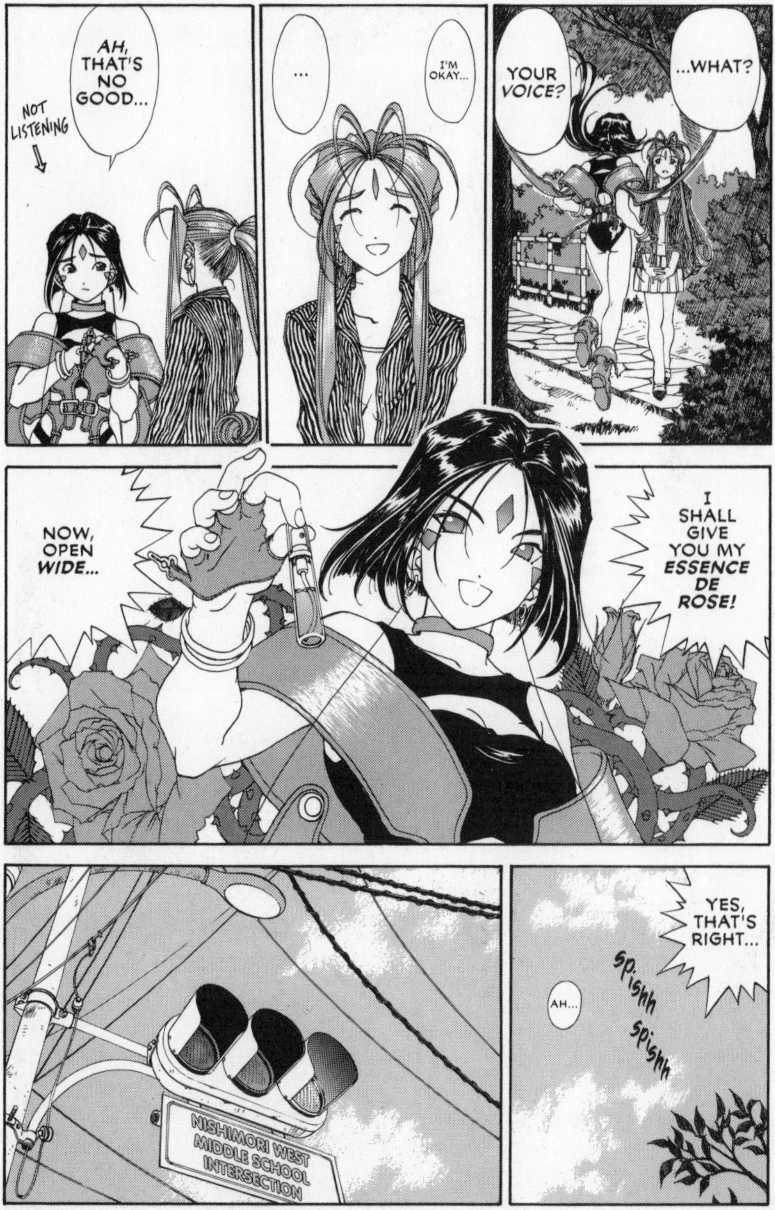
...WHAT?
YOUR VOICE?
I'M OKAY...
...
AH, THAT'S NO GOOD...
NOT LISTENING
I SHALL GIVE YOU MY ESSENCE DE ROSE!
NOW, OPEN WIDE...
YES, THAT'S RIGHT...
spishh
spishh
AH...
NISHIMORI WEST MIDDLE SCHOOL INTERSECTION

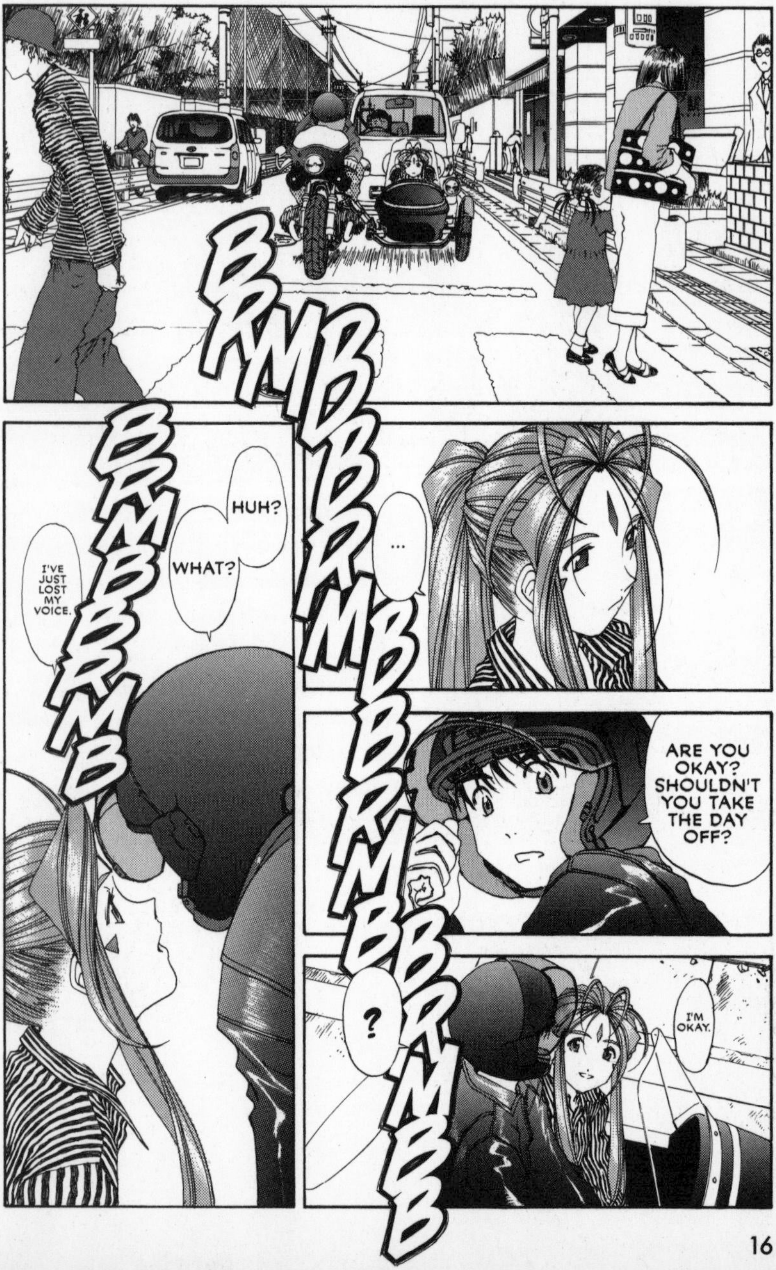
BRMB
BRMBBRMBBRMBB
...
ARE YOU OKAY? SHOULDN'T YOU TAKE THE DAY OFF?
?
I'M OKAY.
HUH?
WHAT?
I'VE JUST LOST MY VOICE.
BRMBBRMB

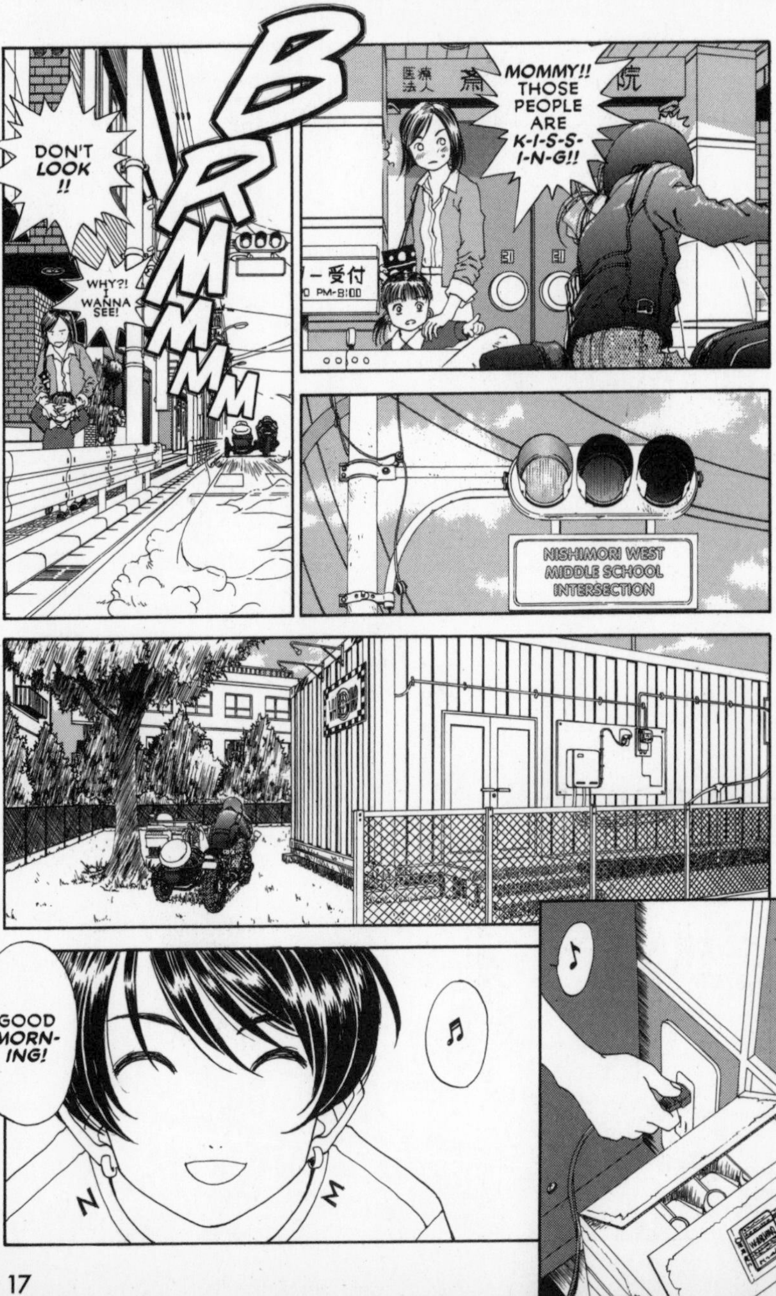
MOMMY!! THOSE PEOPLE ARE K-I-S-S-I-N-G!!
NISHIMORI WEST MIDDLE SCHOOL INTERSECTION
BRMMMMMM
DON'T LOOK!!
WHY?! I WANNA SEE!
♪
GOOD MORNING!
♪
N
M

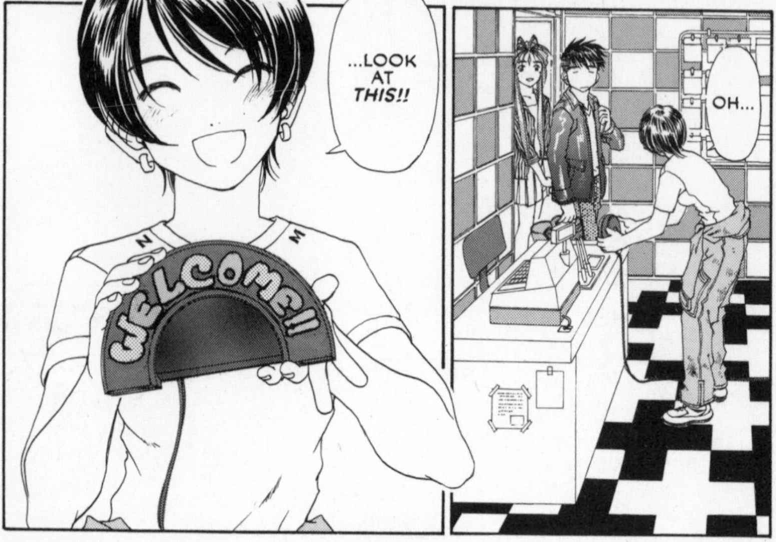
OH...
...LOOK AT THIS!!
WELCOME!!

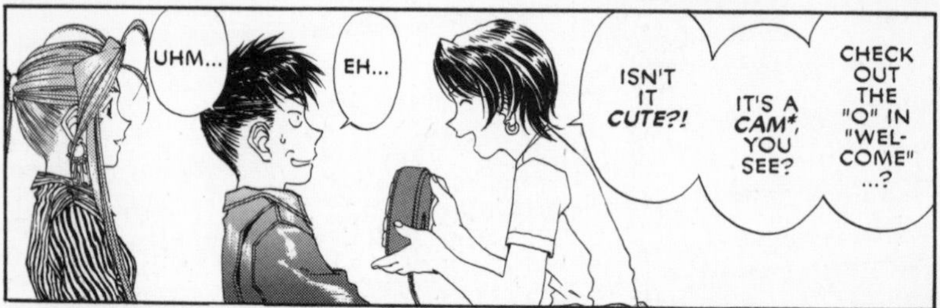
CHECK OUT THE "O" IN "WEL-COME" ...?
IT'S A CAM*, YOU SEE?
ISN'T IT CUTE?!
EH...
UHM...

*Not "cam" as in "camera," but "cam" as in "rotating wheel or shaft that strikes a lever at one or more points along a circular path."

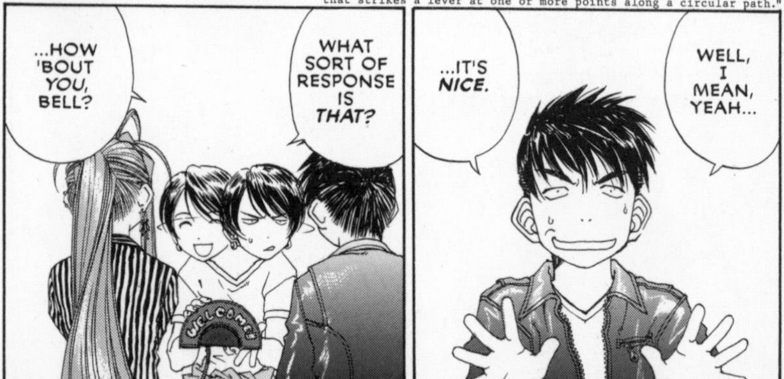
WELL, I MEAN, YEAH...
...IT'S NICE.
WHAT SORT OF RESPONSE IS THAT?
...HOW 'BOUT YOU, BELL?
WELCOME!!

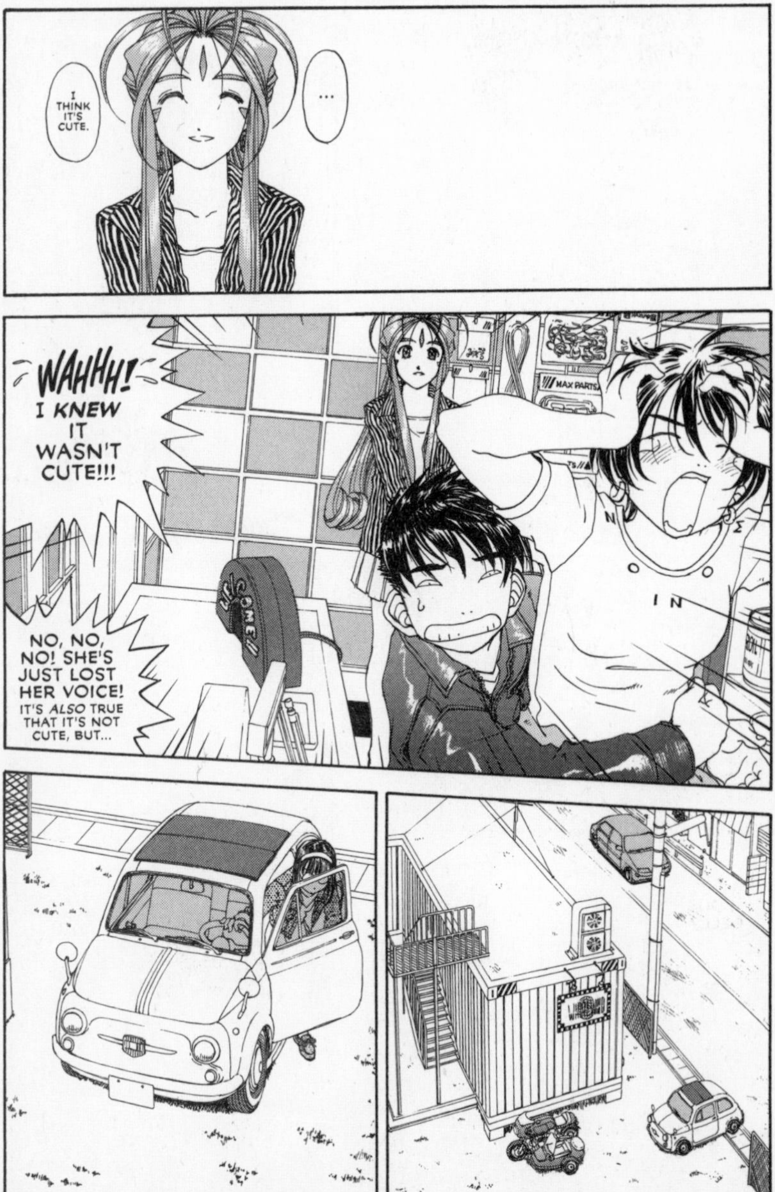
...
I THINK IT'S CUTE.
MAX PARTS
WAHHH! I KNEW IT WASN'T CUTE!!!
NO, NO, NO! SHE'S JUST LOST HER VOICE! IT'S *ALSO* TRUE THAT IT'S NOT CUTE, BUT...

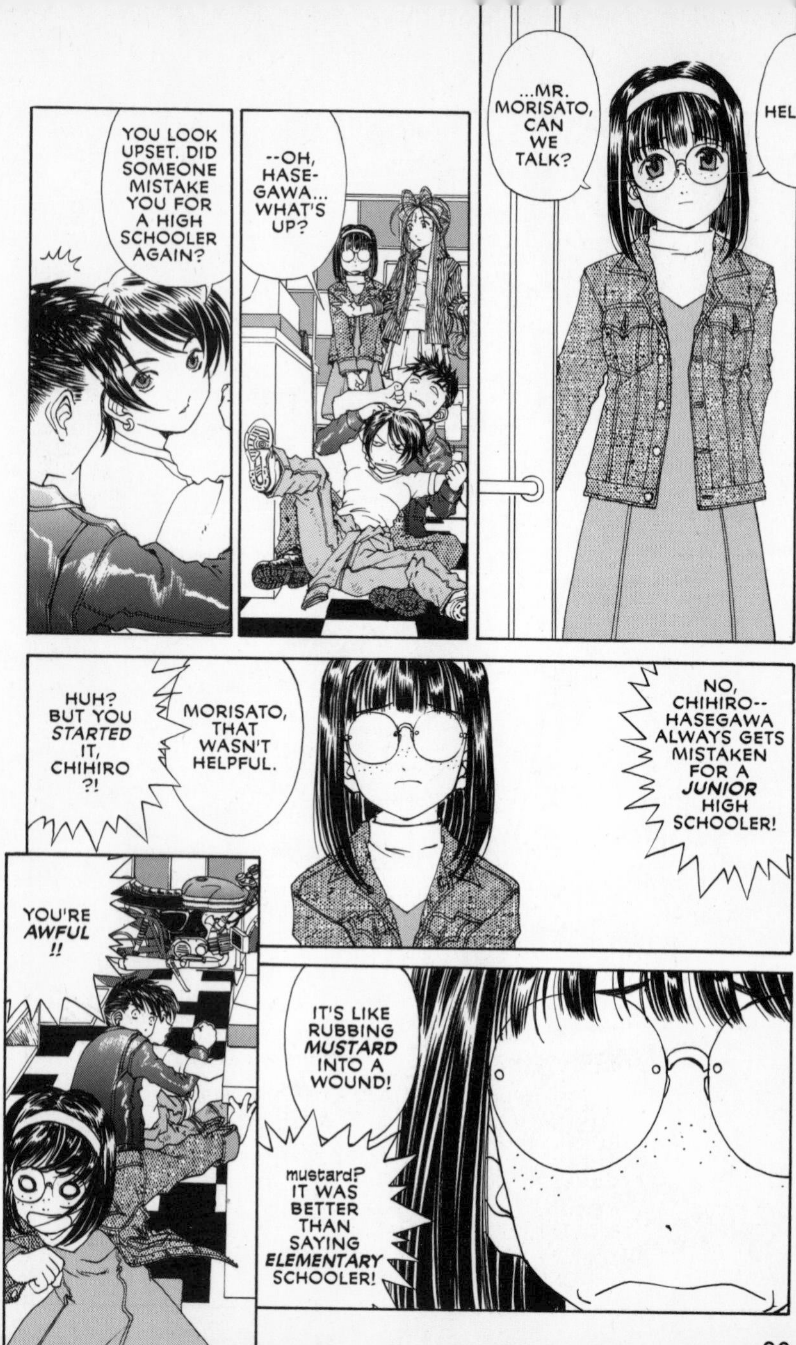
HELLO...
...MR. MORISATO, CAN WE TALK?
--OH, HASEGAWA... WHAT'S UP?
YOU LOOK UPSET. DID SOMEONE MISTAKE YOU FOR A HIGH SCHOOLER AGAIN?
NO, CHIHIRO-- HASEGAWA ALWAYS GETS MISTAKEN FOR A *JUNIOR* HIGH SCHOOLER!
MORISATO, THAT WASN'T HELPFUL.
HUH? BUT YOU *STARTED* IT, CHIHIRO?!
IT'S LIKE RUBBING *MUSTARD* INTO A WOUND!
mustard? IT WAS BETTER THAN SAYING *ELEMENTARY* SCHOOLER!
YOU'RE *AWFUL* !!

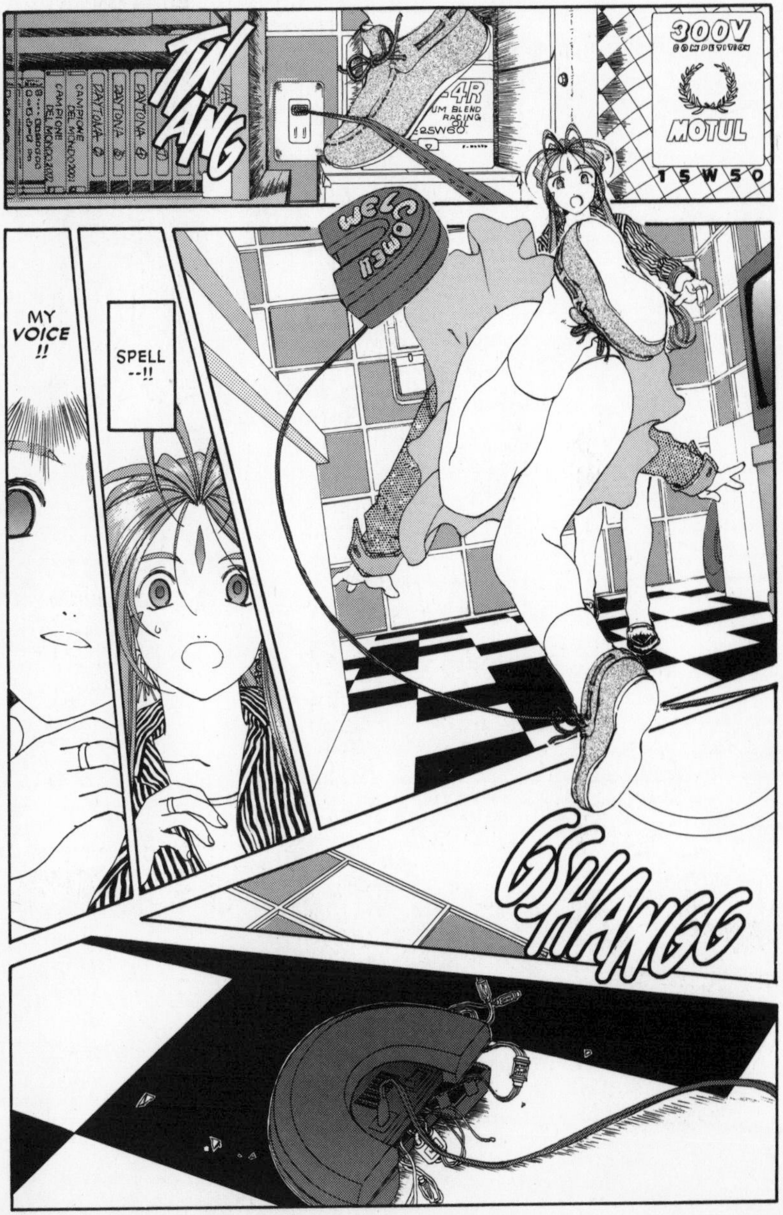

300V
COMPETITION
MOTUL
15W50
TWANG
WELCOME!!
SPELL --!!
MY VOICE !!
GSHANGG

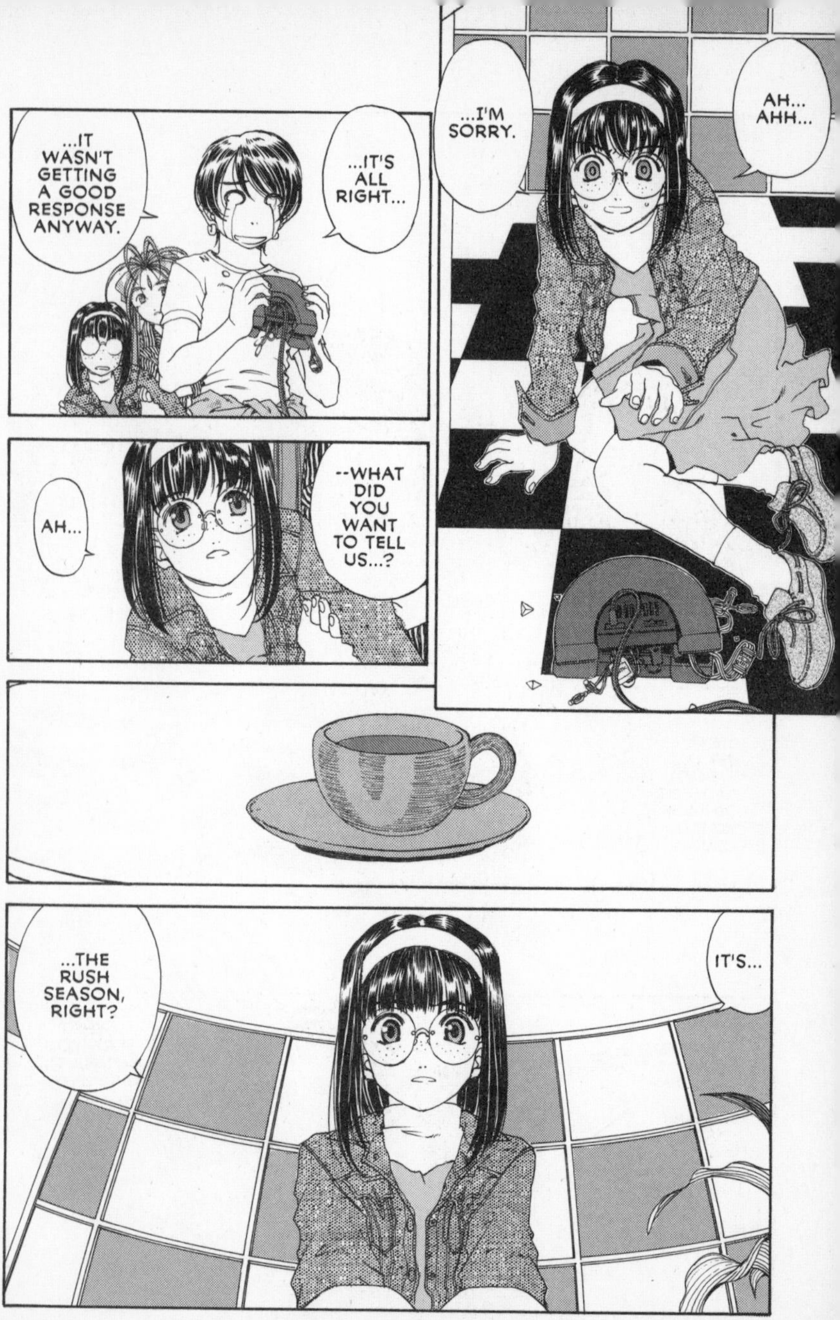
AH... AHH...
...I'M SORRY.
...IT'S ALL RIGHT...
...IT WASN'T GETTING A GOOD RESPONSE ANYWAY.
--WHAT DID YOU WANT TO TELL US...?
AH...
IT'S...
...THE RUSH SEASON, RIGHT?

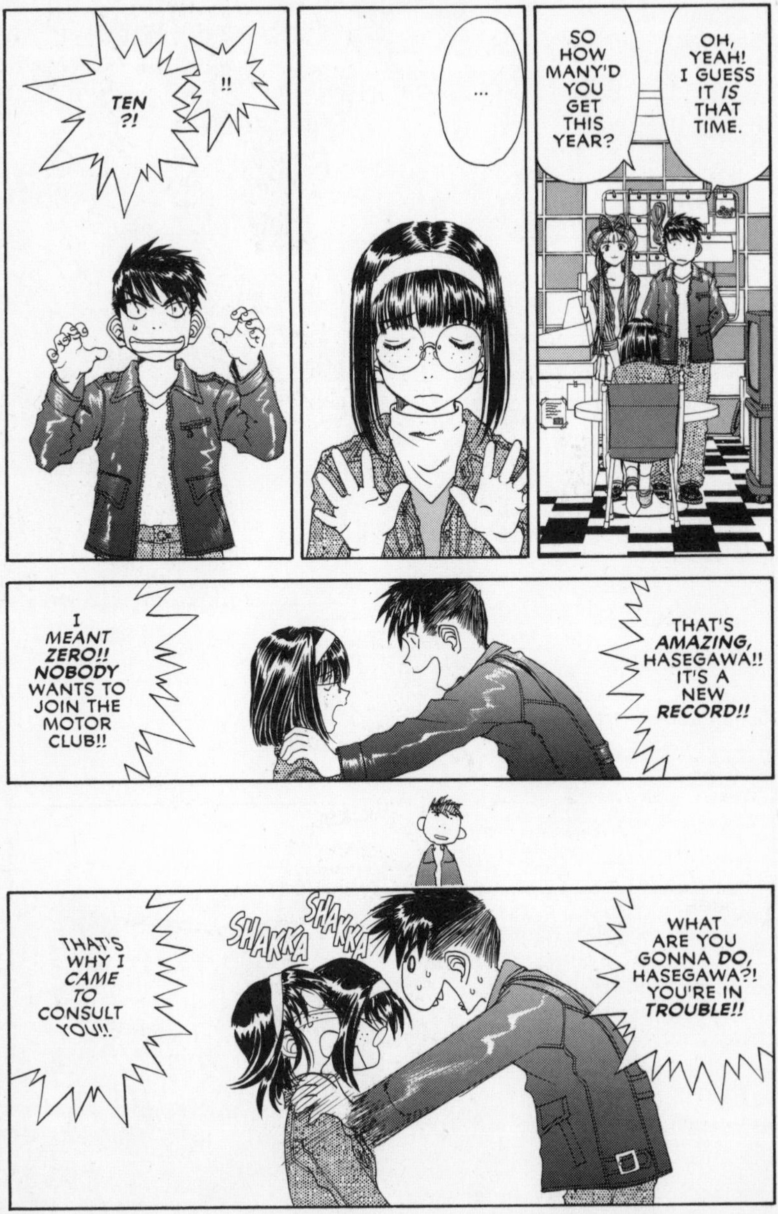
OH, YEAH! I GUESS IT *IS* THAT TIME.
SO HOW MANY'D YOU GET THIS YEAR?
...
!!
TEN ?!
THAT'S *AMAZING,* HASEGAWA!! IT'S A NEW *RECORD!!*
I MEANT *ZERO!! NOBODY* WANTS TO JOIN THE MOTOR CLUB!!
WHAT ARE YOU GONNA *DO,* HASEGAWA?! YOU'RE IN *TROUBLE!!*
SHAKKA
SHAKKA
THAT'S WHY I *CAME TO* CONSULT YOU!!.

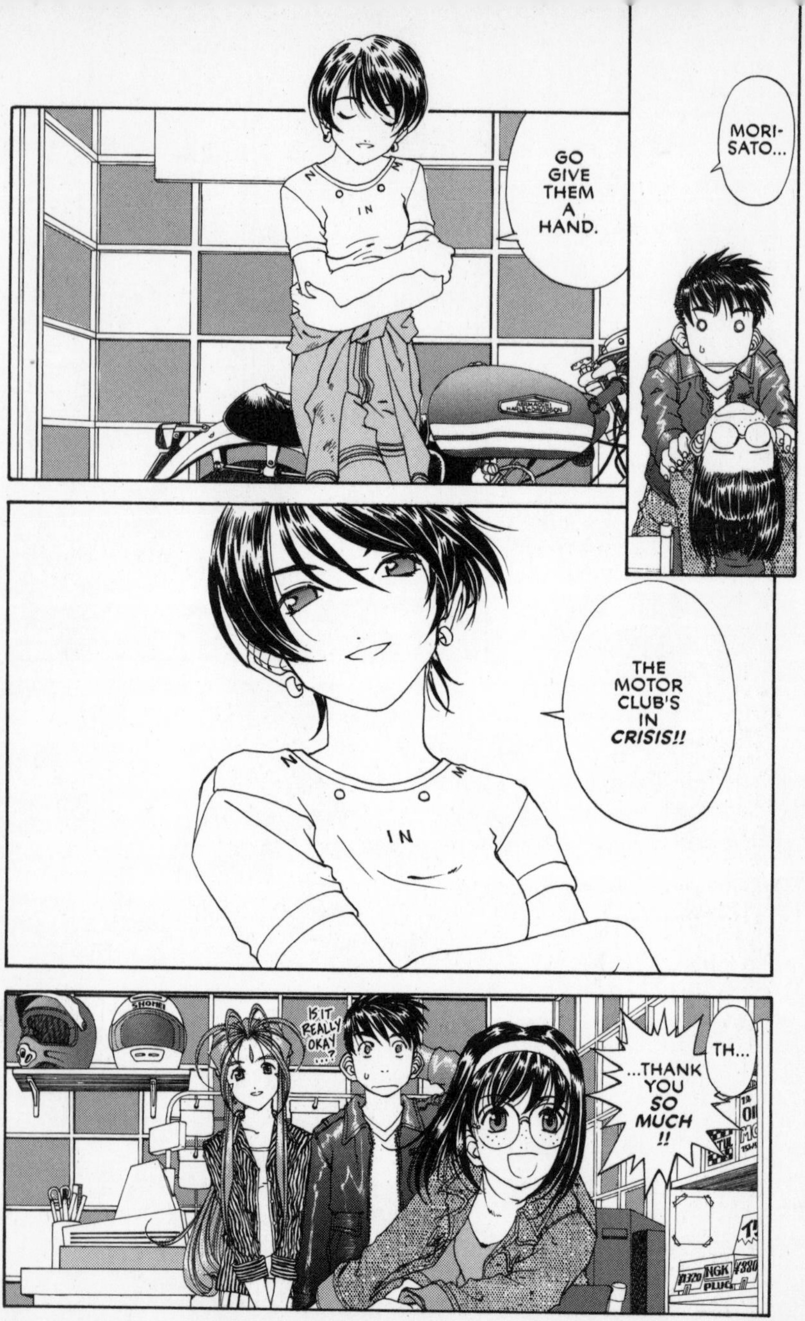
MORI-SATO...
GO GIVE THEM A HAND.
THE MOTOR CLUB'S IN *CRISIS!!*
TH...
...THANK YOU *SO MUCH* !!
IS IT REALLY OKAY ...?
SHOEI
NGK PLUG

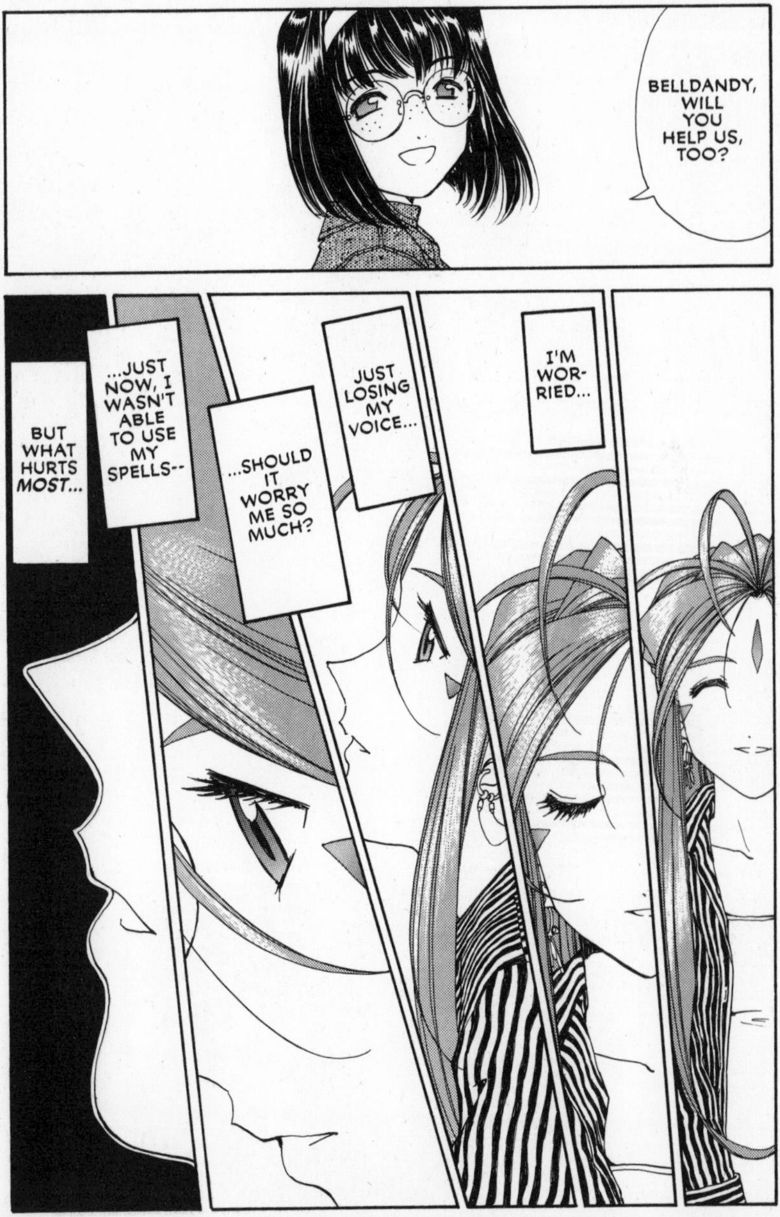
BELLDANDY, WILL YOU HELP US, TOO?
I'M WOR-RIED...
JUST LOSING MY VOICE...
...SHOULD IT WORRY ME SO MUCH?
...JUST NOW, I WASN'T ABLE TO USE MY SPELLS--
BUT WHAT HURTS *MOST*...

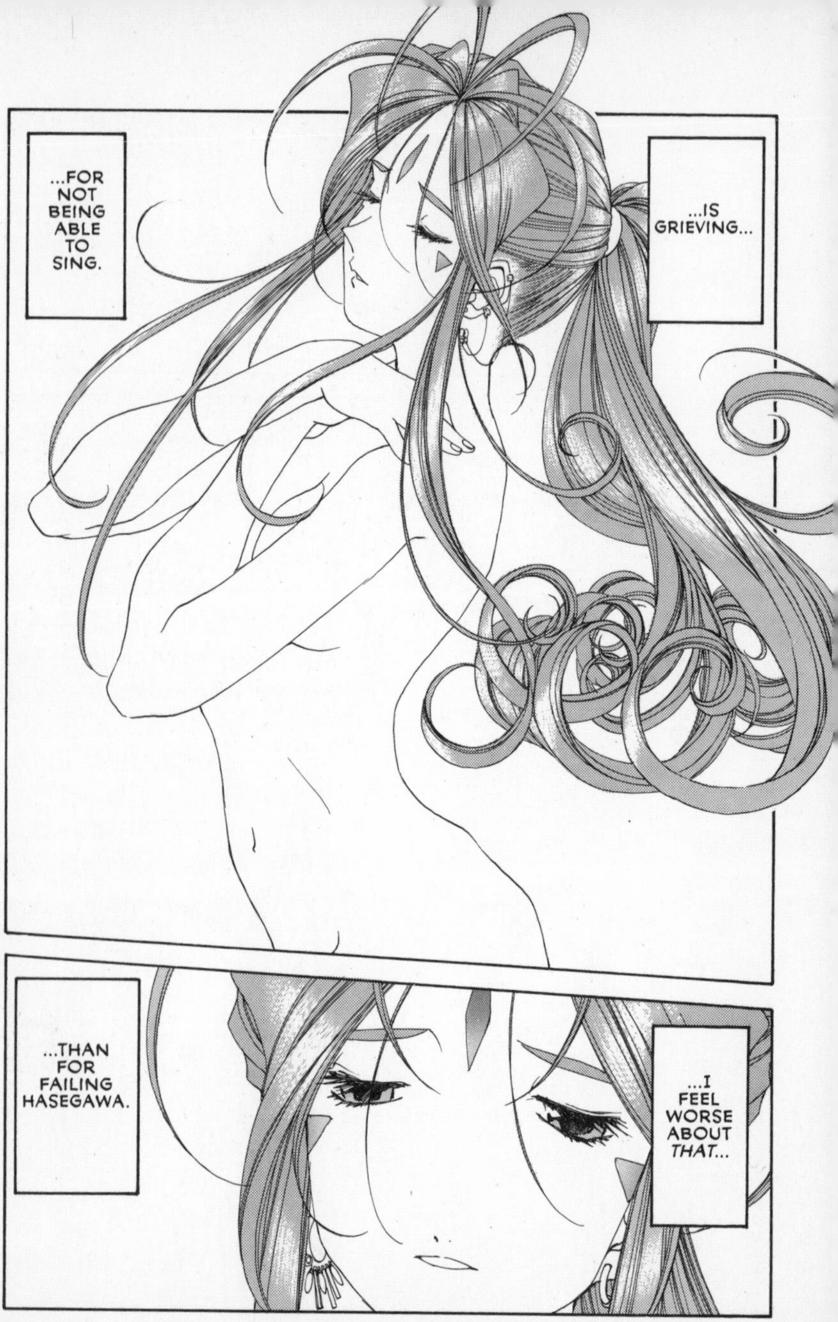
...IS GRIEVING...
...FOR NOT BEING ABLE TO SING.
...I FEEL WORSE ABOUT *THAT*...
...THAN FOR FAILING HASEGAWA.

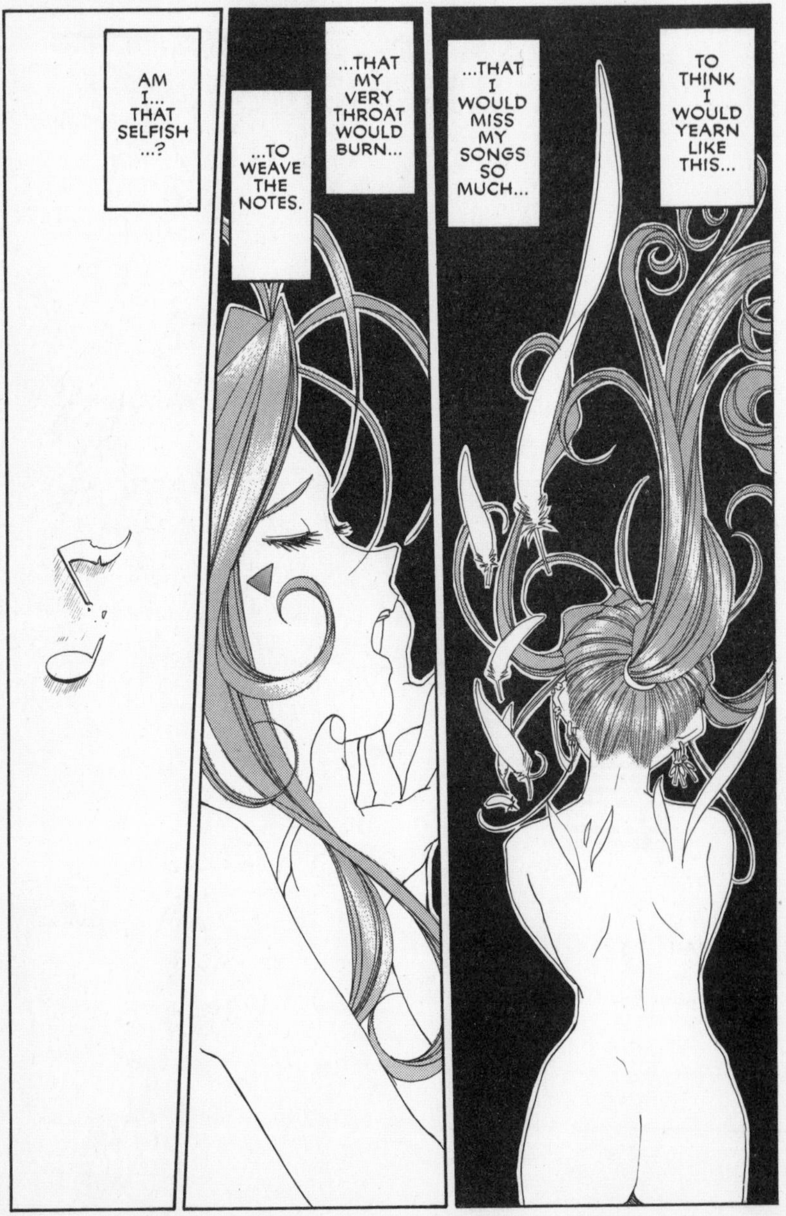
TO THINK I WOULD YEARN LIKE THIS...
...THAT I WOULD MISS MY SONGS SO MUCH...
...THAT MY VERY THROAT WOULD BURN...
...TO WEAVE THE NOTES.
AM I... THAT SELFISH ...?

OH MY GODDESS!
BELLDANDY

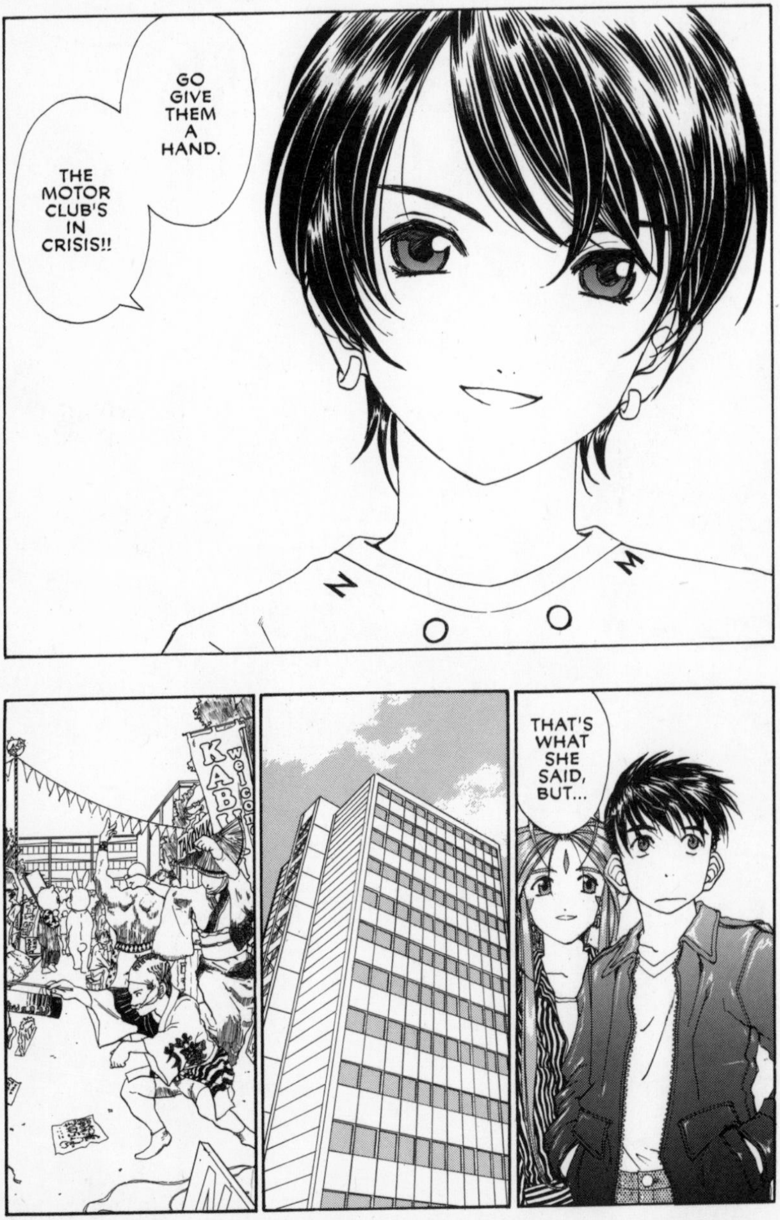
GO GIVE THEM A HAND.
THE MOTOR CLUB'S IN CRISIS!!
THAT'S WHAT SHE SAID, BUT...

CHAPTER 178

Those Who Guard and Those Who Plunder

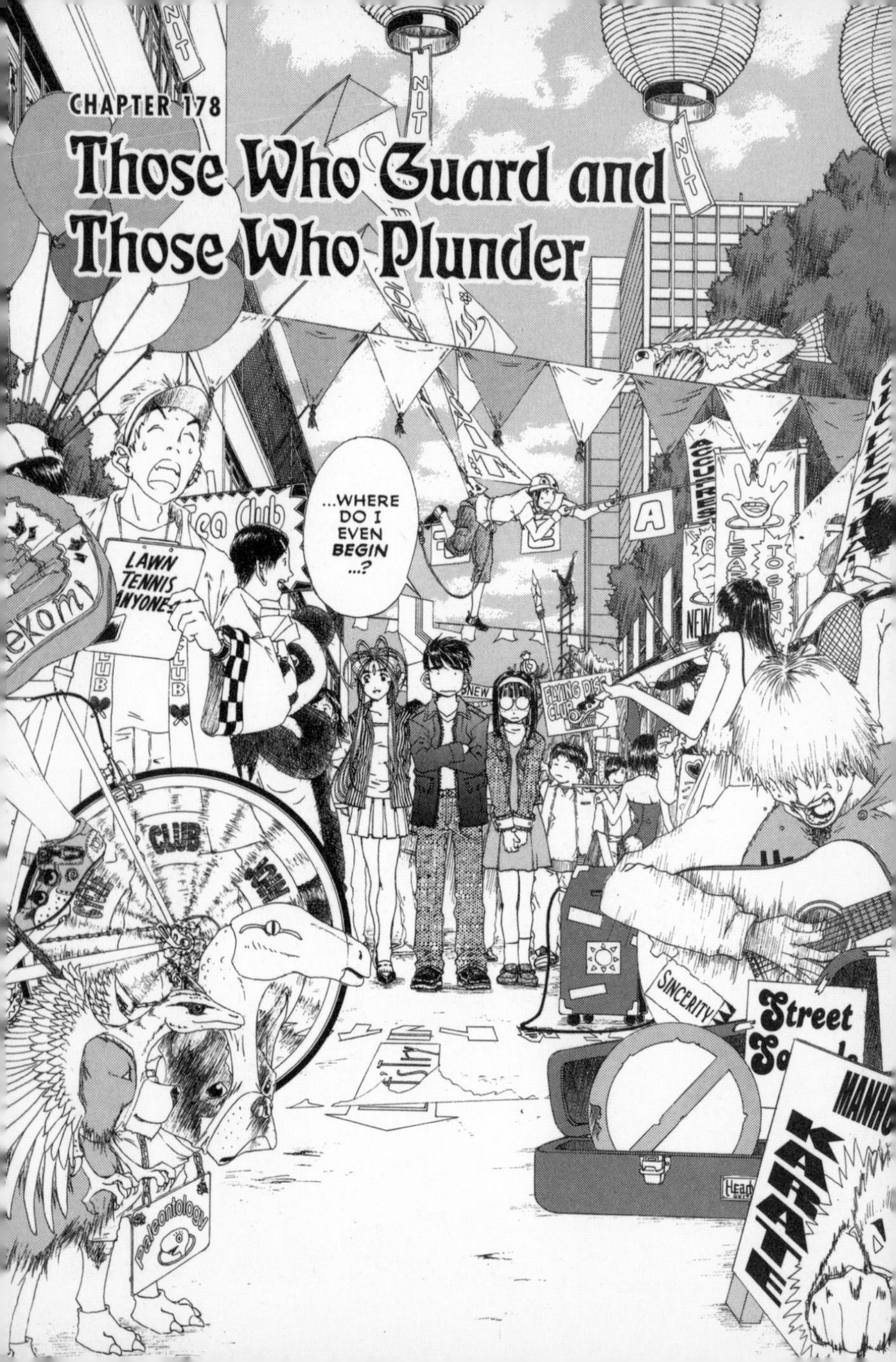
...WHERE DO I EVEN BEGIN ...?
NIT
Tea Club
LAWN TENNIS ANYONE?
CLUB
A
FLYING DISC CLUB
NEW
SINCERITY
Street
paleontology
KARATE

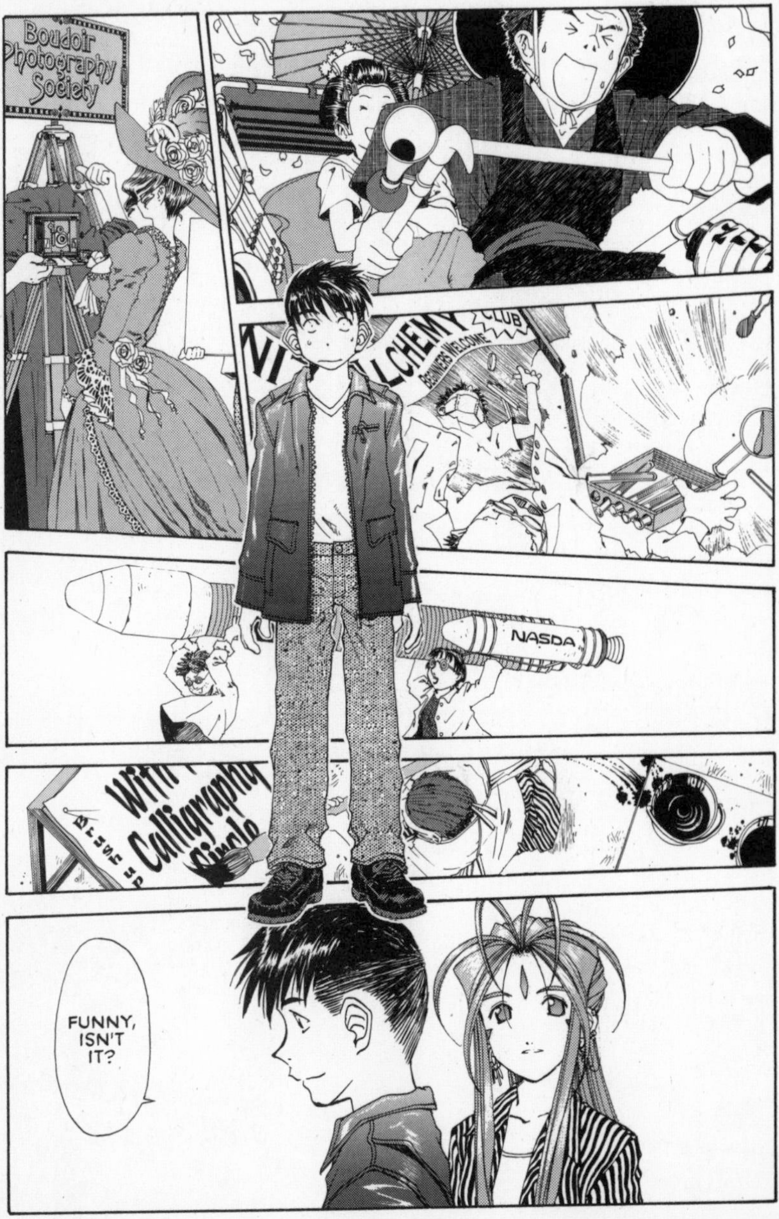
Boudoir Photography Society
ALCHEMY
CLUB
BEGINNERS WELCOME
NASDA
Calligraphy Circle
FUNNY, ISN'T IT?

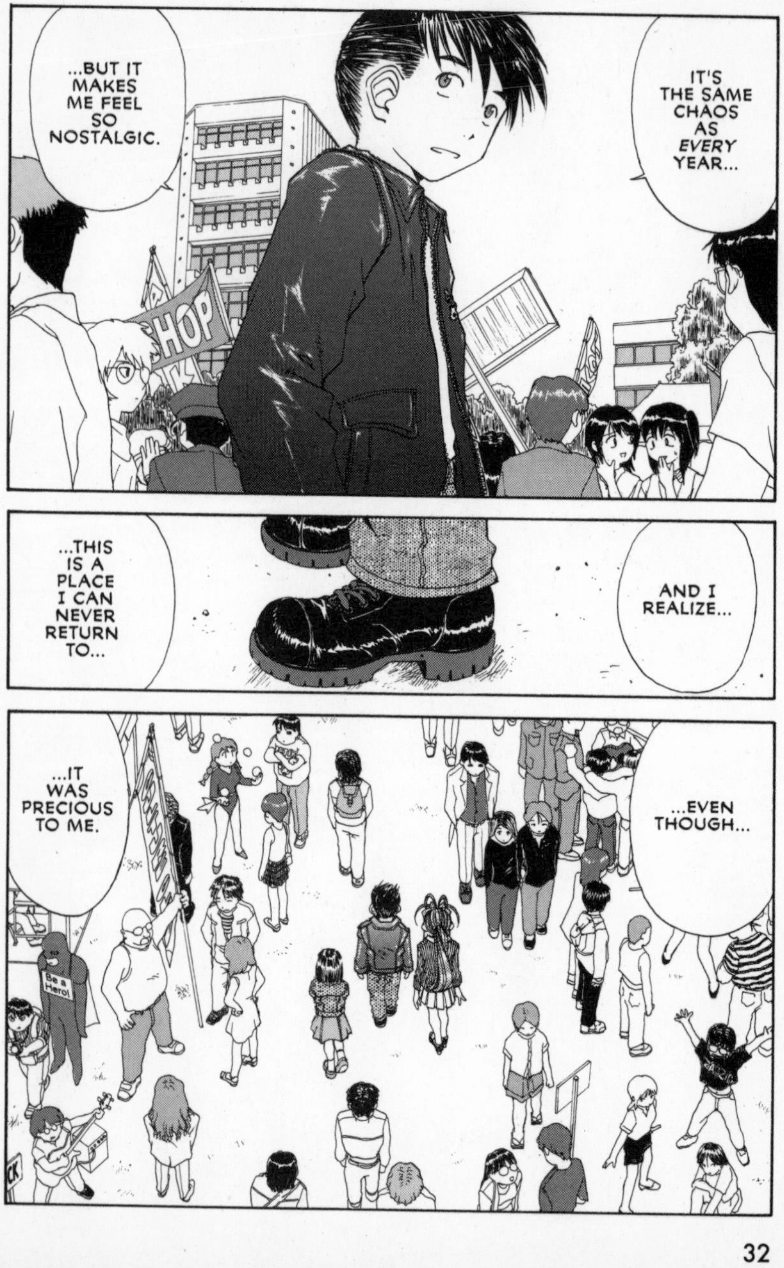
IT'S THE SAME CHAOS AS *EVERY* YEAR...
...BUT IT MAKES ME FEEL SO NOSTALGIC.
SHOP
AND I REALIZE...
...THIS IS A PLACE I CAN NEVER RETURN TO...
...EVEN THOUGH...
...IT WAS PRECIOUS TO ME.
Be a Hero!

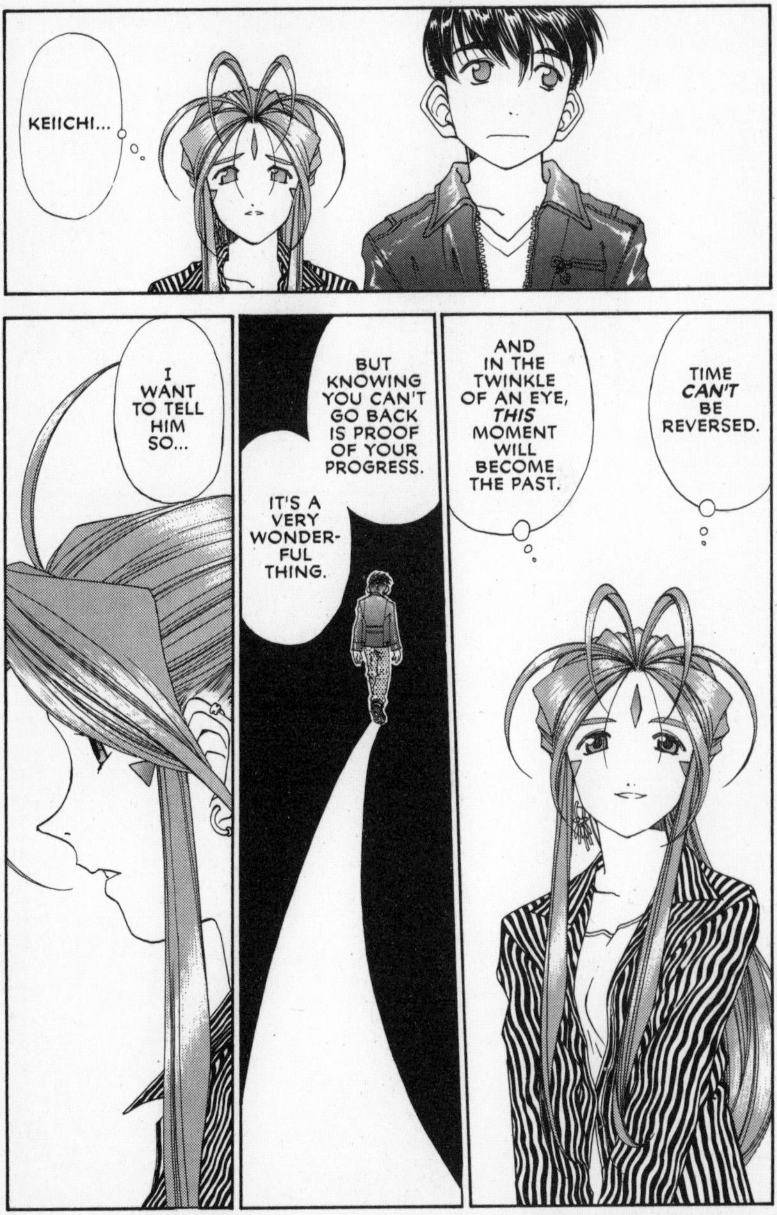
KEIICHI...
TIME CAN'T BE REVERSED.
AND IN THE TWINKLE OF AN EYE, THIS MOMENT WILL BECOME THE PAST.
BUT KNOWING YOU CAN'T GO BACK IS PROOF OF YOUR PROGRESS.
IT'S A VERY WONDERFUL THING.
I WANT TO TELL HIM SO...

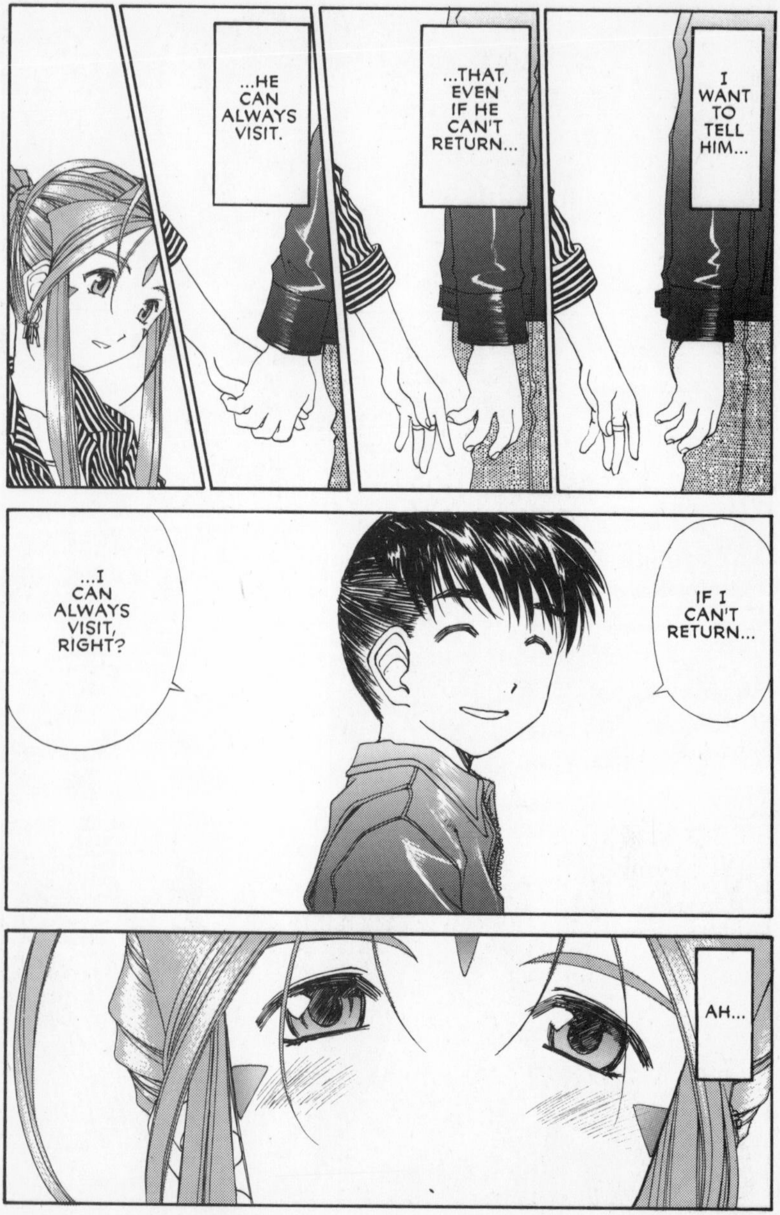
I WANT TO TELL HIM...
...THAT, EVEN IF HE CAN'T RETURN...
...HE CAN ALWAYS VISIT.
IF I CAN'T RETURN...
...I CAN ALWAYS VISIT, RIGHT?
AH...

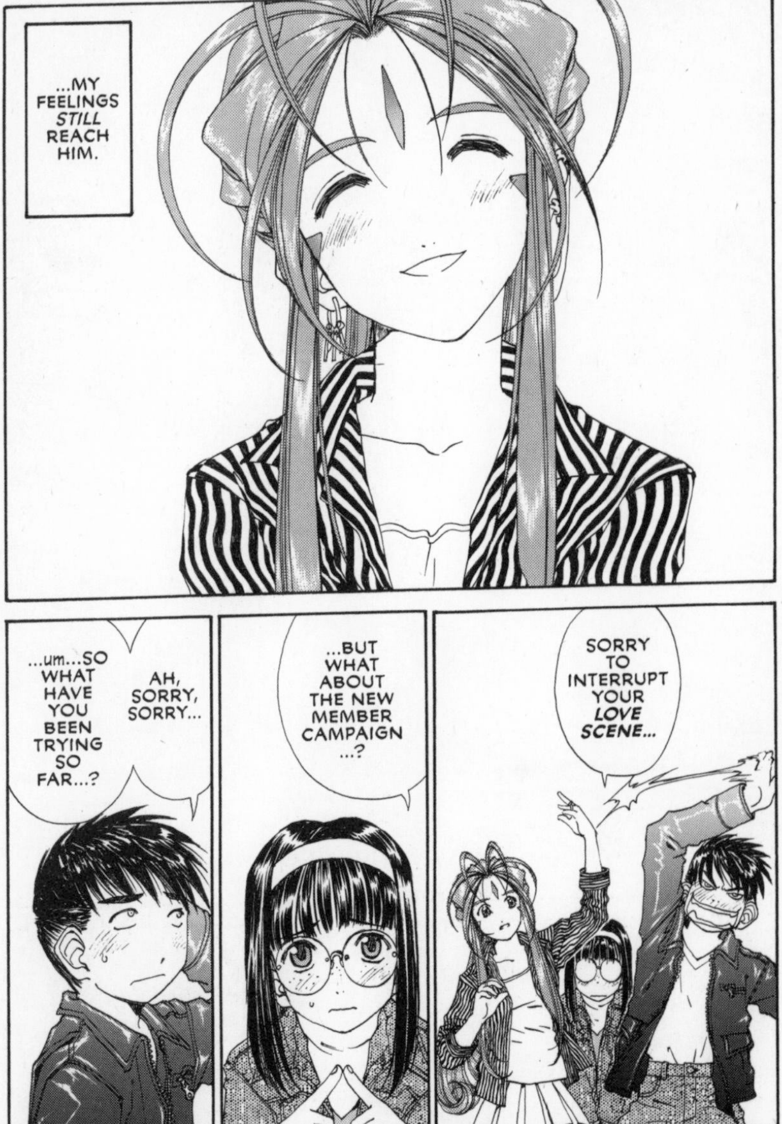
...MY FEELINGS *STILL* REACH HIM.
SORRY TO INTERRUPT YOUR *LOVE SCENE*...
...BUT WHAT ABOUT THE NEW MEMBER CAMPAIGN ...?
AH, SORRY, SORRY...
...um...SO WHAT HAVE YOU BEEN TRYING SO FAR...?

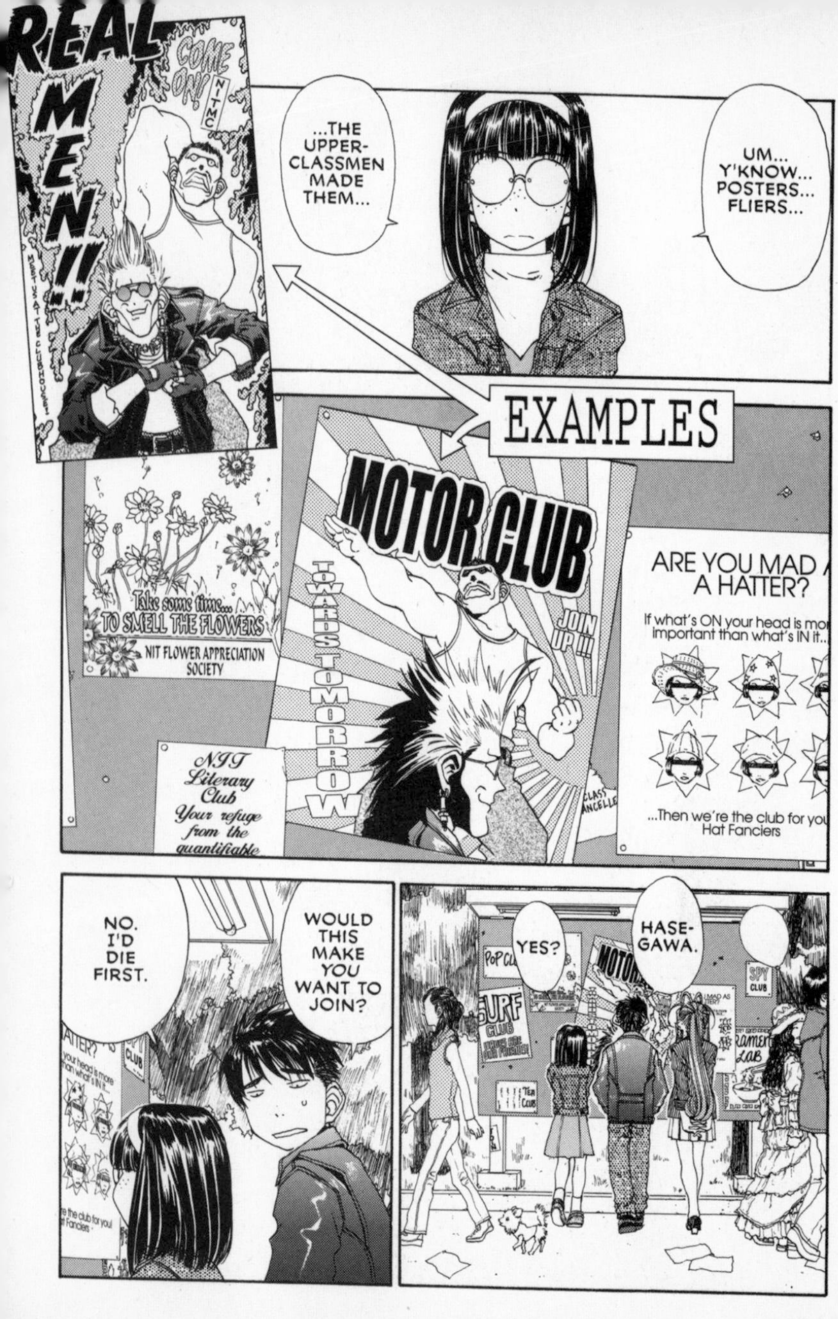

UM... Y'KNOW... POSTERS... FLIERS...
...THE UPPER-CLASSMEN MADE THEM...
REAL MEN!!
COME ON!
NITMC
MEET US AT THE CLUBHOUSE!
EXAMPLES
MOTOR CLUB
TOWARDS TOMORROW
JOIN UP!!!
ARE YOU MAD A
A HATTER?
If what's ON your head is mo
important than what's IN it..
...Then we're the club for yo
Hat Fanciers
Take some time... TO SMELL THE FLOWERS
NIT FLOWER APPRECIATION SOCIETY
NIT Literary Club Your refuge from the quantifiable
HASE-GAWA.
YES?
SPY CLUB
SURF CLUB
WOULD THIS MAKE YOU WANT TO JOIN?
NO. I'D DIE FIRST.

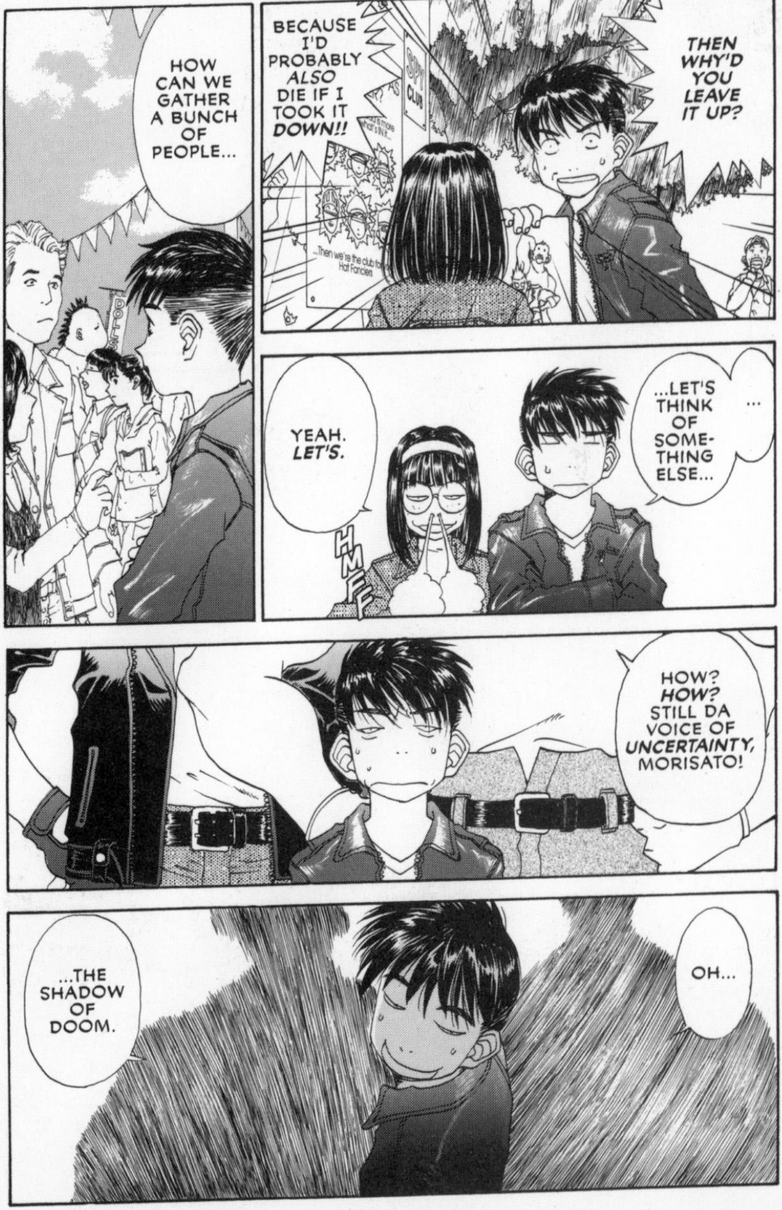

THEN WHY'D YOU LEAVE IT UP?
BECAUSE I'D PROBABLY *ALSO* DIE IF I TOOK IT *DOWN!!*
SPY CLUB
...Then we're the club for Hat Fanciers
...
...LET'S THINK OF SOMETHING ELSE...
YEAH. *LET'S.*
HMFF
HOW CAN WE GATHER A BUNCH OF PEOPLE...
HOW? *HOW?* STILL DA VOICE OF *UNCERTAINTY,* MORISATO!
OH...
...THE SHADOW OF DOOM.

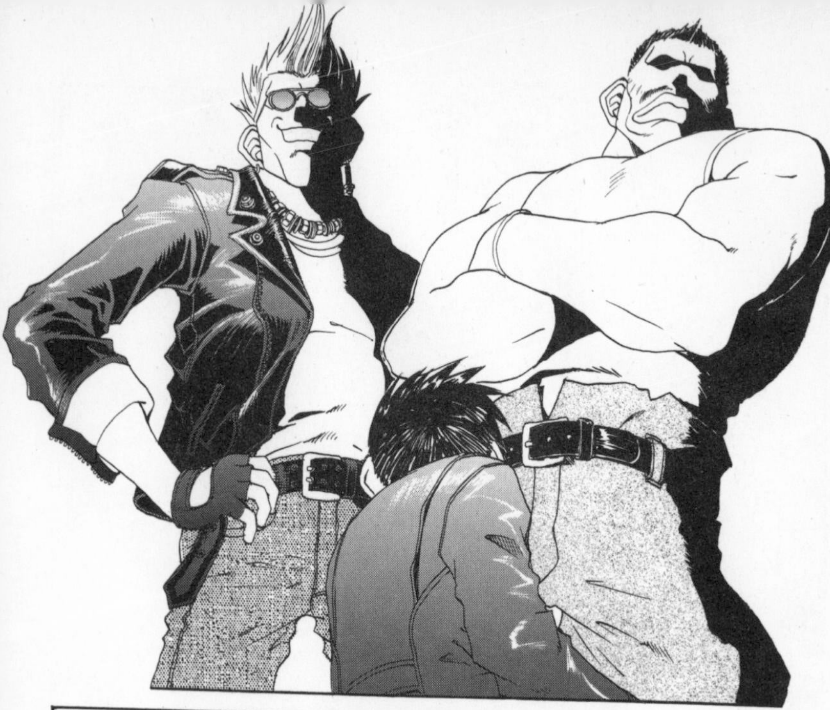

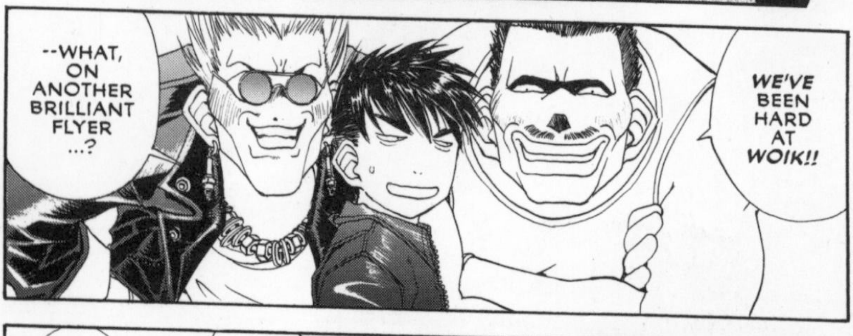
WE'VE BEEN HARD AT WOIK!!
--WHAT, ON ANOTHER BRILLIANT FLYER ...?

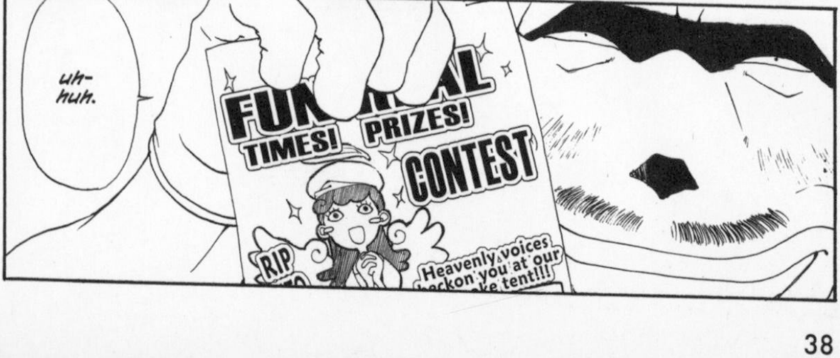
uh-huh.
TIMES! PRIZES!
CONTEST
RIP
Heavenly voices

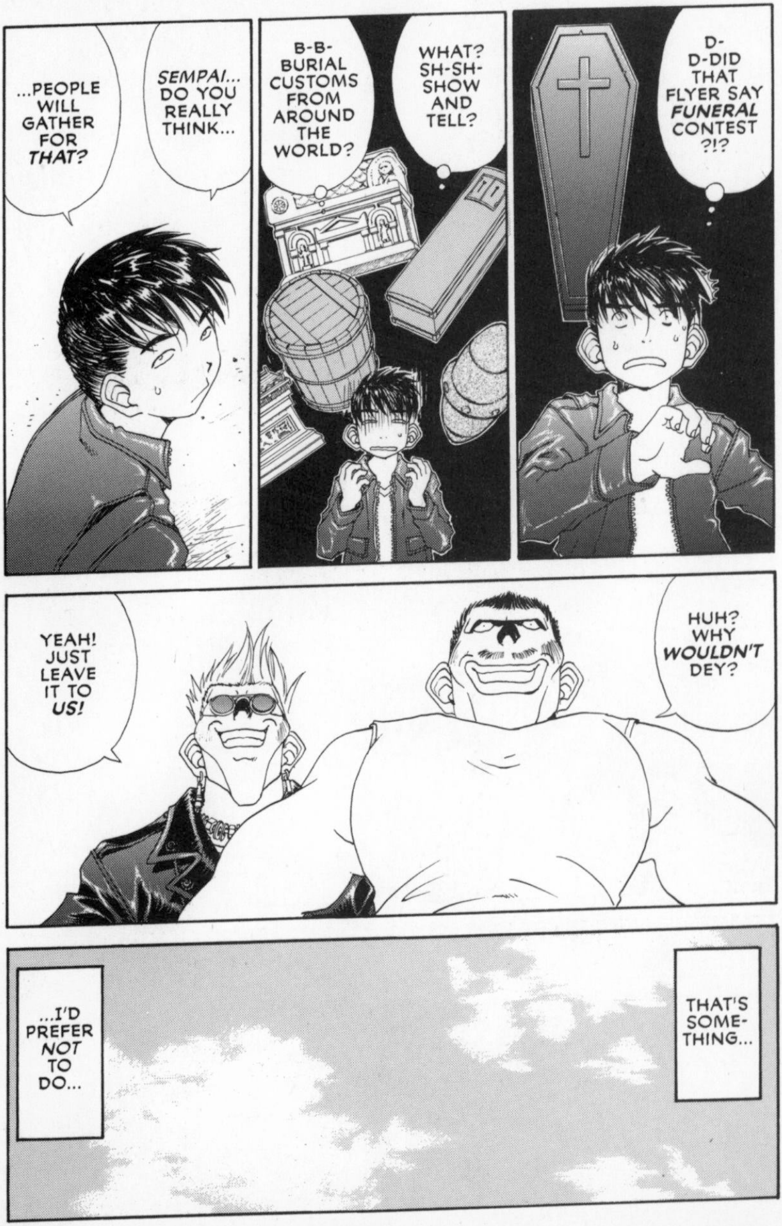
D-D-DID THAT FLYER SAY *FUNERAL* CONTEST?!?
WHAT? SH-SH-SHOW AND TELL?
B-B-BURIAL CUSTOMS FROM AROUND THE WORLD?
SEMPAI... DO YOU REALLY THINK...
...PEOPLE WILL GATHER FOR *THAT?*
HUH? WHY *WOULDN'T* DEY?
YEAH! JUST LEAVE IT TO *US!*
THAT'S SOME-THING...
...I'D PREFER *NOT* TO DO...

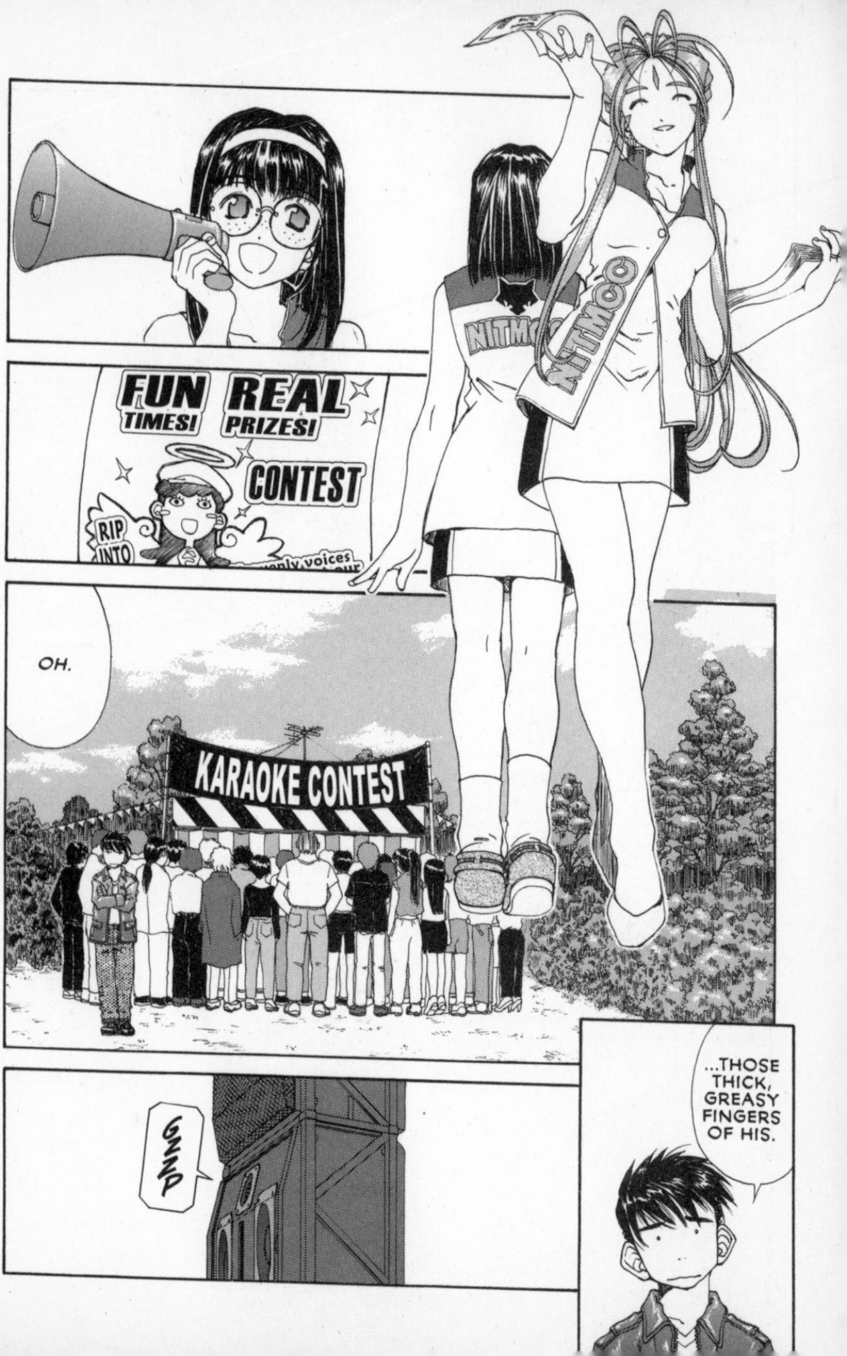
NITMOCO
NITMOCO
FUN TIMES!
REAL PRIZES!
CONTEST
RIP INTO
OH.
KARAOKE CONTEST
...THOSE THICK, GREASY FINGERS OF HIS.
GZZP

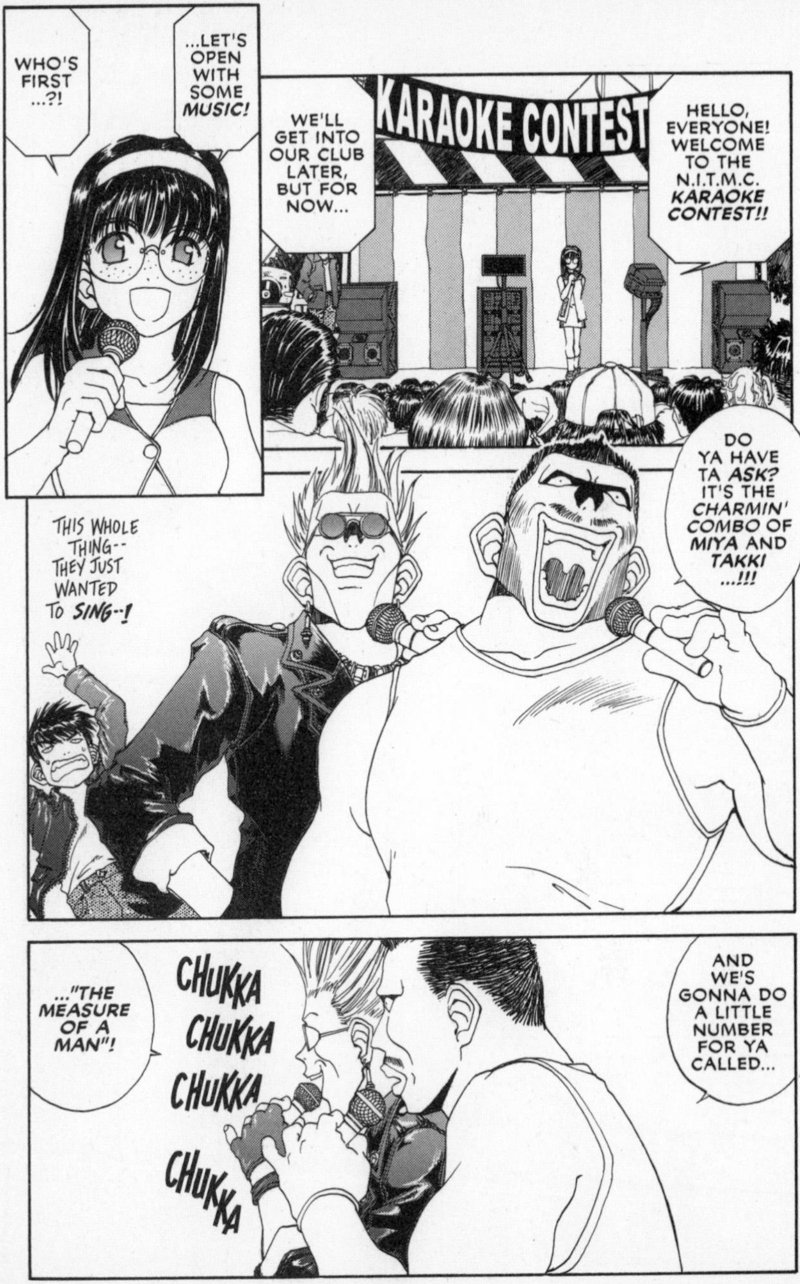
KARAOKE CONTEST
HELLO, EVERYONE! WELCOME TO THE N.I.T.M.C. KARAOKE CONTEST!!
WE'LL GET INTO OUR CLUB LATER, BUT FOR NOW...
...LET'S OPEN WITH SOME MUSIC!
WHO'S FIRST ...?!
DO YA HAVE TA ASK? IT'S THE CHARMIN' COMBO OF MIYA AND TAKKI ...!!!
THIS WHOLE THING-- THEY JUST WANTED TO SING--!
AND WE'S GONNA DO A LITTLE NUMBER FOR YA CALLED...
CHUKKA
CHUKKA
CHUKKA
CHUKKA
..."THE MEASURE OF A MAN"!

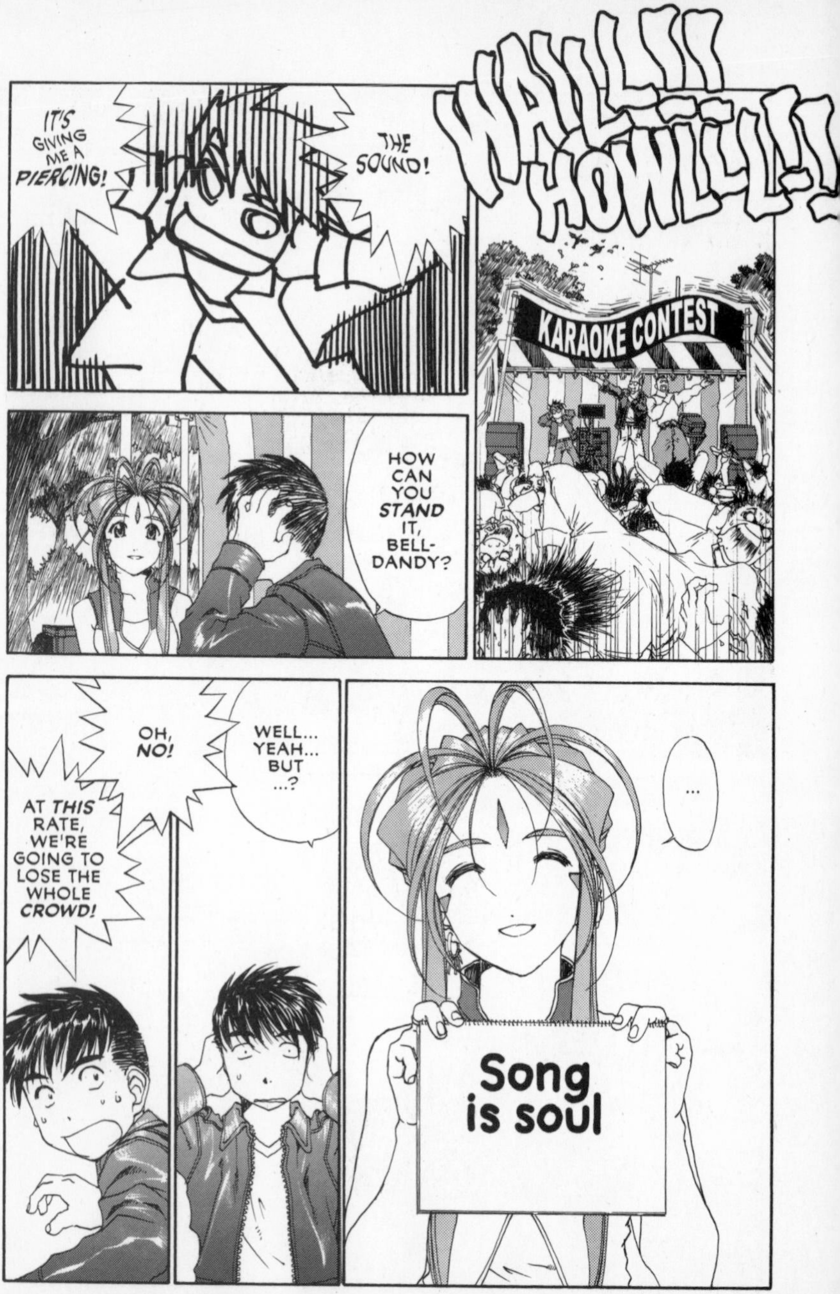
WAILLL HOWLLL!!
KARAOKE CONTEST
THE SOUND!
IT'S GIVING ME A PIERCING!
HOW CAN YOU STAND IT, BELL-DANDY?
...
Song is soul
WELL... YEAH... BUT ...?
OH, NO!
AT THIS RATE, WE'RE GOING TO LOSE THE WHOLE CROWD!

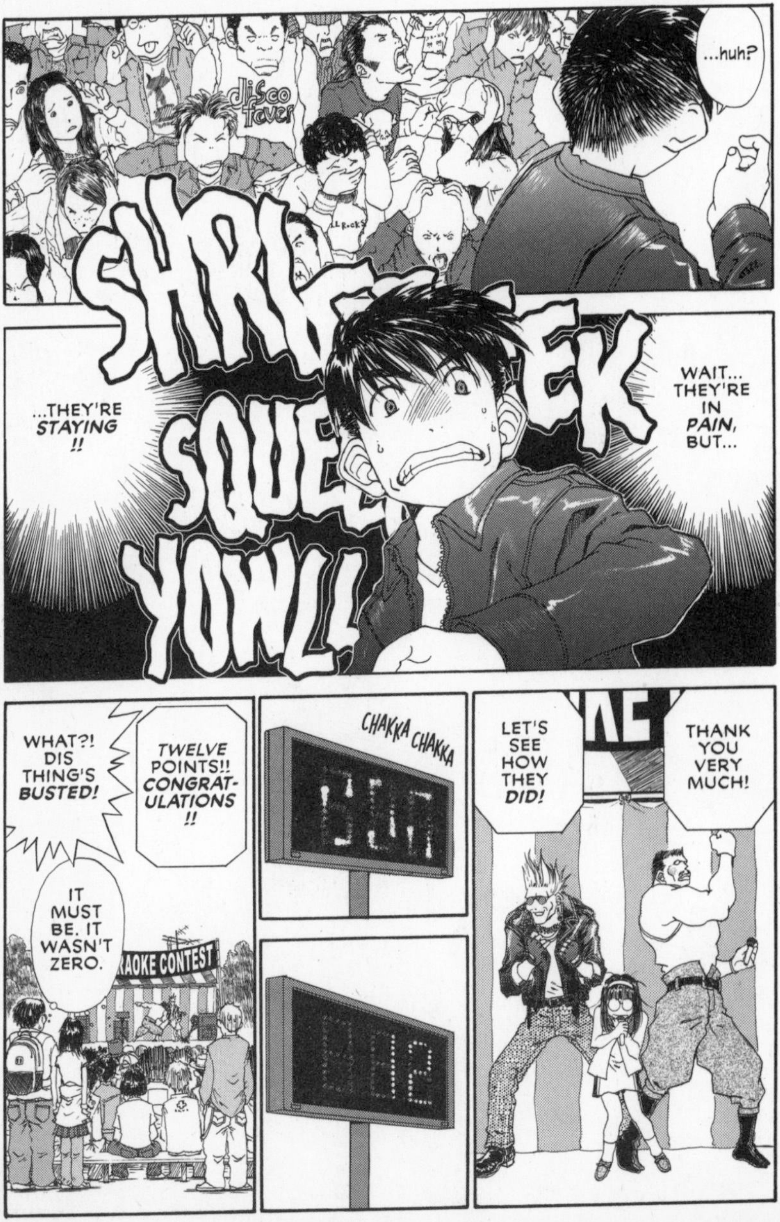
...huh?
SHRI
EK
SQUE
YOWL!
WAIT... THEY'RE IN PAIN, BUT...
...THEY'RE STAYING!!
THANK YOU VERY MUCH!
LET'S SEE HOW THEY DID!
CHAKKA CHAKKA
TWELVE POINTS!! CONGRAT-ULATIONS!!
WHAT?! DIS THING'S BUSTED!
IT MUST BE. IT WASN'T ZERO.
RAOKE CONTEST

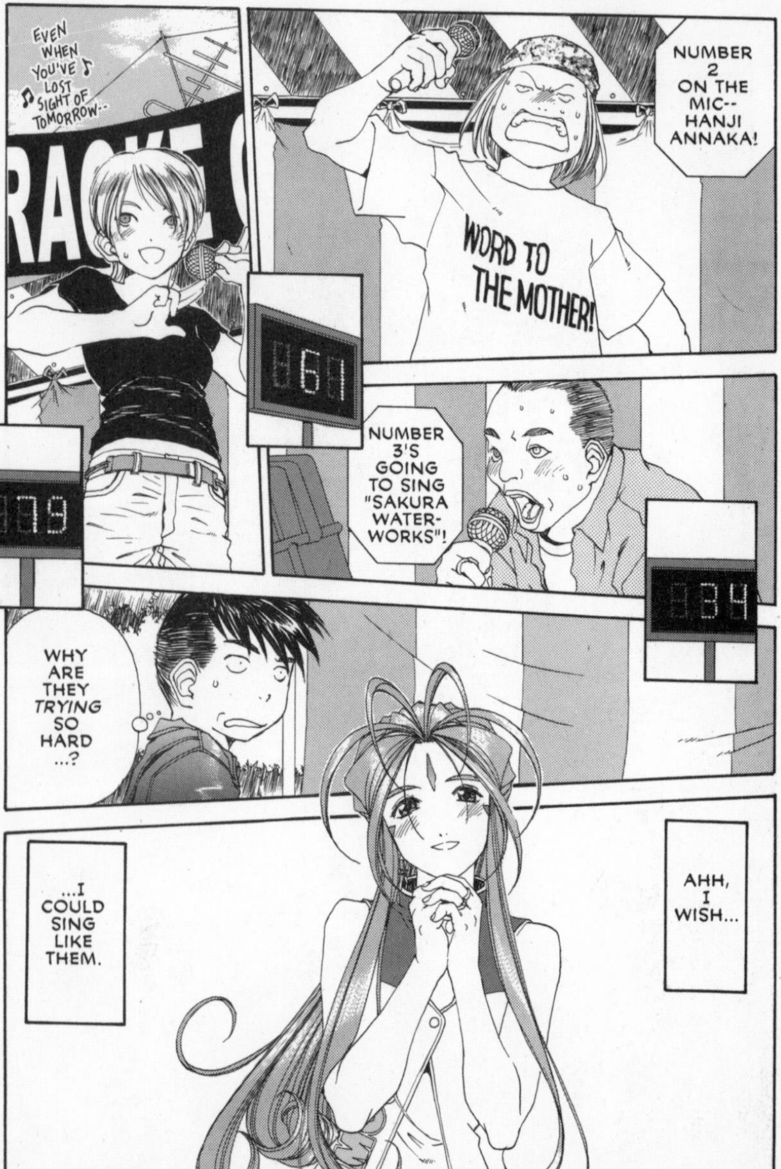
NUMBER 2 ON THE MIC-- HANJI ANNAKA!
WORD TO THE MOTHER!
NUMBER 3'S GOING TO SING "SAKURA WATER-WORKS"!
EVEN WHEN YOU'VE LOST SIGHT OF TOMORROW--
WHY ARE THEY *TRYING* SO HARD ...?
AHH, I WISH...
...I COULD SING LIKE THEM.

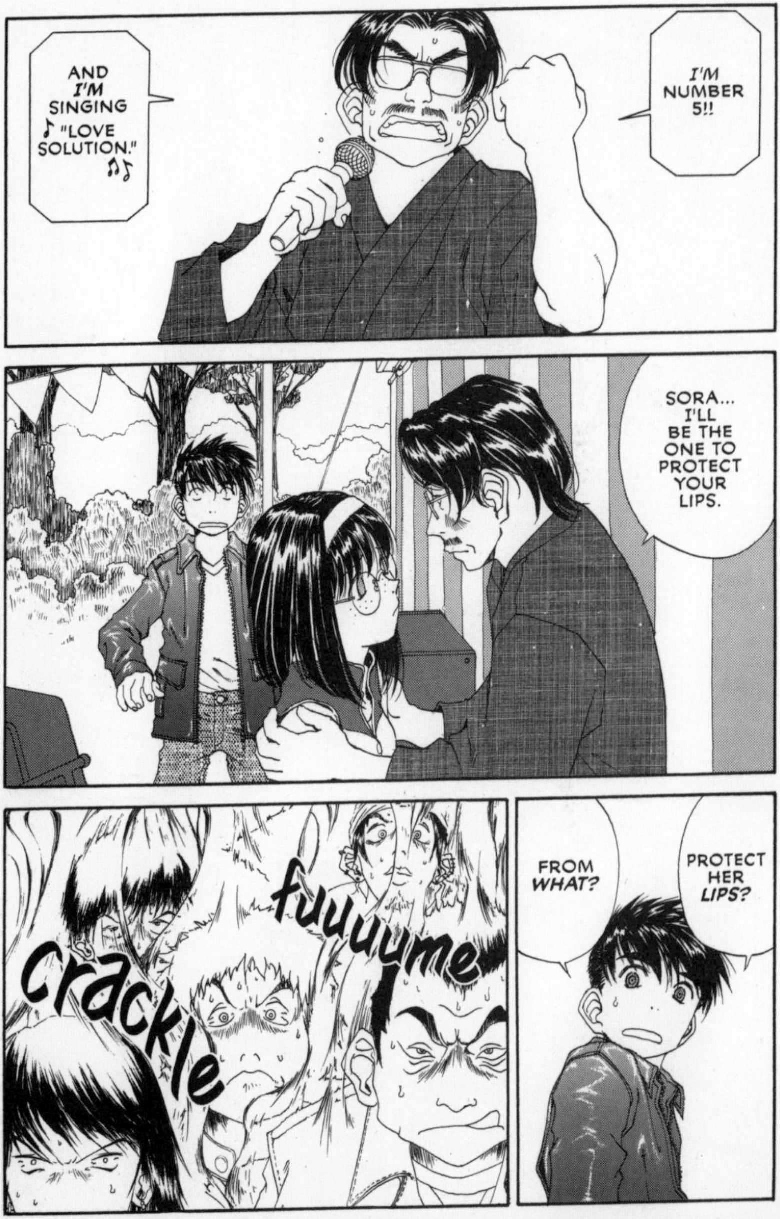
I'M NUMBER 5!!
AND I'M SINGING ♪ "LOVE SOLUTION." ♫♪
SORA... I'LL BE THE ONE TO PROTECT YOUR LIPS.
PROTECT HER LIPS?
FROM WHAT?
fuuuume
crackle

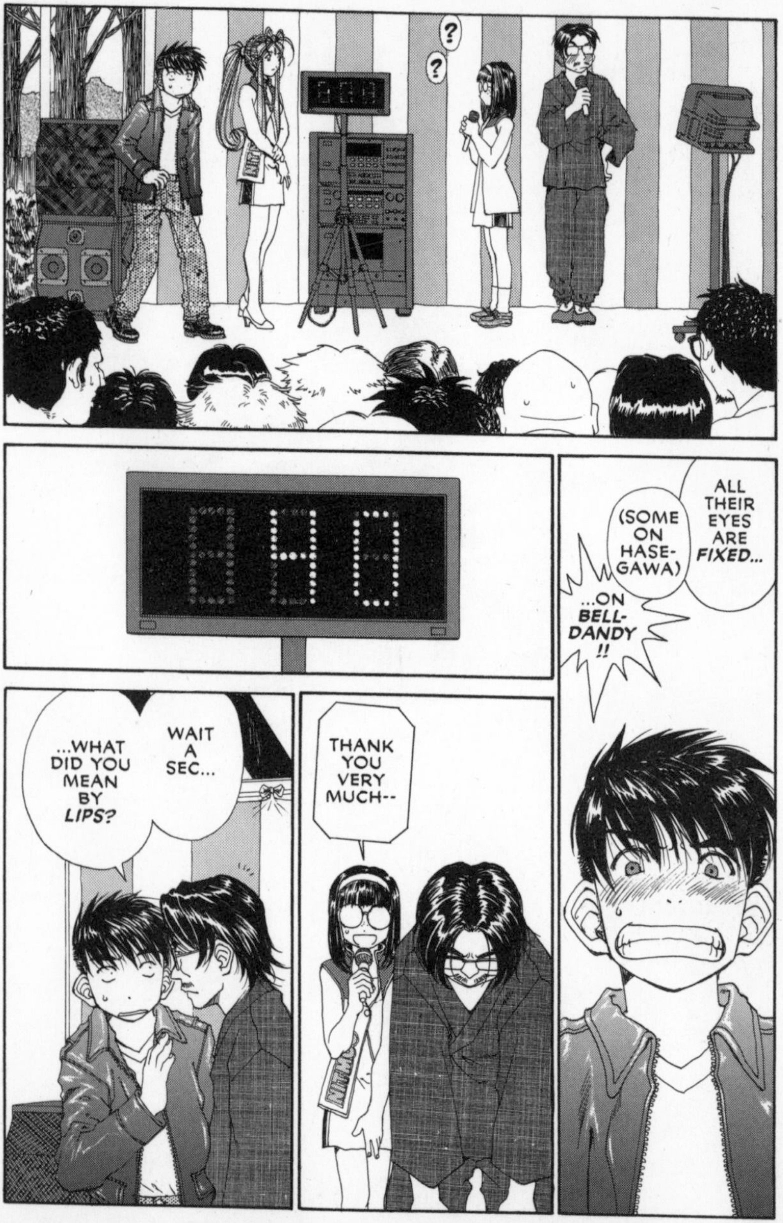
?
?
ALL THEIR EYES ARE *FIXED*...
(SOME ON HASE-GAWA)
...ON *BELL-DANDY* !!
THANK YOU VERY MUCH--
WAIT A SEC...
...WHAT DID YOU MEAN BY *LIPS?*

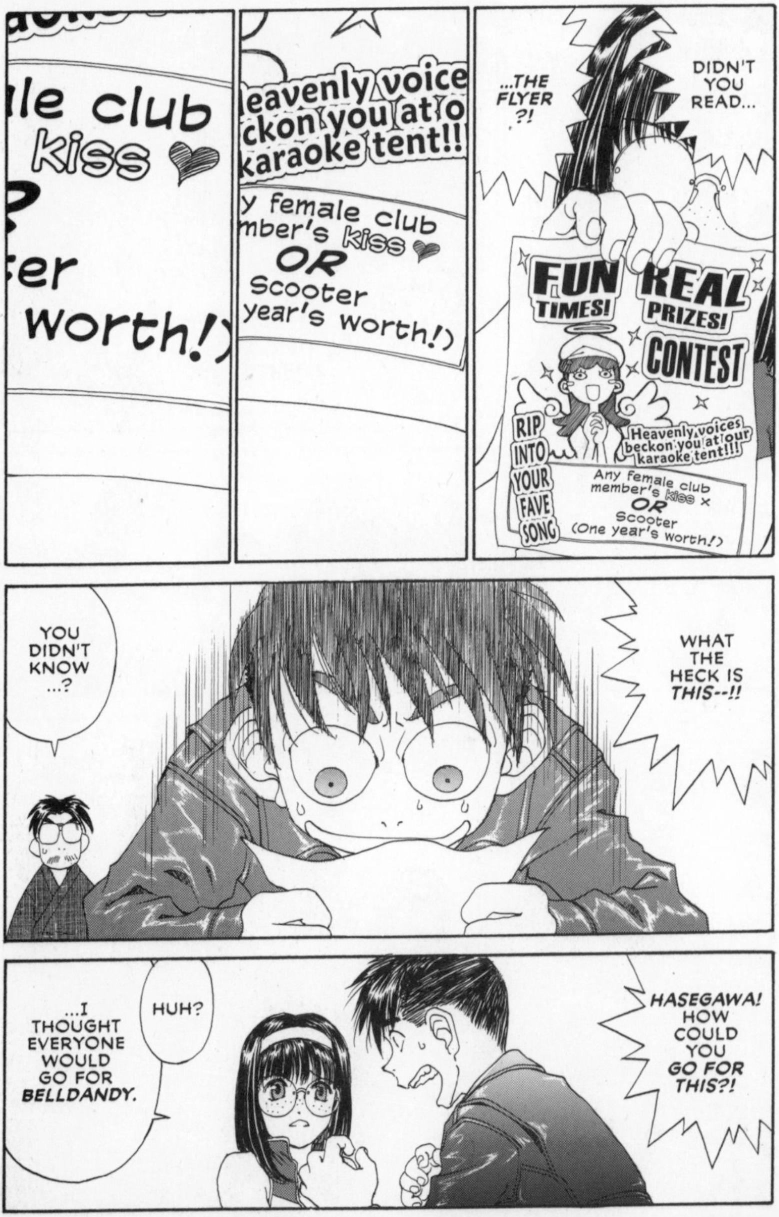

DIDN'T YOU READ...
...THE FLYER?!
FUN TIMES!
REAL PRIZES!
CONTEST
RIP INTO YOUR FAVE SONG
Heavenly voices beckon you at our karaoke tent!!!
Any female club member's kiss ×
OR
Scooter (One year's worth!)
leavenly voice
ckon you at o
karaoke tent!!
y female club
mber's kiss
OR
Scooter
year's worth!)
ale club
kiss
?
ter
worth!)
WHAT THE HECK IS THIS--!!
YOU DIDN'T KNOW ...?
HASEGAWA! HOW COULD YOU GO FOR THIS?!
HUH?
...I THOUGHT EVERYONE WOULD GO FOR BELLDANDY.

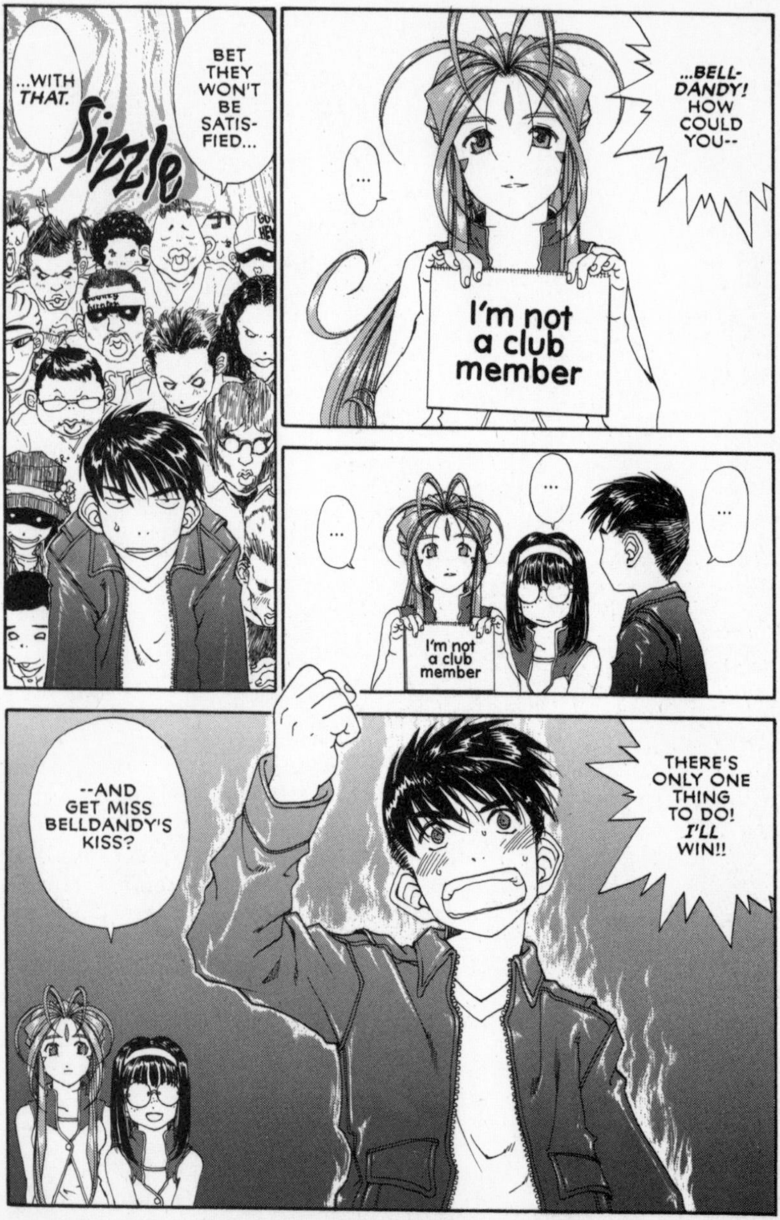
...BELL-DANDY! HOW COULD YOU--
...
I'm not a club member
...
...
...
I'm not a club member
BET THEY WON'T BE SATIS-FIED...
...WITH THAT.
Sizzle
THERE'S ONLY ONE THING TO DO! I'LL WIN!!
--AND GET MISS BELLDANDY'S KISS?

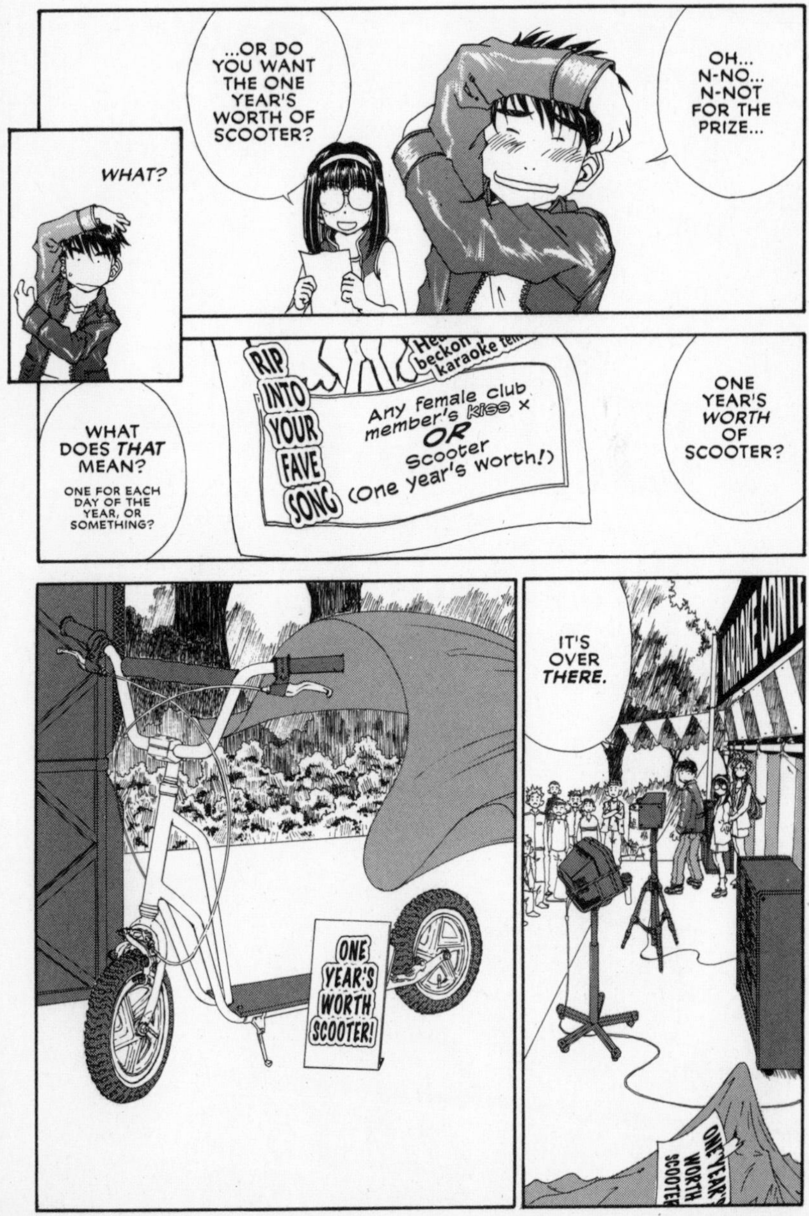
OH... N-NO... N-NOT FOR THE PRIZE...
...OR DO YOU WANT THE ONE YEAR'S WORTH OF SCOOTER?
WHAT?
ONE YEAR'S WORTH OF SCOOTER?
RIP INTO YOUR FAVE SONG
Any female club member's kiss × OR Scooter (One year's worth!)
WHAT DOES THAT MEAN?
ONE FOR EACH DAY OF THE YEAR, OR SOMETHING?
IT'S OVER THERE.
ONE YEAR'S WORTH SCOOTER!

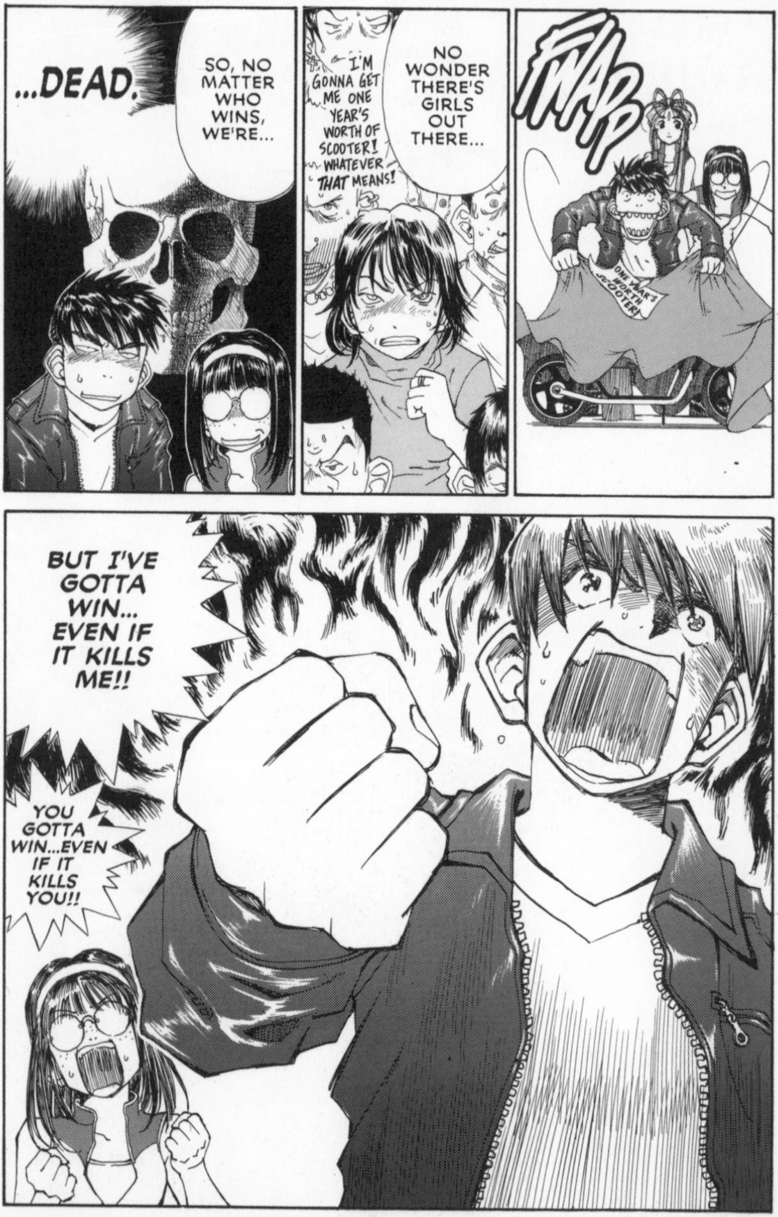
FWAP
ONE YEAR'S WORTH SCOOTER!
NO WONDER THERE'S GIRLS OUT THERE...
I'M GONNA GET ME ONE YEAR'S WORTH OF SCOOTER! WHATEVER THAT MEANS!
SO, NO MATTER WHO WINS, WE'RE...
...DEAD.
BUT I'VE GOTTA WIN... EVEN IF IT KILLS ME!!
YOU GOTTA WIN...EVEN IF IT KILLS YOU!!

CHAPTER 179

What Can I Do For You

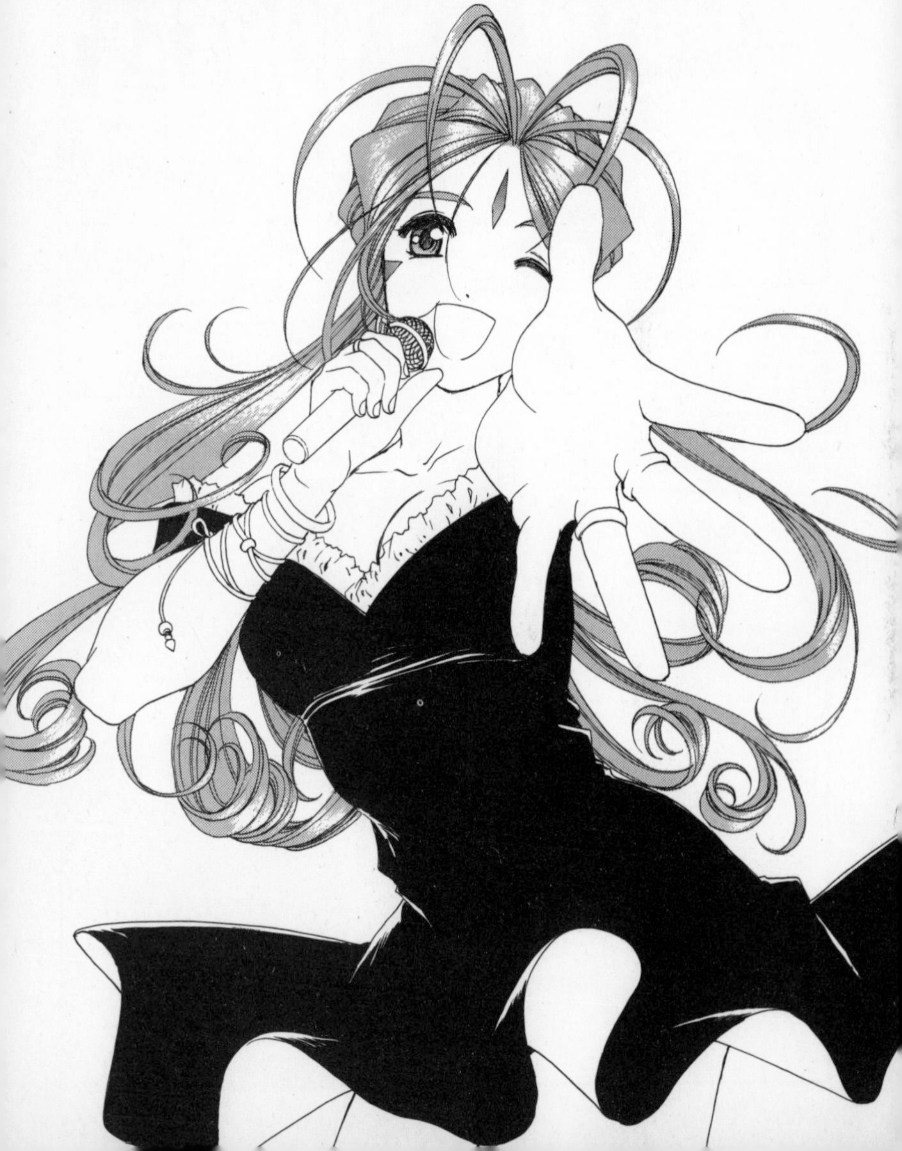

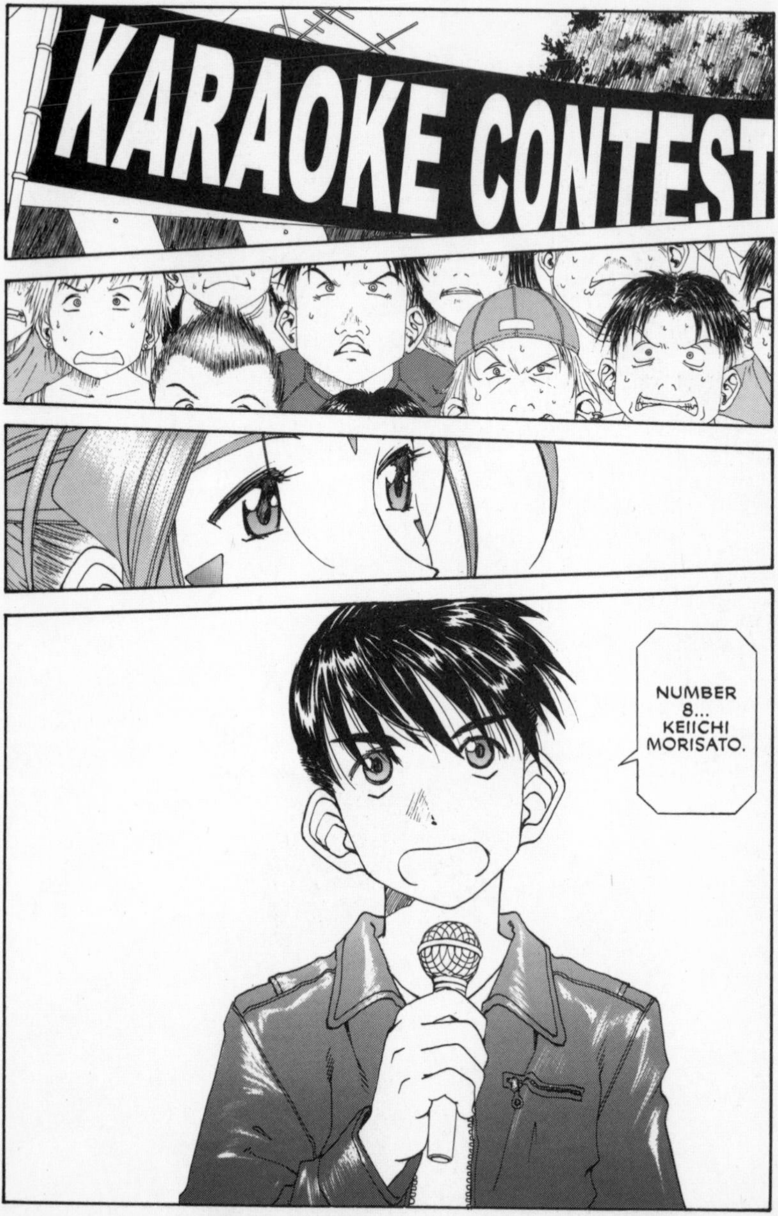
KARAOKE CONTEST
NUMBER 8... KEIICHI MORISATO.

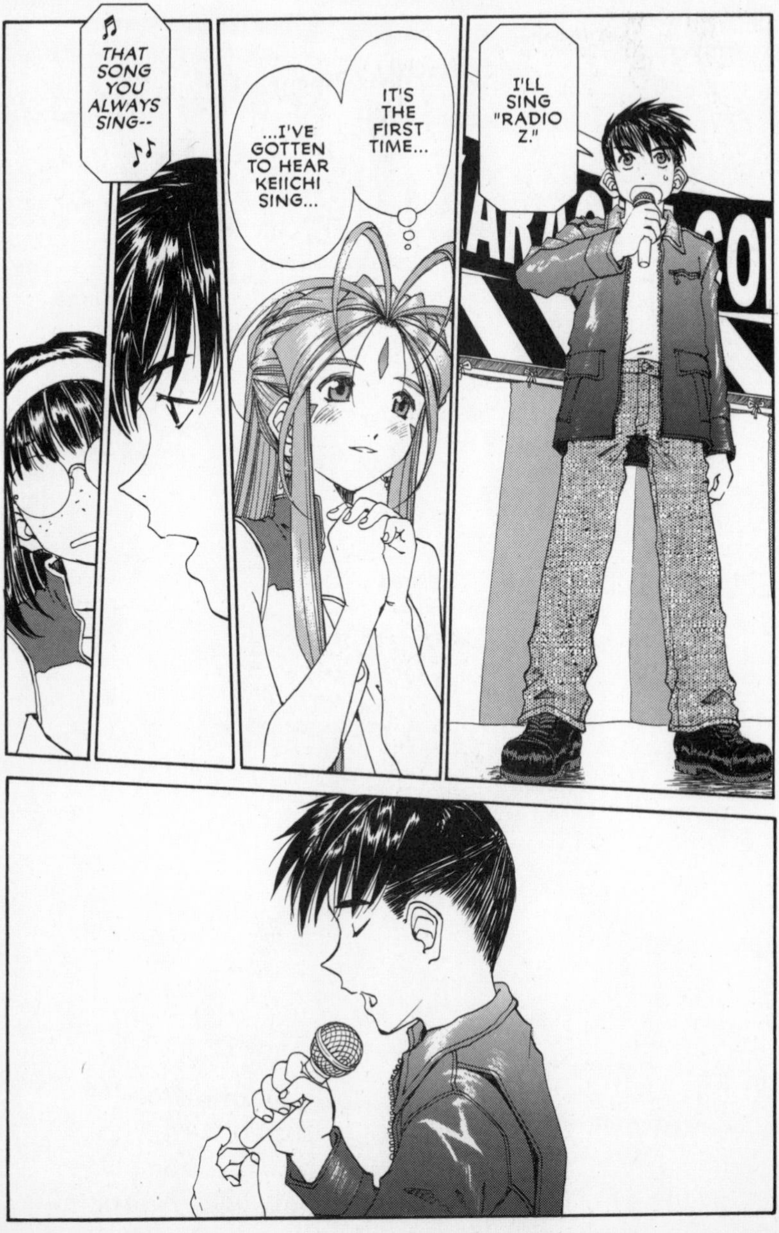
I'LL SING "RADIO Z."
IT'S THE FIRST TIME...
...I'VE GOTTEN TO HEAR KEIICHI SING...
♪ THAT SONG YOU ALWAYS SING-- ♪♪

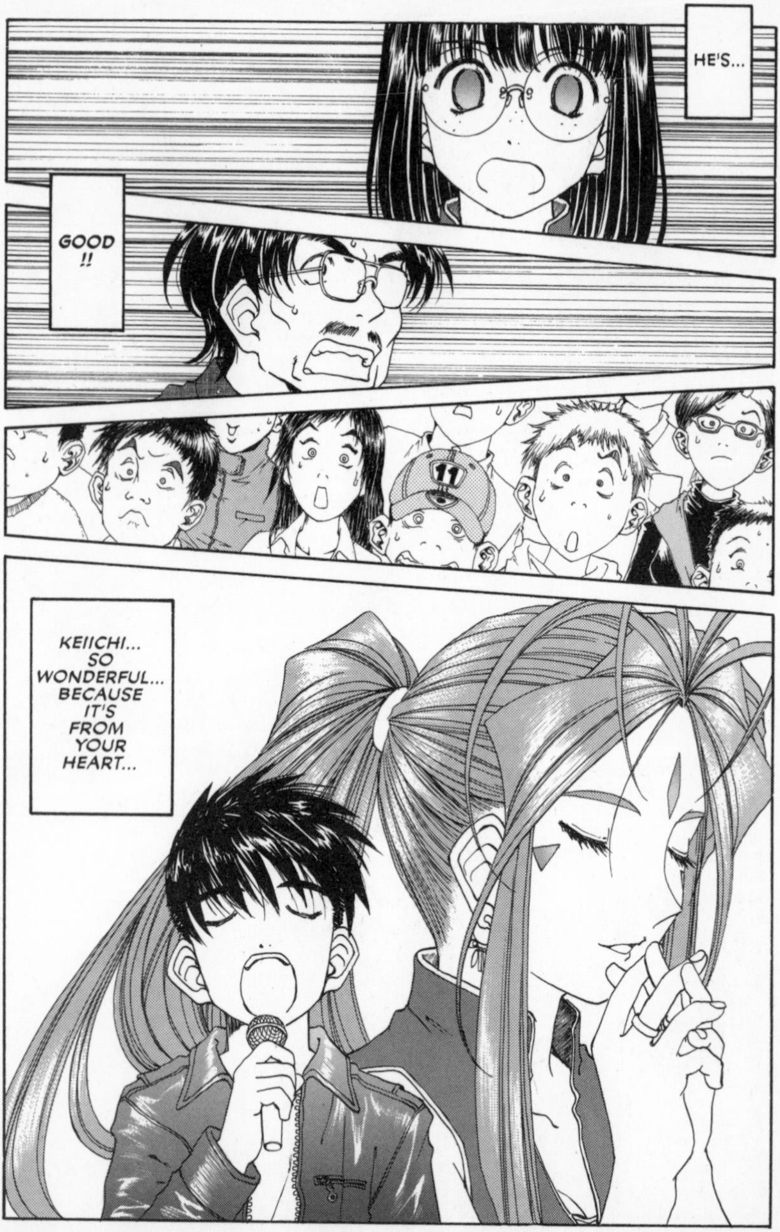
HE'S...
GOOD !!
KEIICHI... SO WONDERFUL... BECAUSE IT'S FROM YOUR HEART...

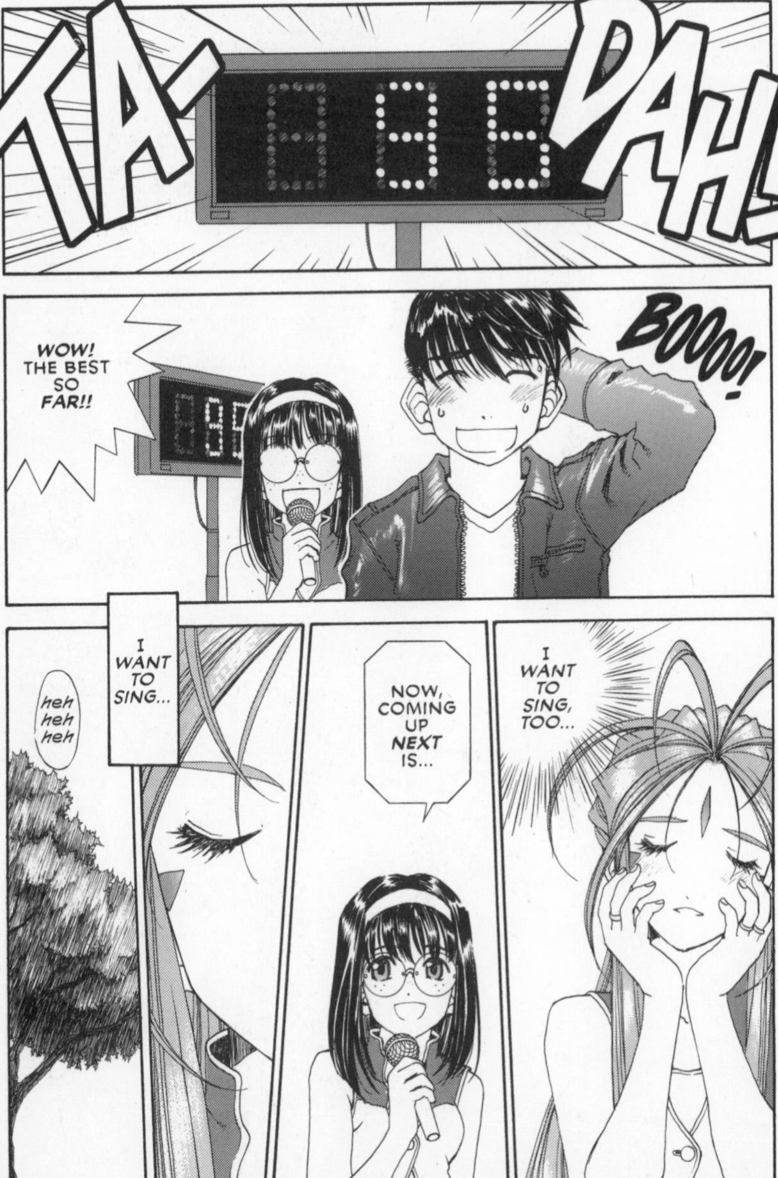
TA-DAH!
BOOOOO!
WOW! THE BEST SO FAR!!
I WANT TO SING, TOO...
NOW, COMING UP NEXT IS...
I WANT TO SING...
heh heh heh

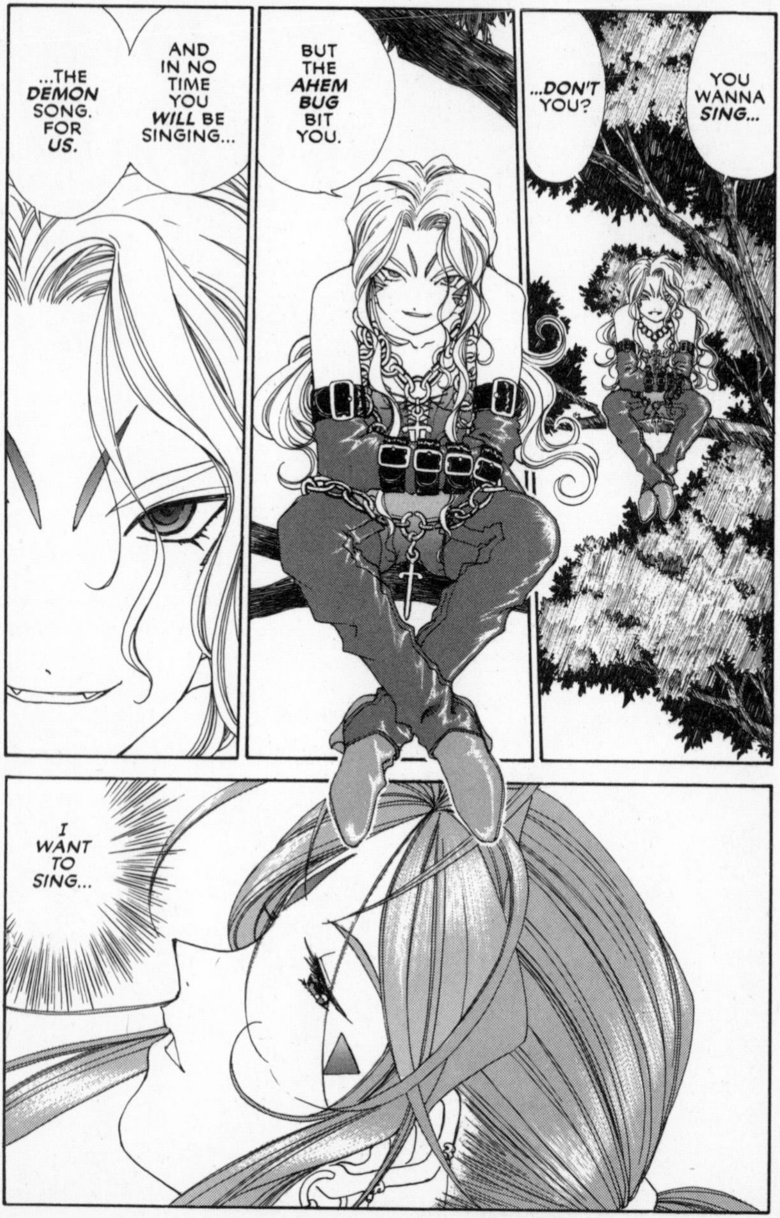
YOU WANNA *SING*...
...*DON'T* YOU?
BUT THE *AHEM BUG* BIT YOU.
AND IN NO TIME YOU *WILL* BE SINGING...
...THE *DEMON* SONG. FOR *US.*
I WANT TO SING...

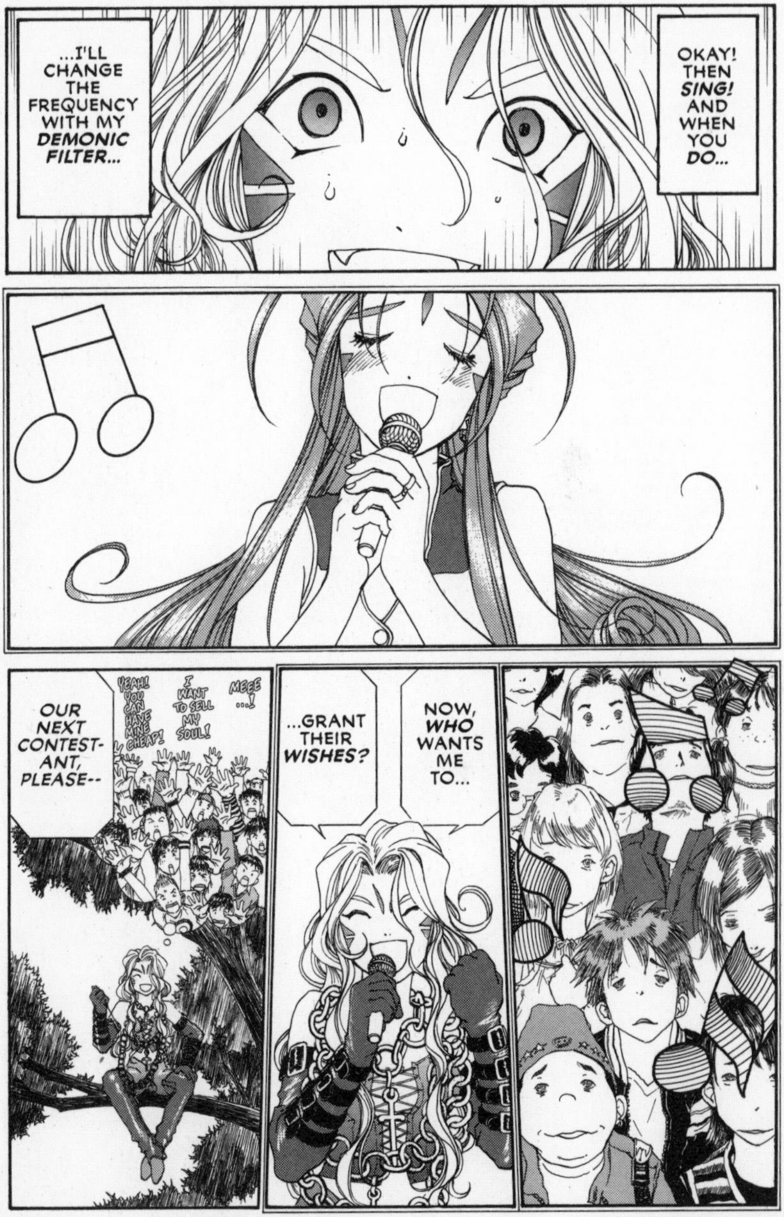
OKAY! THEN *SING!* AND WHEN YOU *DO...*
...I'LL CHANGE THE FREQUENCY WITH MY *DEMONIC FILTER...*
NOW, *WHO* WANTS ME TO...
...GRANT THEIR *WISHES?*
MEEE ...!
I WANT TO SELL MY SOUL!
YEAH! YOU CAN HAVE MINE CHEAP!
OUR NEXT CONTEST-ANT, PLEASE--

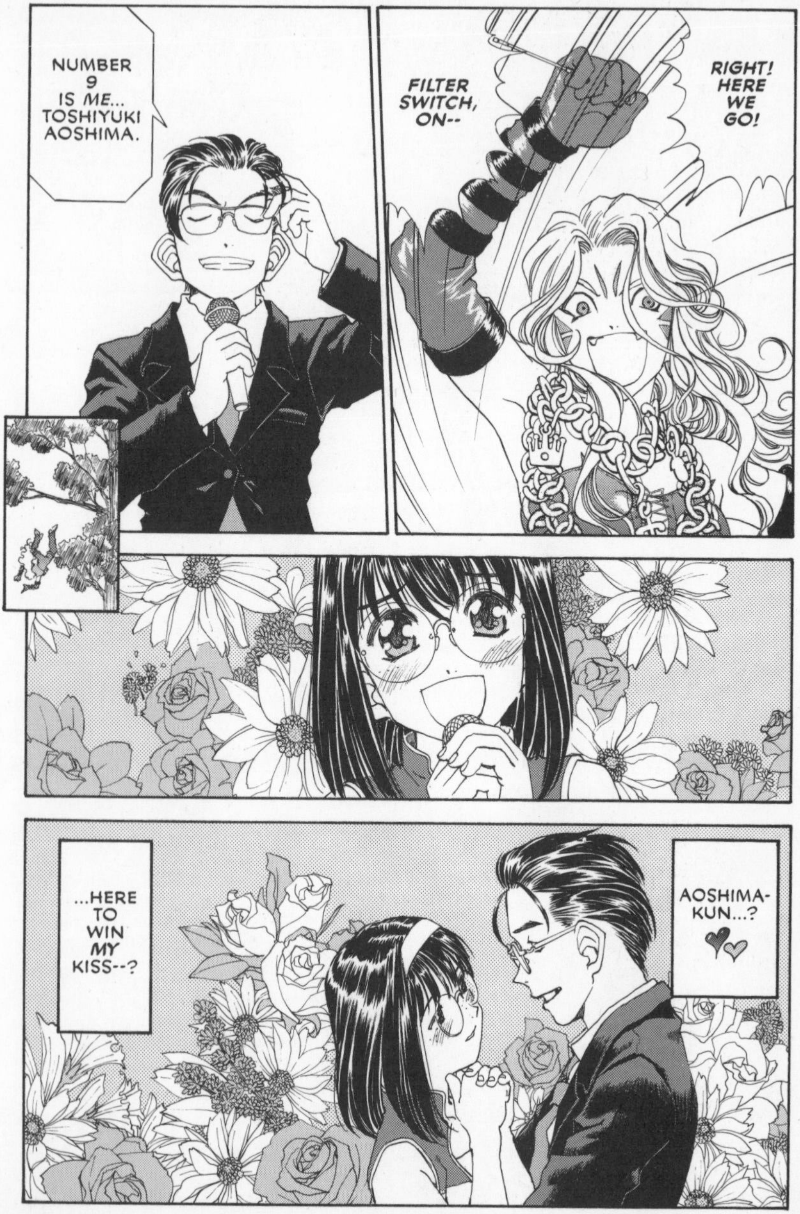
RIGHT! HERE WE GO!
FILTER SWITCH, ON--
NUMBER 9 IS *ME*... TOSHIYUKI AOSHIMA.
AOSHIMA-KUN...? ♥♥
...HERE TO WIN *MY* KISS--?

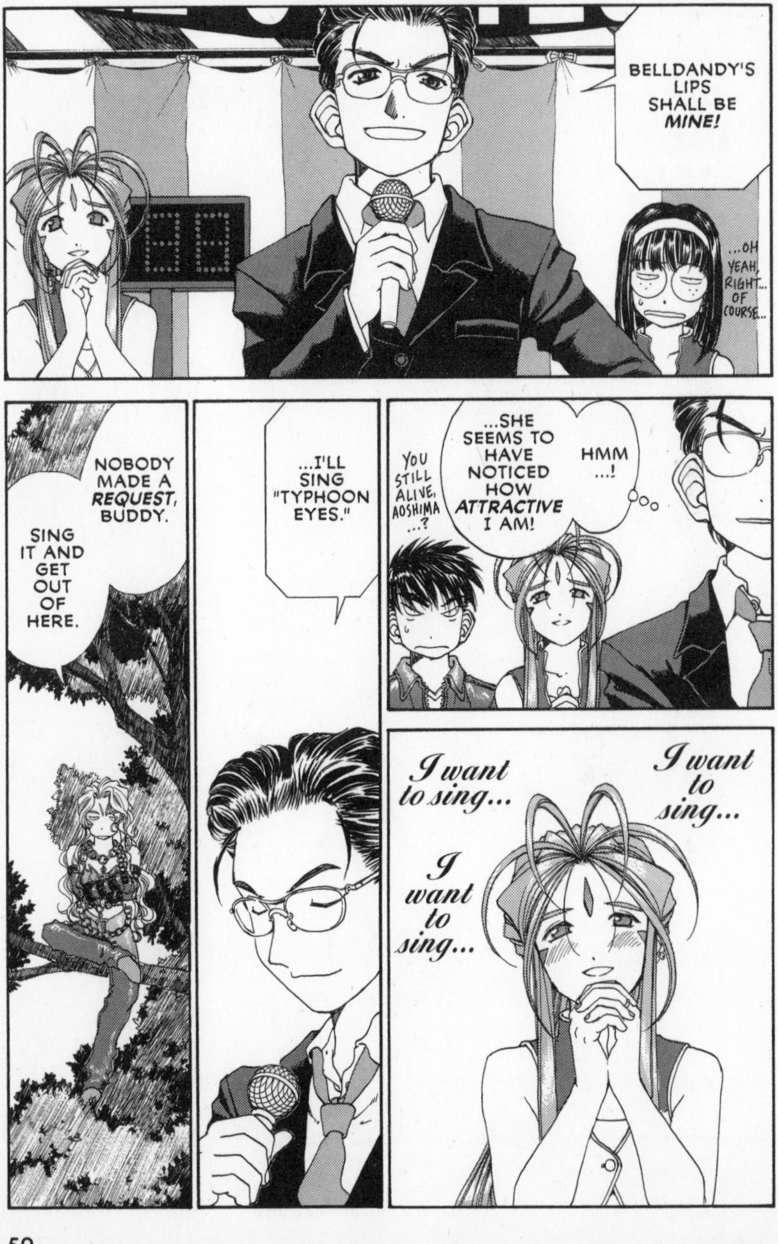
BELLDANDY'S LIPS SHALL BE *MINE!*
...OH YEAH, RIGHT... OF COURSE...
HMM ...!
...SHE SEEMS TO HAVE NOTICED HOW *ATTRACTIVE* I AM!
YOU STILL ALIVE, AOSHIMA ...?
I want to sing...
I want to sing...
I want to sing...
...I'LL SING "TYPHOON EYES."
NOBODY MADE A *REQUEST*, BUDDY.
SING IT AND GET OUT OF HERE.

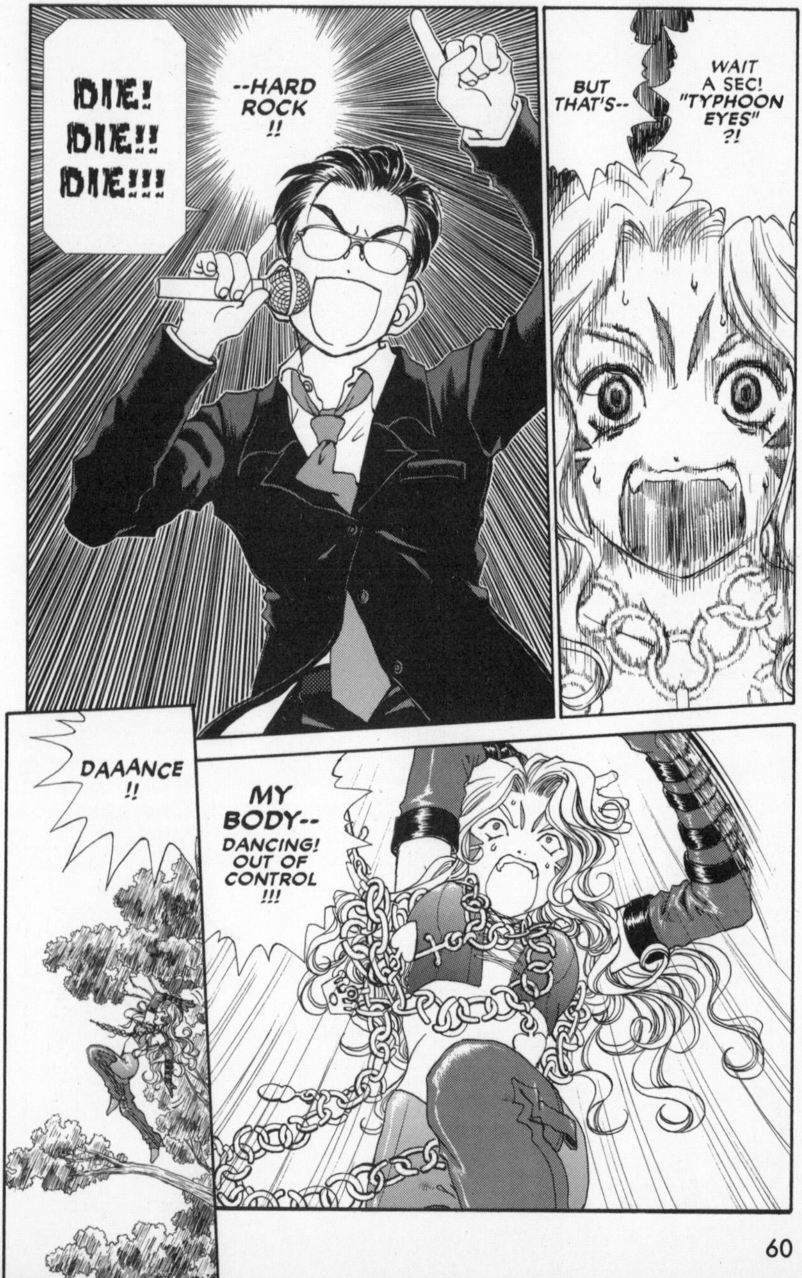
WAIT A SEC! "TYPHOON EYES" ?!
BUT THAT'S--
--HARD ROCK !!
DIE! DIE!! DIE!!!
MY BODY--
DANCING! OUT OF CONTROL !!!
DAAANCE !!

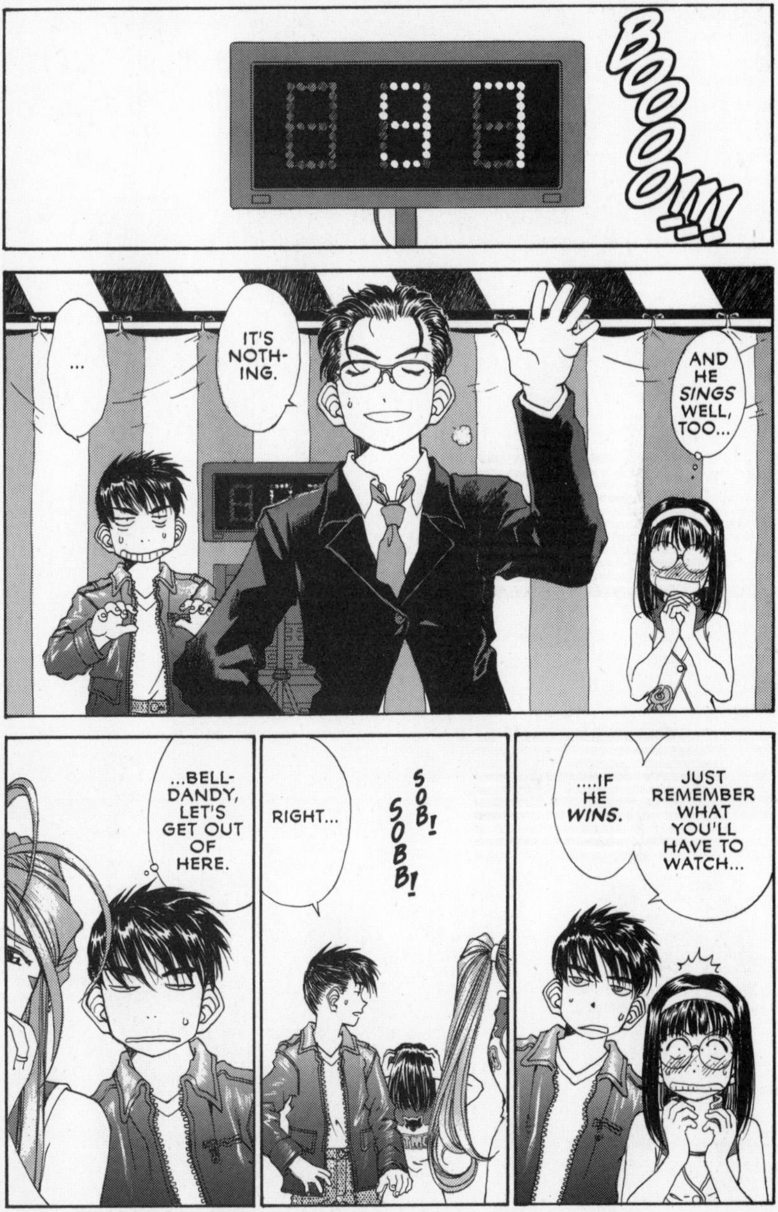
BOOOO!!!
AND HE SINGS WELL, TOO...
IT'S NOTHING.
...
JUST REMEMBER WHAT YOU'LL HAVE TO WATCH...
....IF HE WINS.
SOB! SOBB!
RIGHT...
...BELLDANDY, LET'S GET OUT OF HERE.

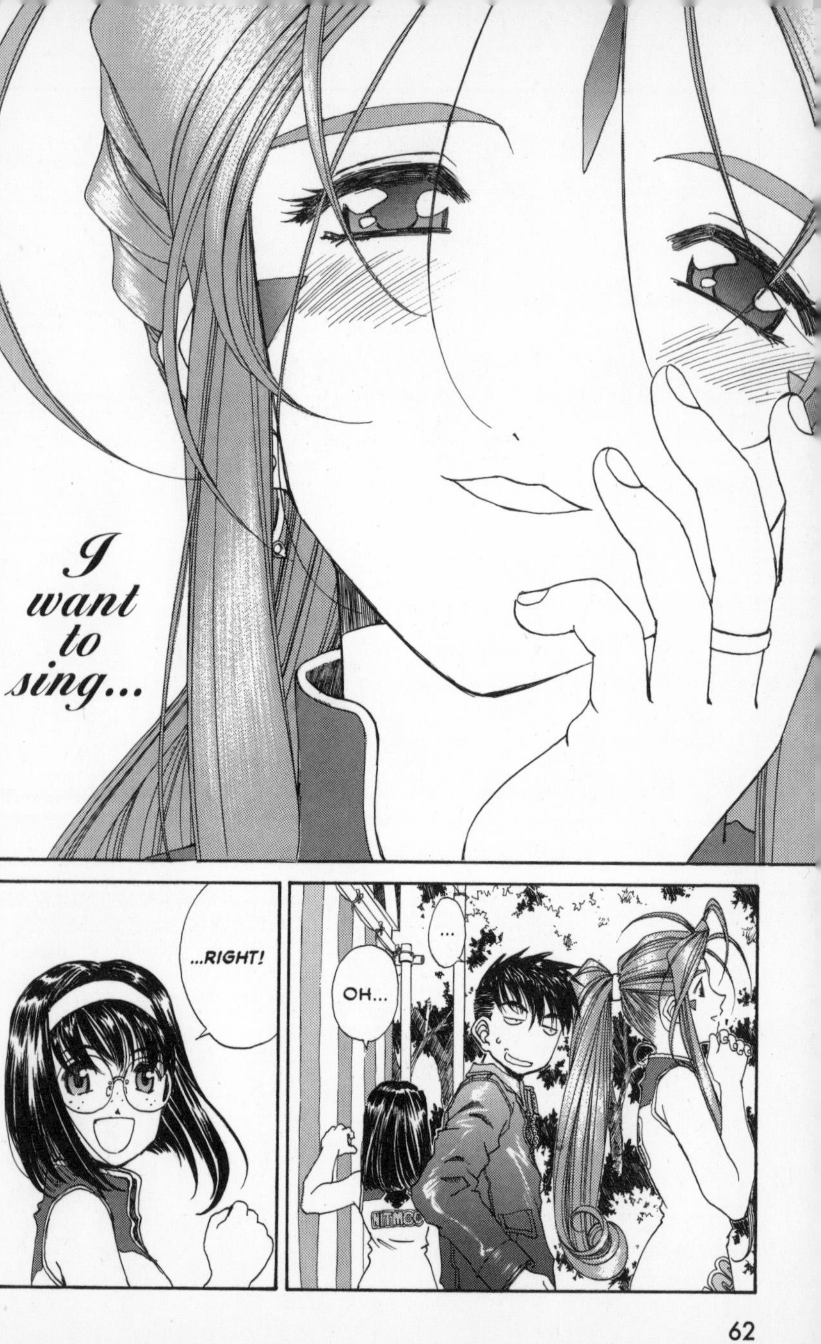
I want to sing...
...
OH...
...RIGHT!

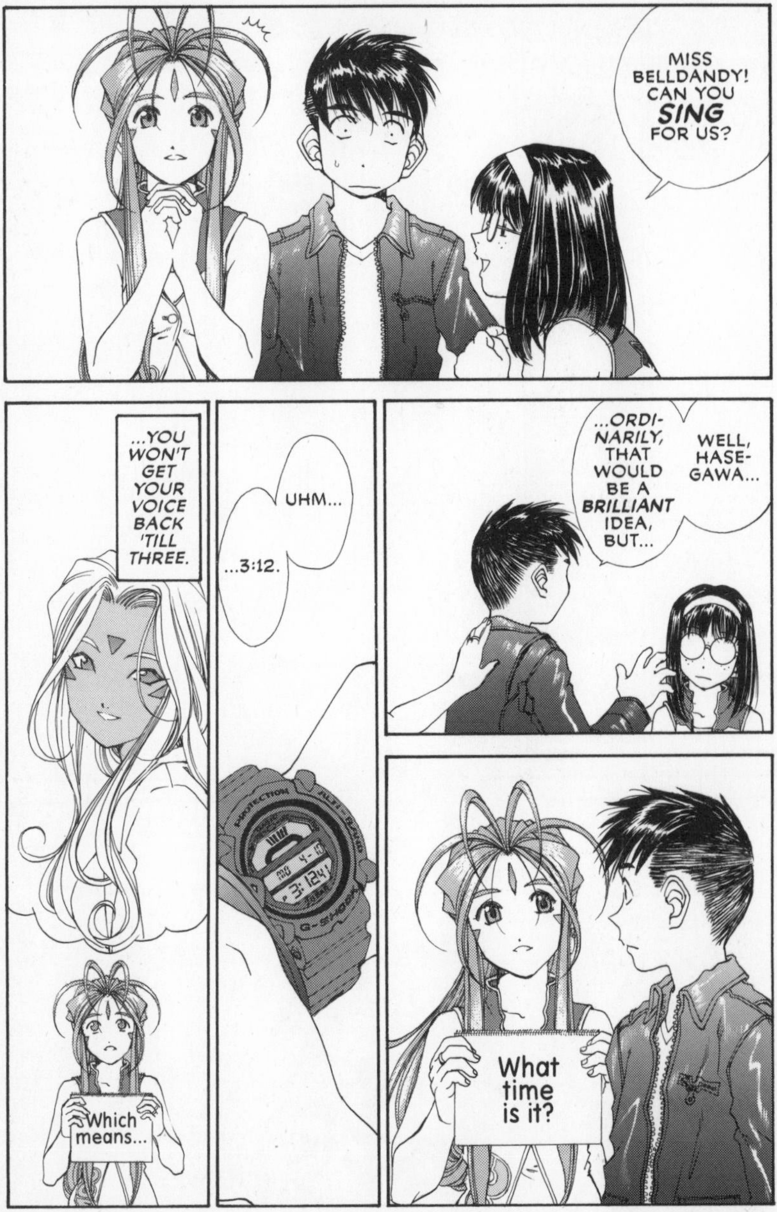
MISS BELLDANDY! CAN YOU *SING* FOR US?
WELL, HASE-GAWA...
...*ORDINARILY*, THAT WOULD BE A *BRILLIANT* IDEA, BUT...
What time is it?
UHM...
...3:12.
...*YOU WON'T GET YOUR VOICE BACK 'TILL THREE.*
Which means...

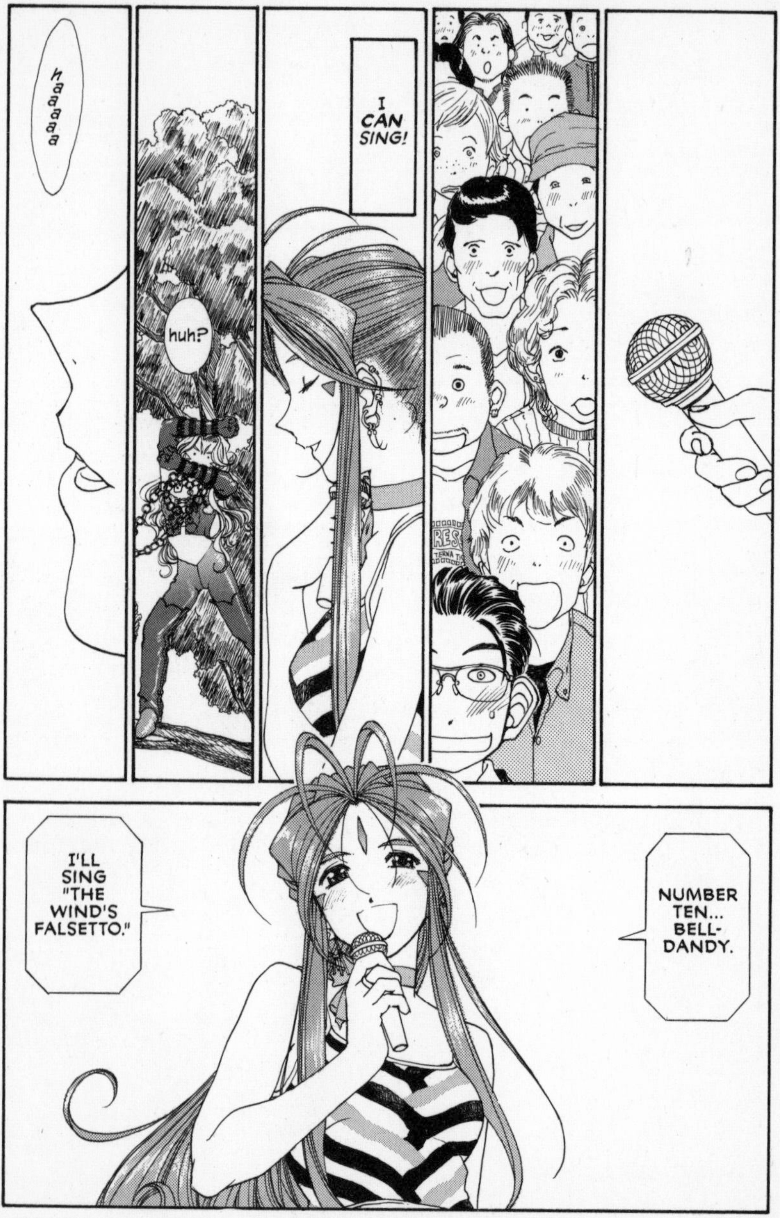
I CAN SING!
huh?
haaaaaa
NUMBER TEN... BELL-DANDY.
I'LL SING "THE WIND'S FALSETTO."

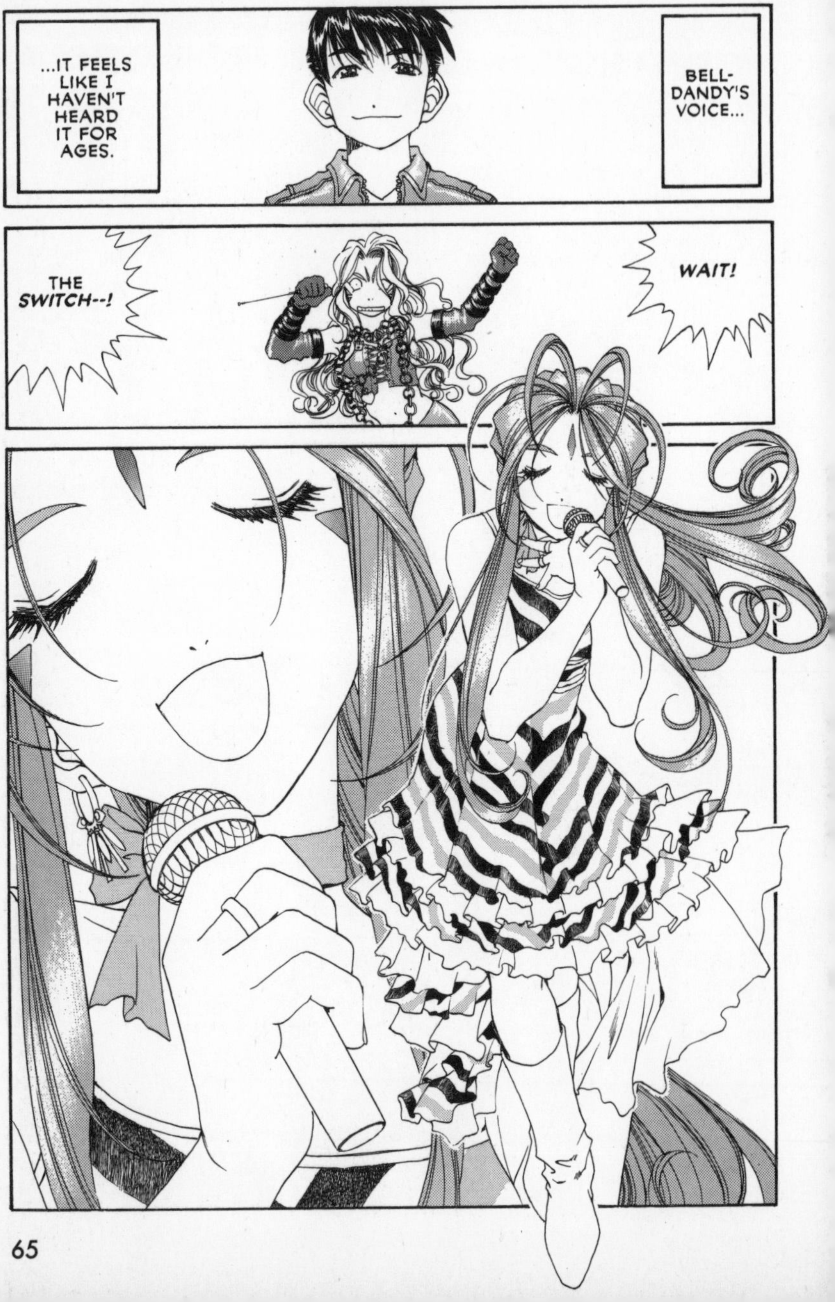
BELL-DANDY'S VOICE...
...IT FEELS LIKE I HAVEN'T HEARD IT FOR AGES.
WAIT!
THE SWITCH--!

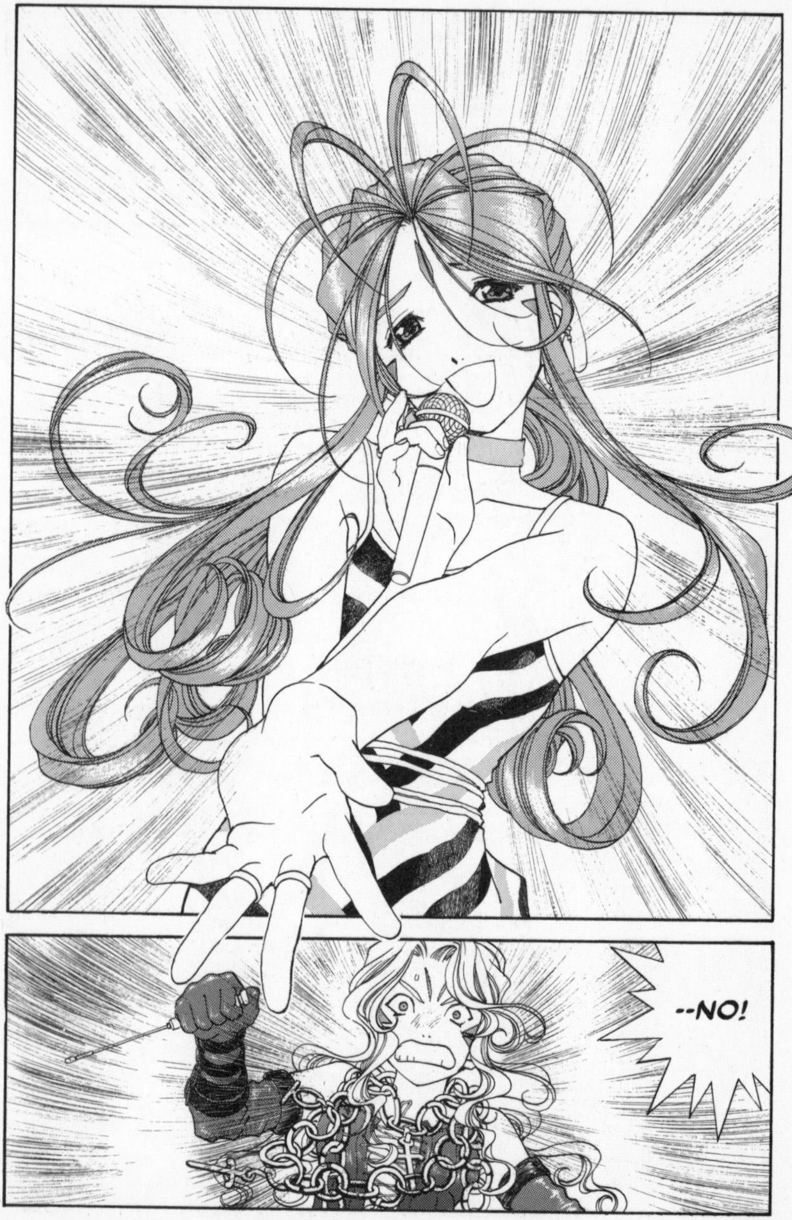
--NO!

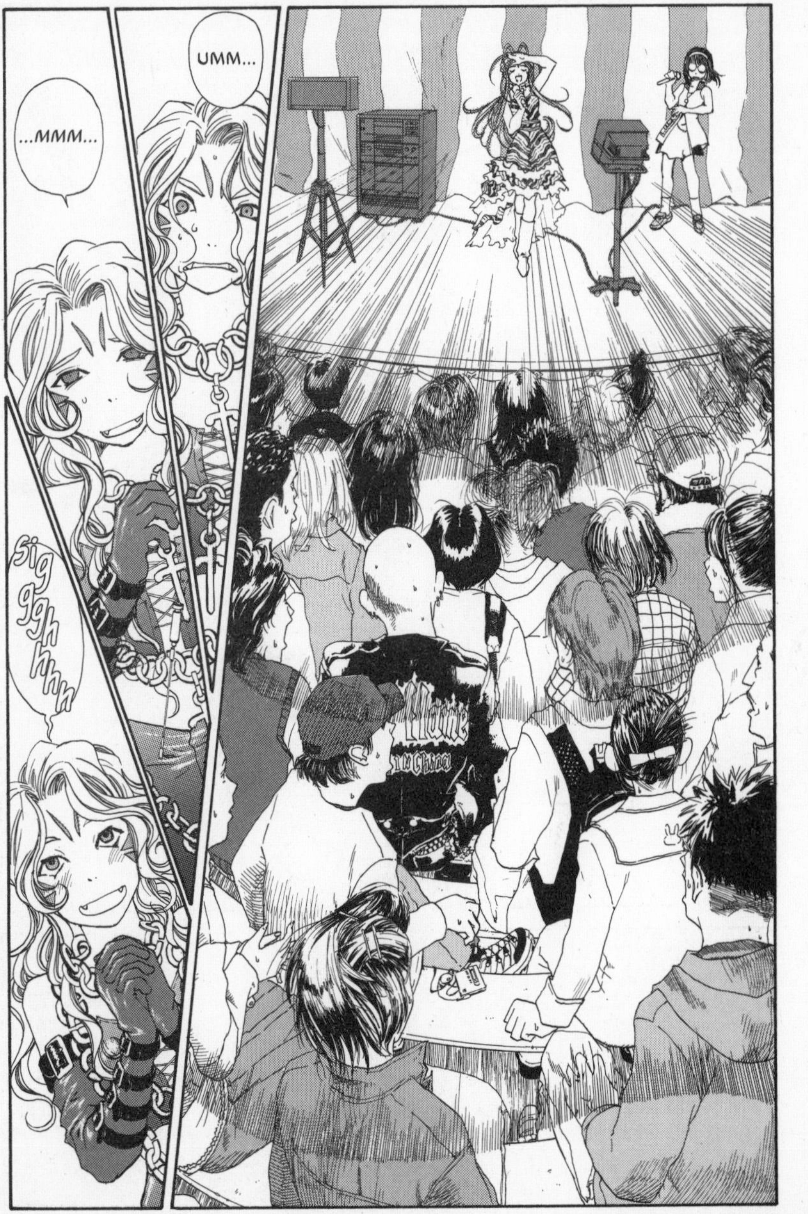
UMM...
...MMM...
siggghhhh

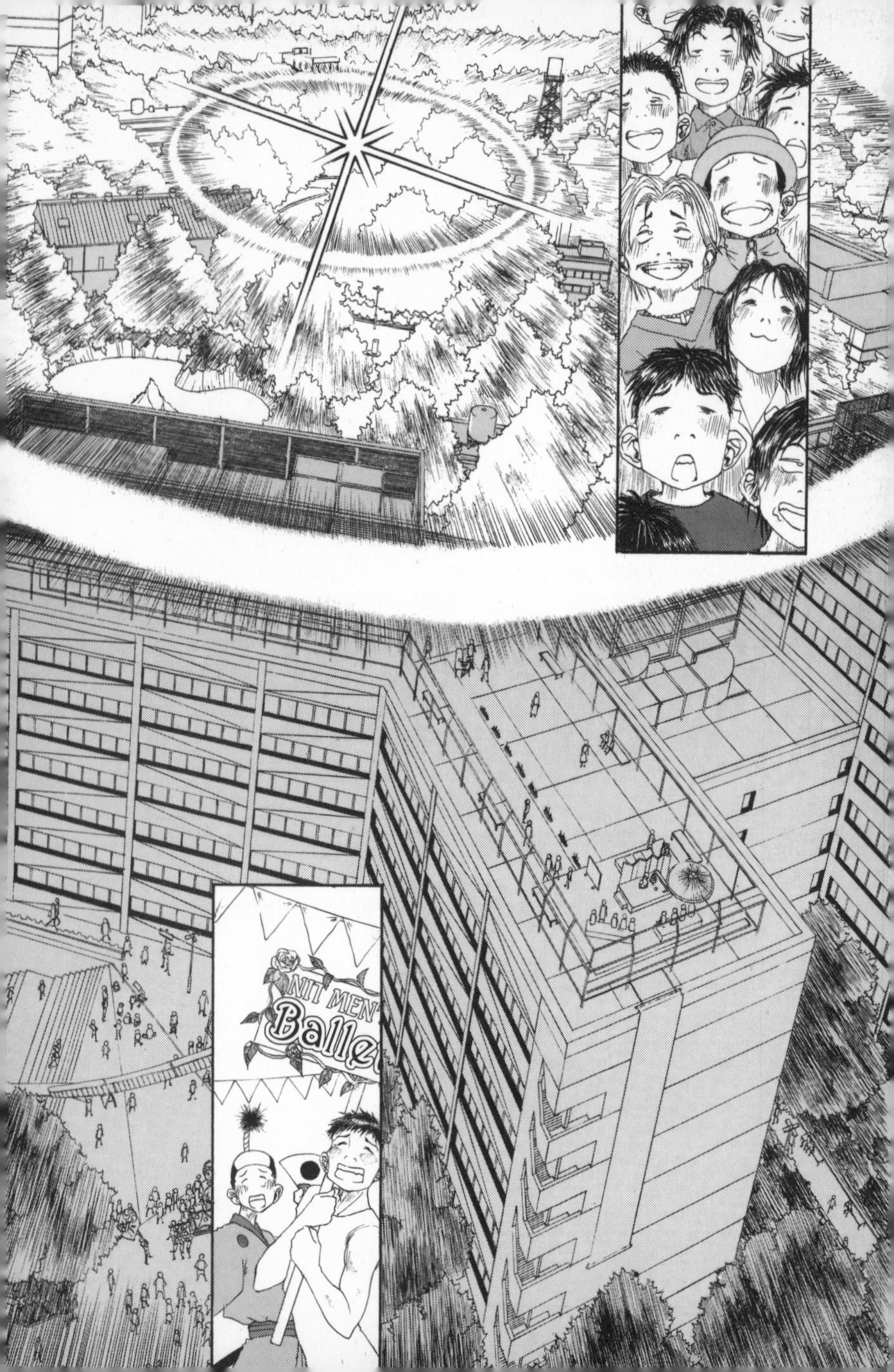
NIT MEN'
Balle

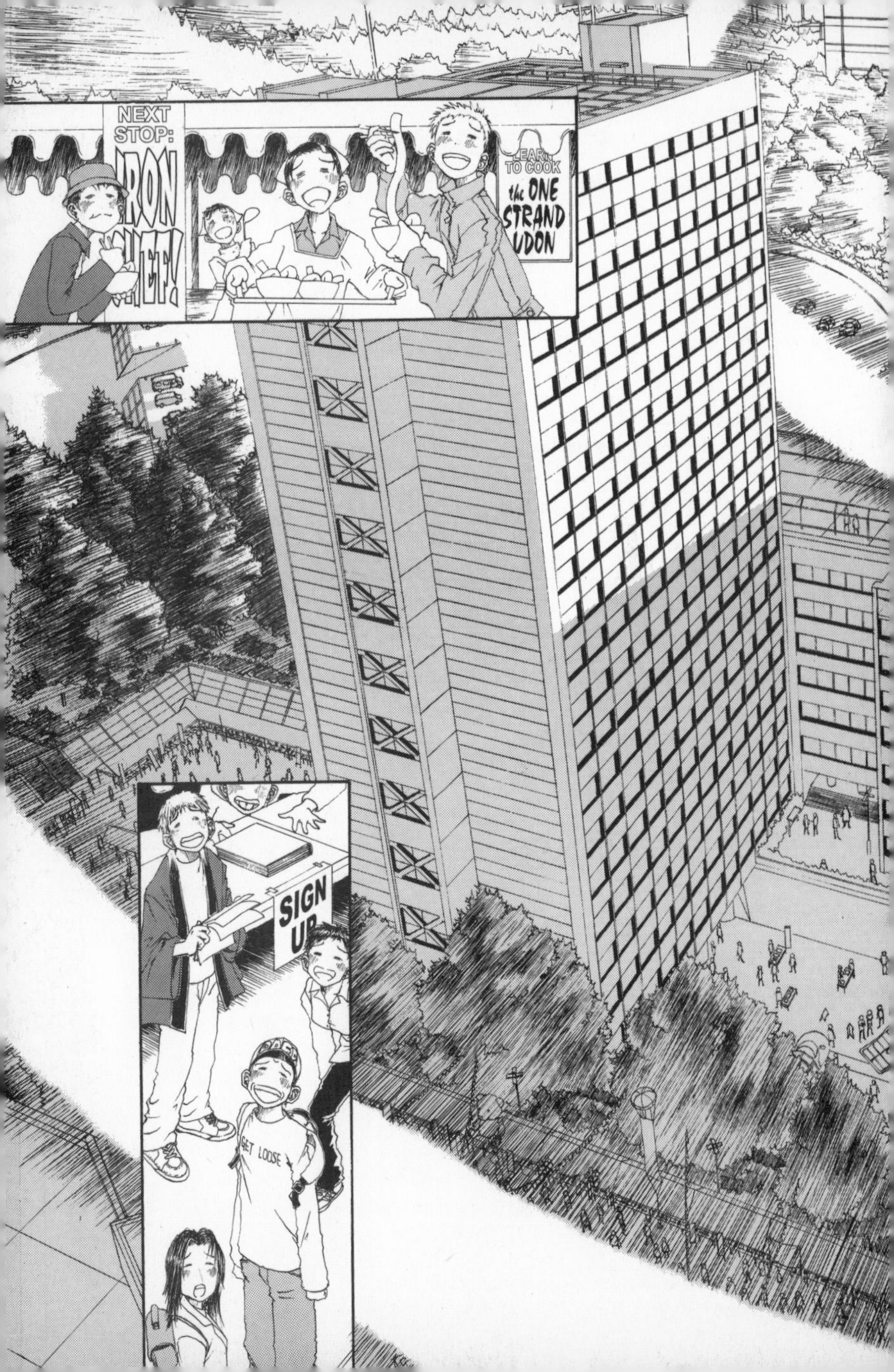
LEARN TO COOK the ONE STRAND UDON
NEXT STOP: IRON CHEF!
SIGN UP
GET LOOSE

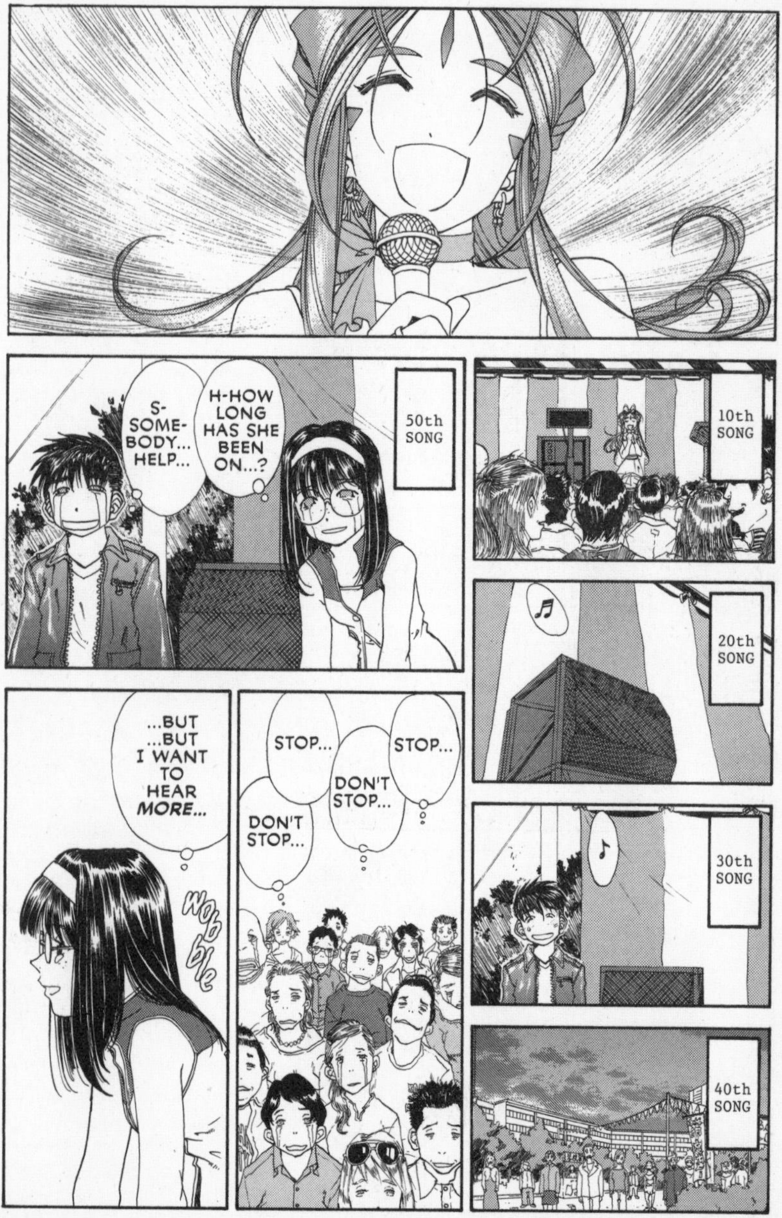
10th SONG
♪
20th SONG
♪
30th SONG
40th SONG
50th SONG
H-HOW LONG HAS SHE BEEN ON...?
S-SOME-BODY... HELP...
STOP...
DON'T STOP...
STOP...
DON'T STOP...
...BUT ...BUT I WANT TO HEAR *MORE...*
wobble

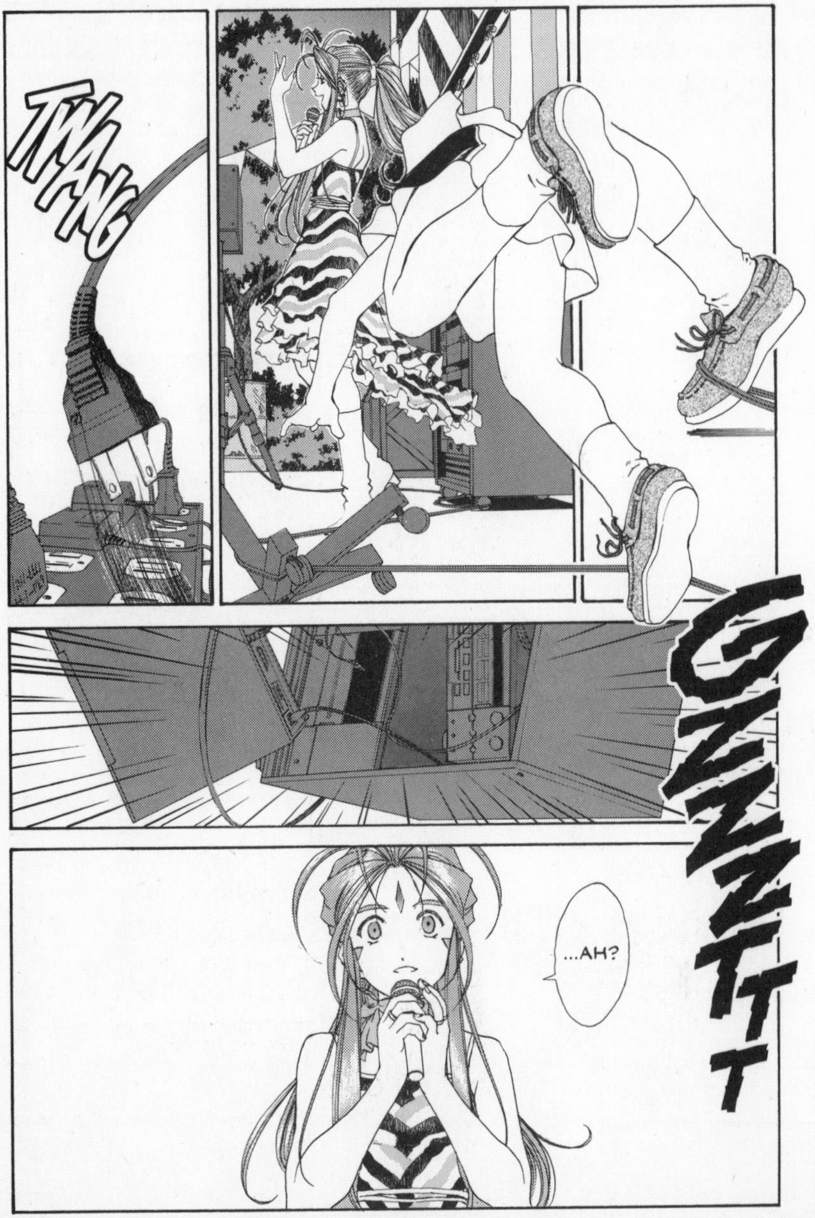

TWANG
GWANTTT
...AH?

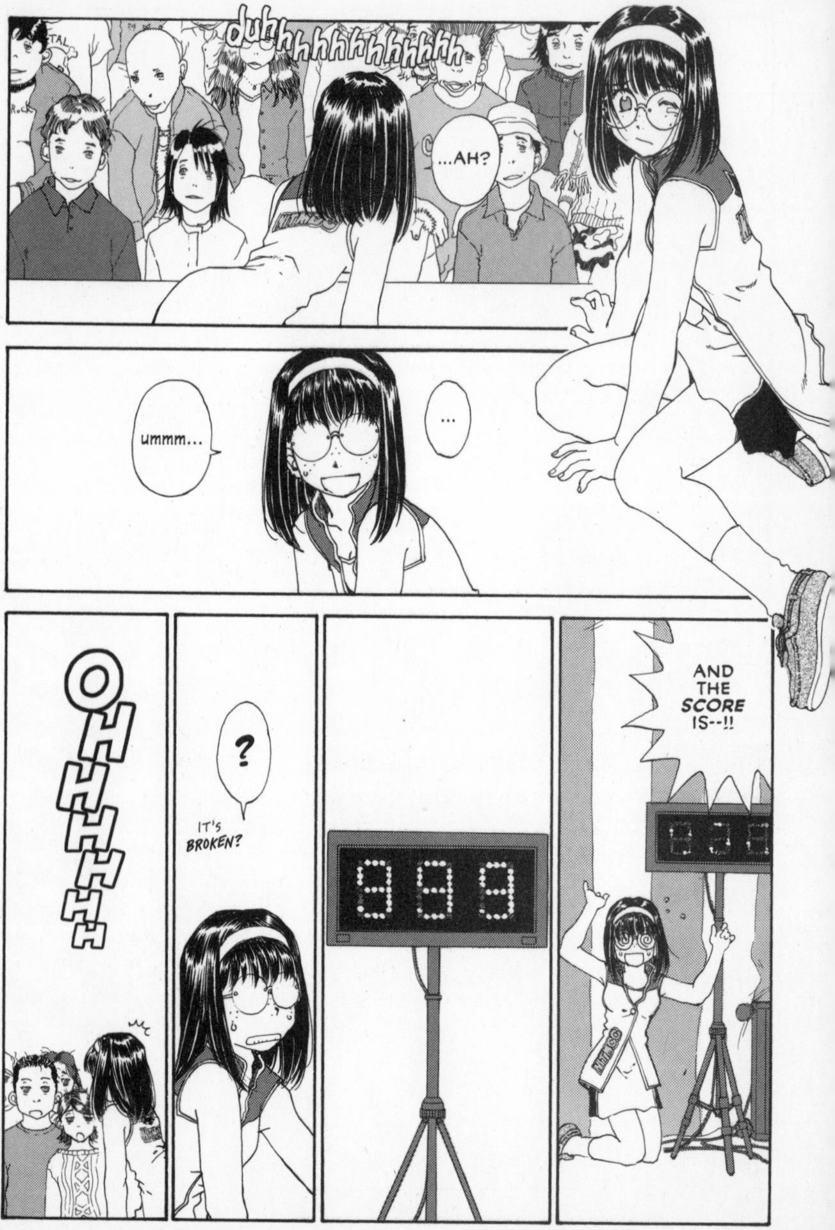

duhhhhhhhhhhhhh
...AH?
...
ummm...
AND THE SCORE IS--!!
999
?
IT'S BROKEN?
OHHHHHHHH

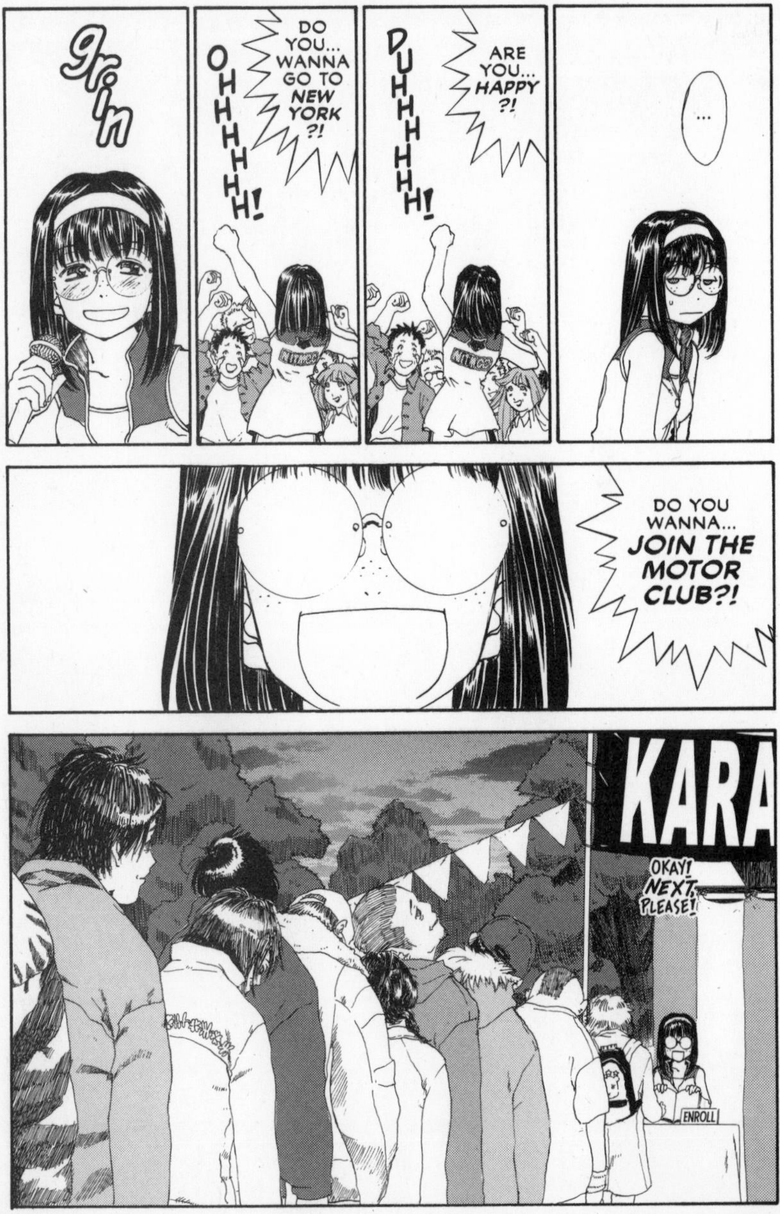
...
ARE YOU... HAPPY?!
DUHHHHHH!
DO YOU... WANNA GO TO NEW YORK?!
OHHHHHH!
grin
DO YOU WANNA... JOIN THE MOTOR CLUB?!
KARA
OKAY! NEXT, PLEASE!
ENROLL

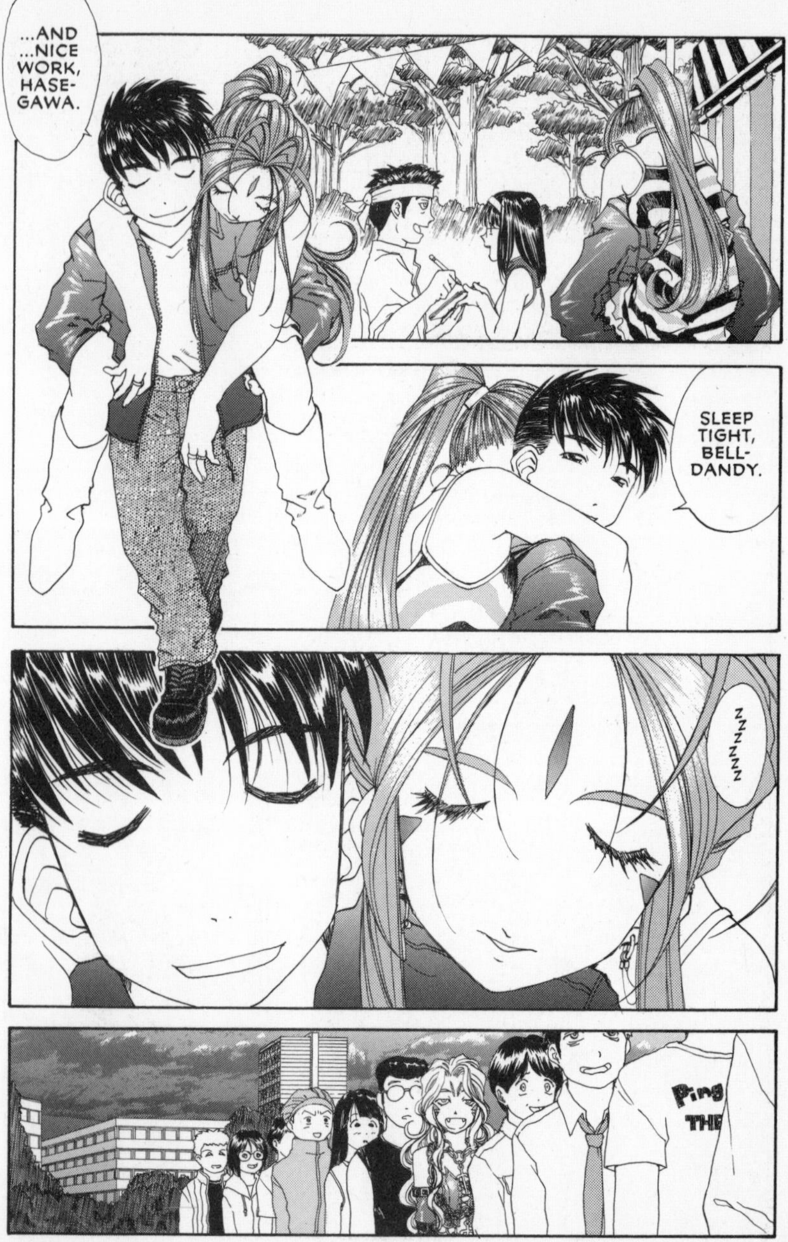
...AND ...NICE WORK, HASE-GAWA.
SLEEP TIGHT, BELL-DANDY.
ZZZZZ
Ping THE

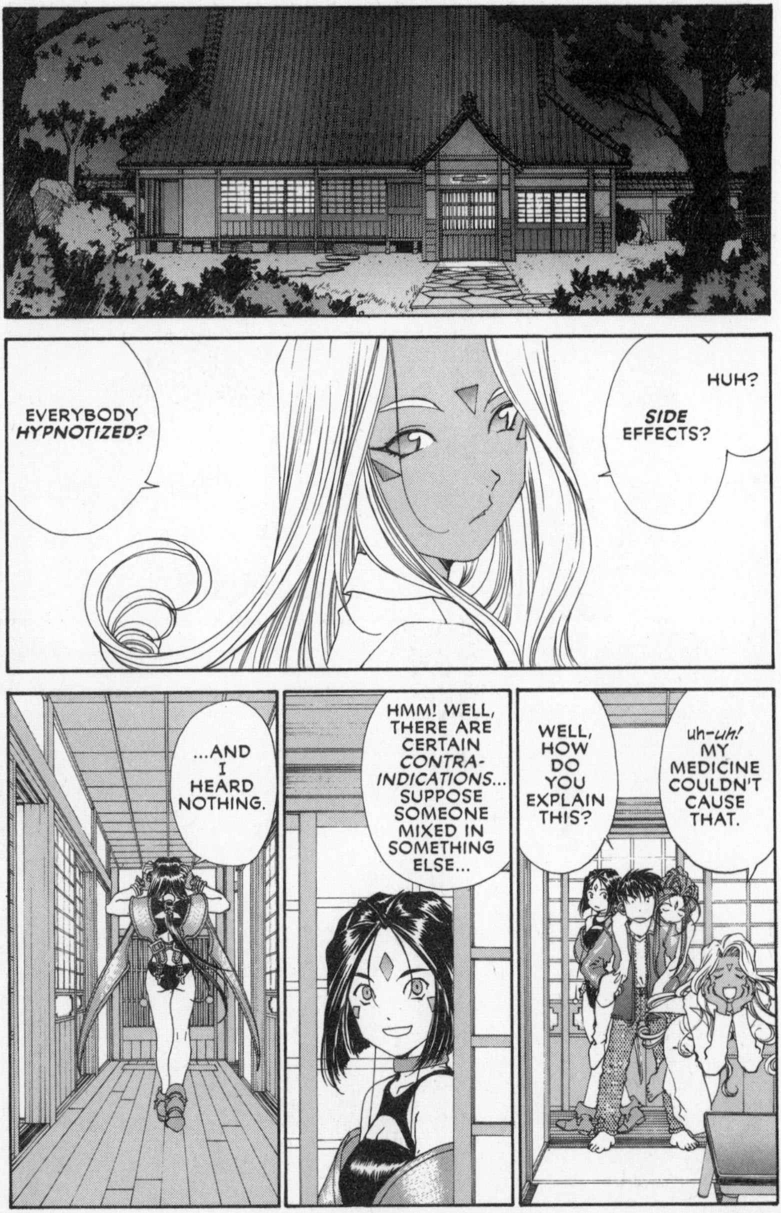
HUH? SIDE EFFECTS?
EVERYBODY HYPNOTIZED?
uh-uh! MY MEDICINE COULDN'T CAUSE THAT.
WELL, HOW DO YOU EXPLAIN THIS?
HMM! WELL, THERE ARE CERTAIN CONTRA-INDICATIONS... SUPPOSE SOMEONE MIXED IN SOMETHING ELSE...
...AND I HEARD NOTHING.

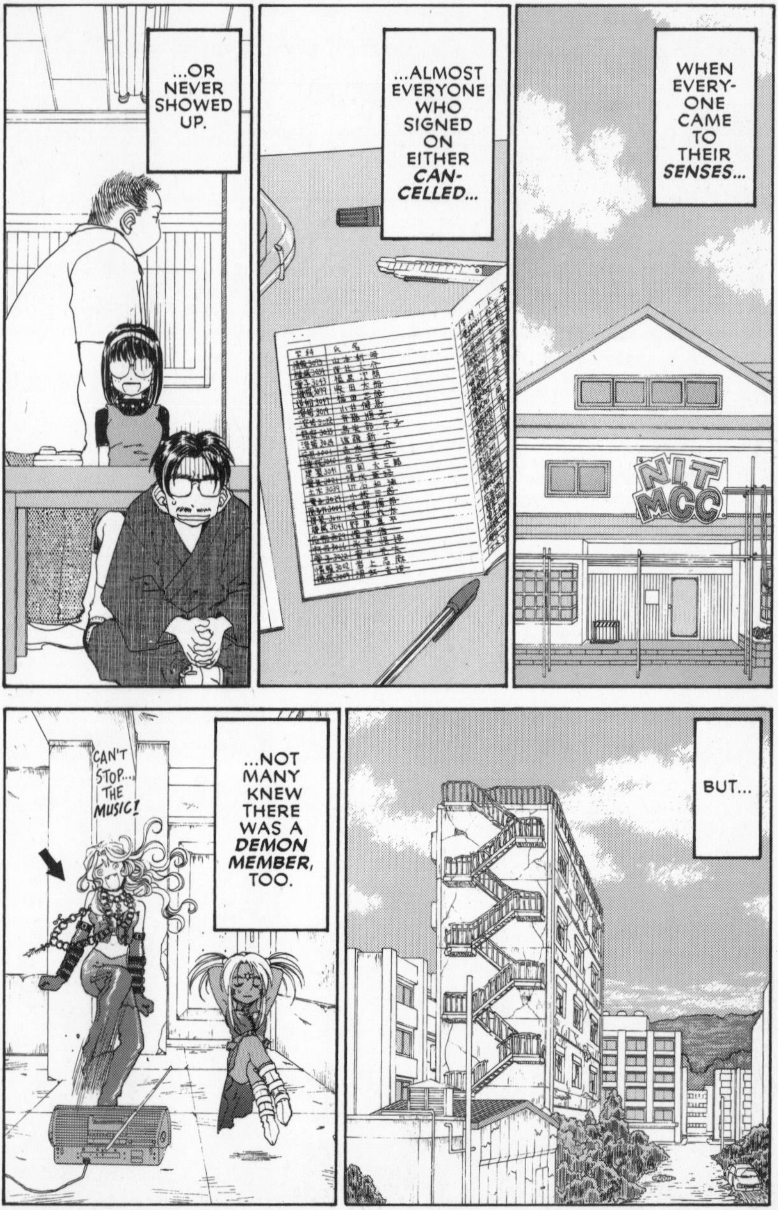
WHEN EVERY-ONE CAME TO THEIR SENSES...
NIT MCC
...ALMOST EVERYONE WHO SIGNED ON EITHER CAN-CELLED...
...OR NEVER SHOWED UP.
BUT...
...NOT MANY KNEW THERE WAS A DEMON MEMBER, TOO.
CAN'T STOP... THE MUSIC!

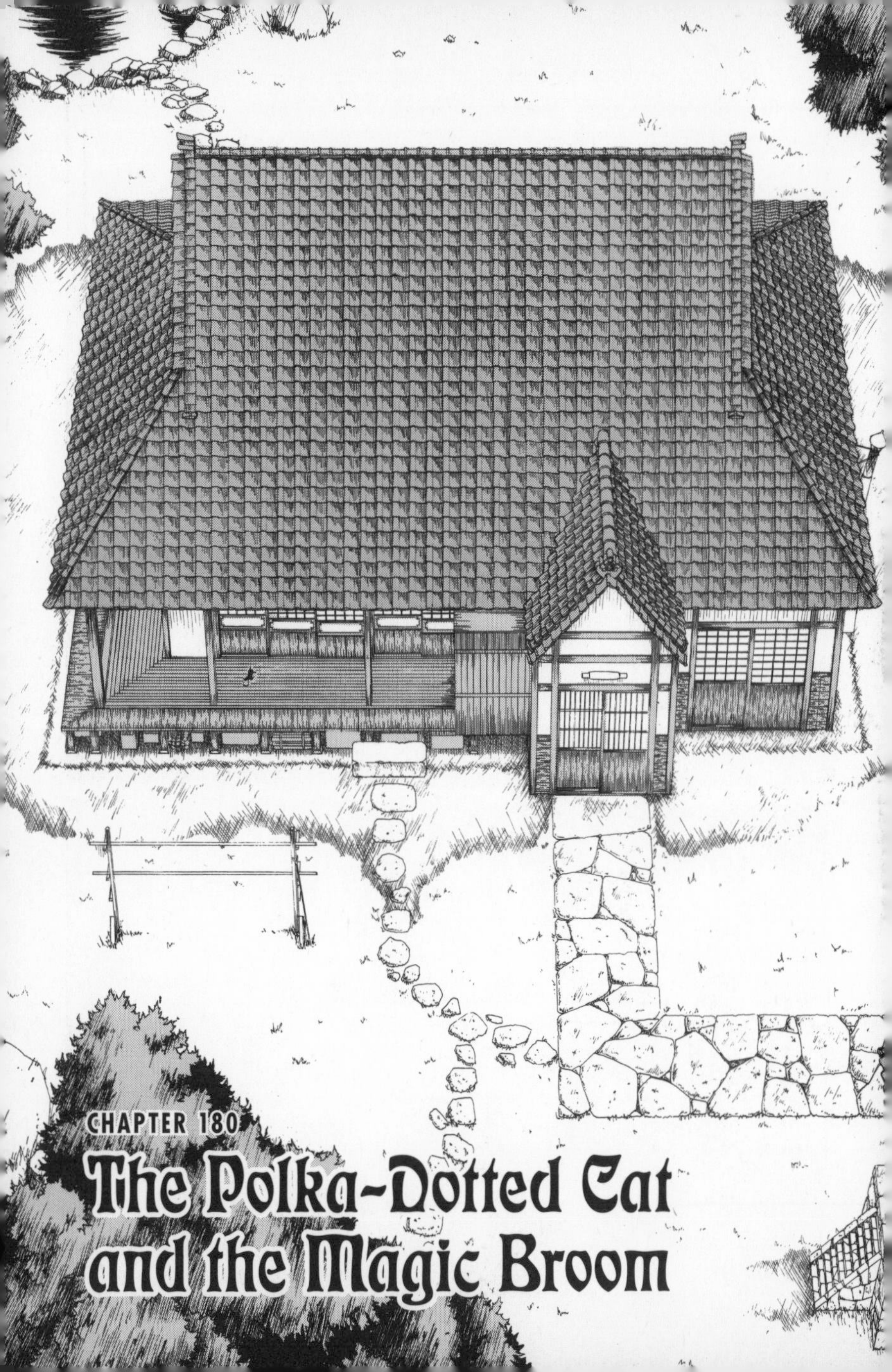

CHAPTER 180

The Polka-Dotted Cat and the Magic Broom

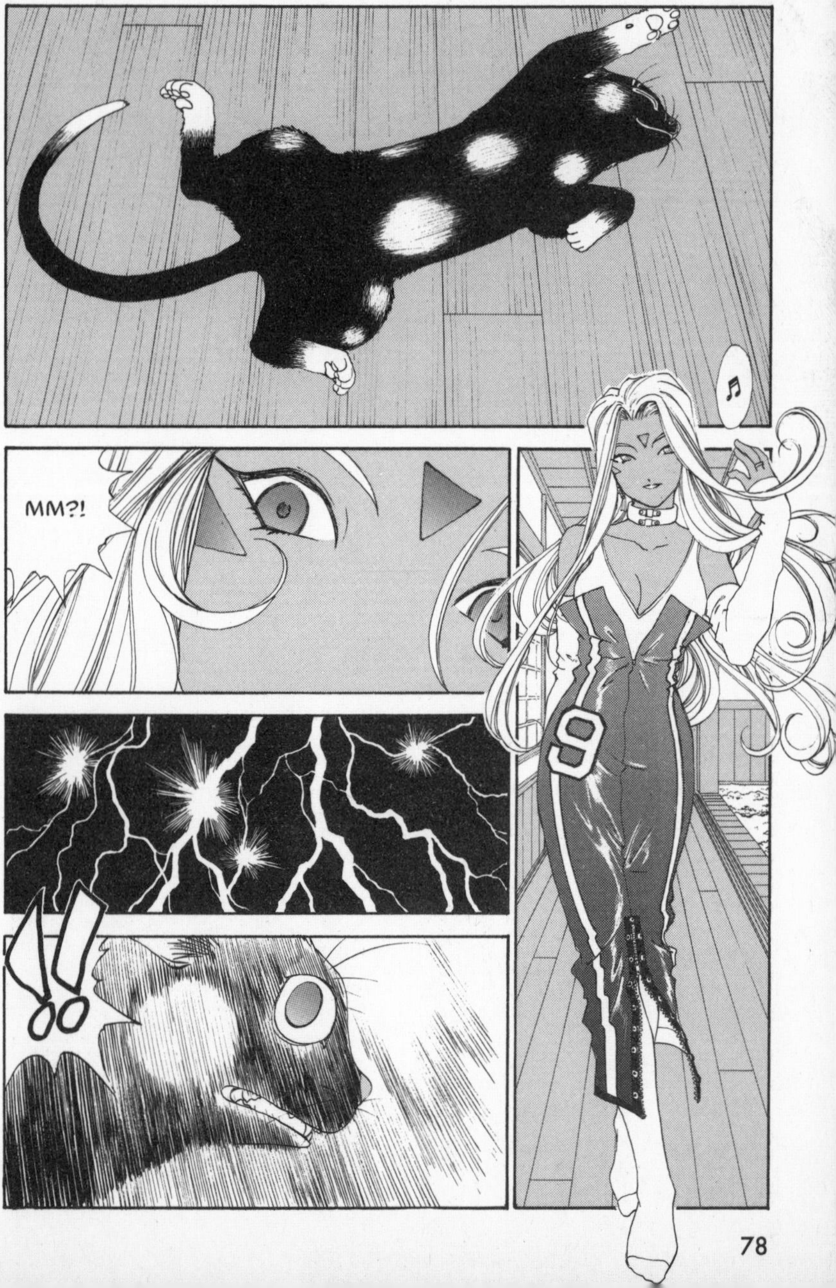
♪
MM?!
!!

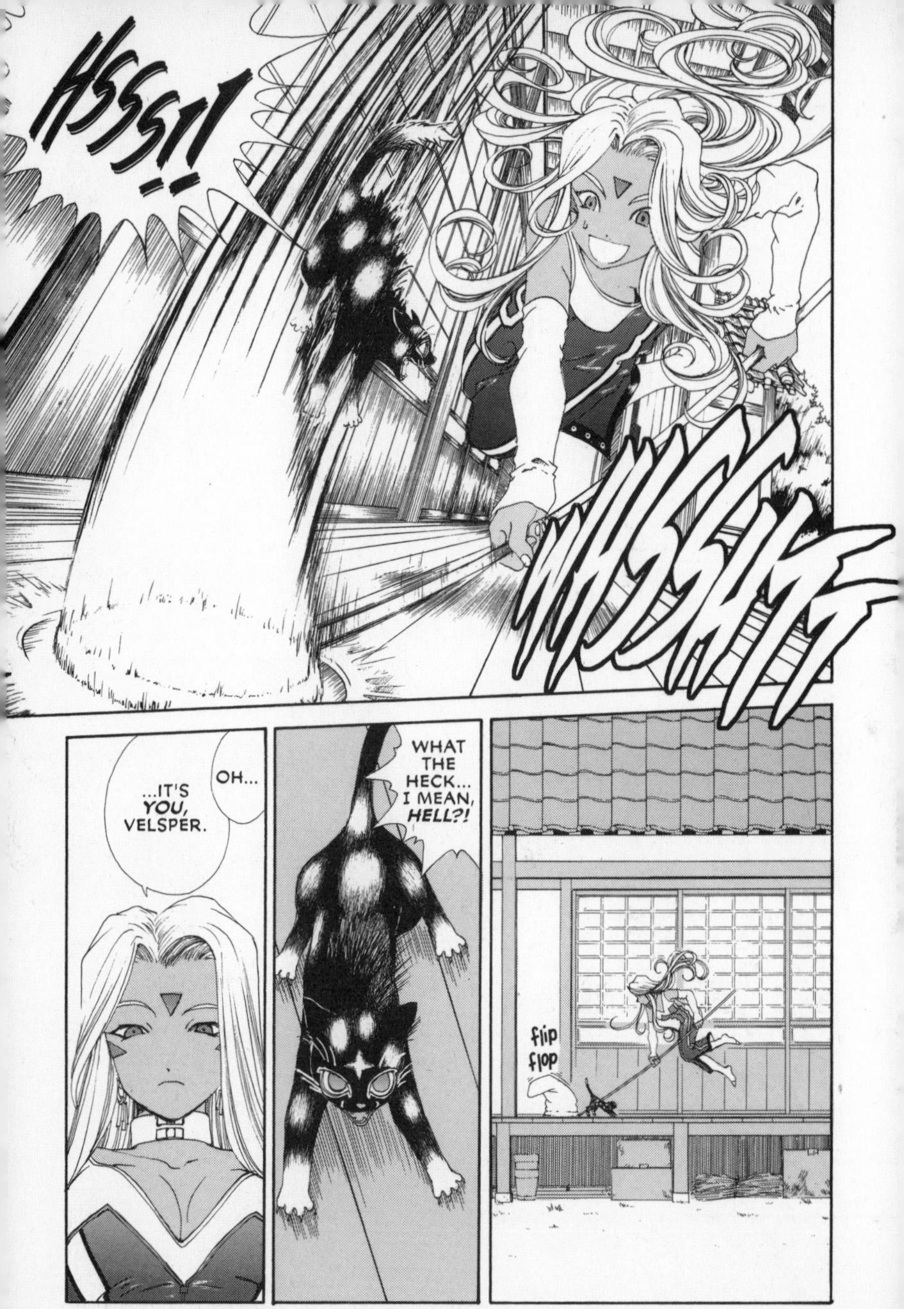

HSSSST!!
WHSSHT
flip flop
WHAT THE HECK... I MEAN, *HELL?!*
OH...
...IT'S *YOU,* VELSPER.

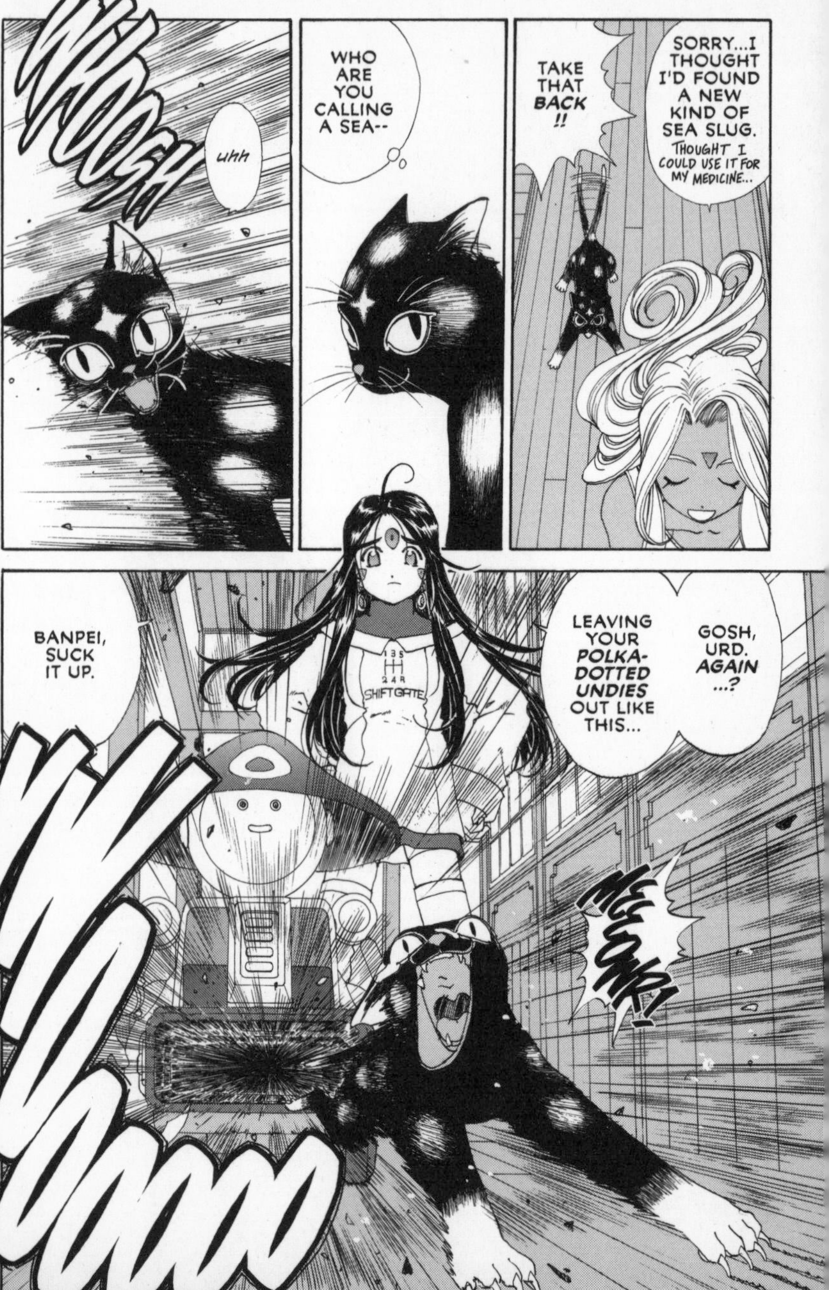
SORRY...I THOUGHT I'D FOUND A NEW KIND OF SEA SLUG. THOUGHT I COULD USE IT FOR MY MEDICINE...
TAKE THAT BACK!!
WHO ARE YOU CALLING A SEA--
WHOOSH
uhh
GOSH, URD. AGAIN ...?
LEAVING YOUR POLKA-DOTTED UNDIES OUT LIKE THIS...
BANPEI, SUCK IT UP.
MEOWR!

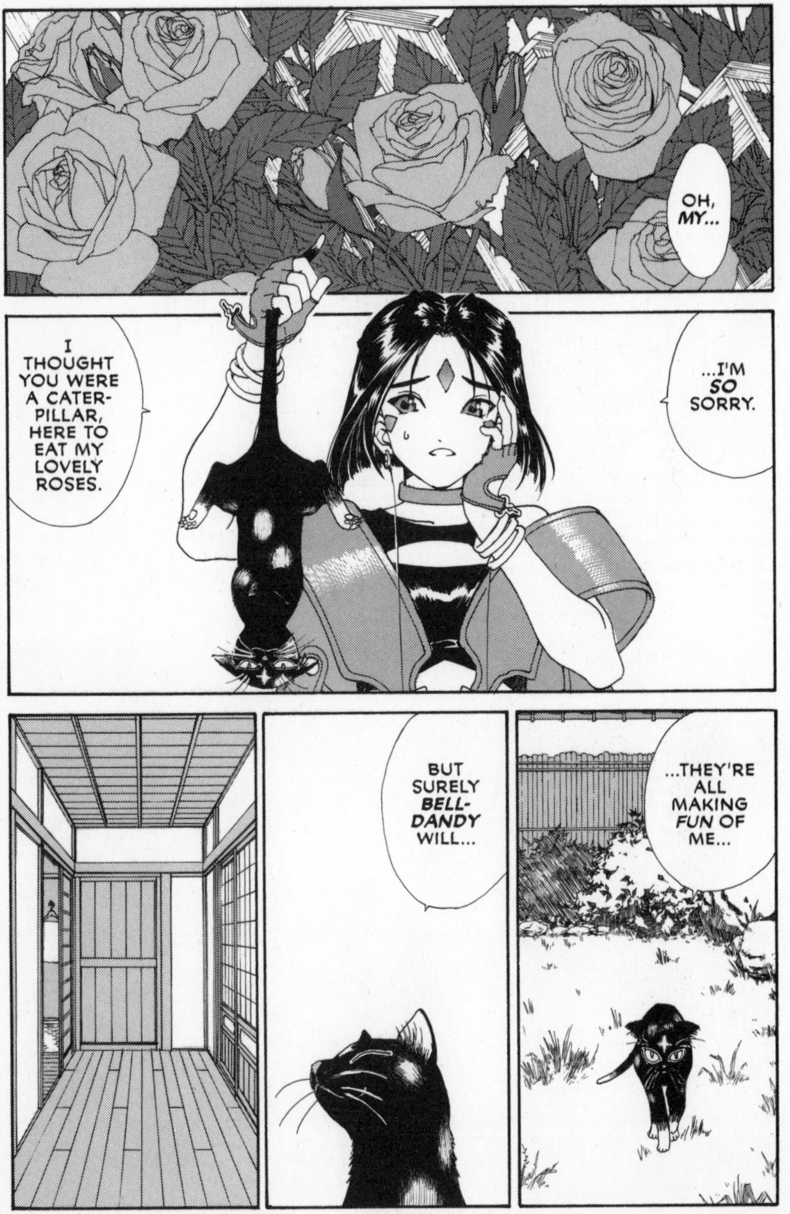
OH, MY...
...I'M SO SORRY.
I THOUGHT YOU WERE A CATER-PILLAR, HERE TO EAT MY LOVELY ROSES.
...THEY'RE ALL MAKING FUN OF ME...
BUT SURELY BELL-DANDY WILL...

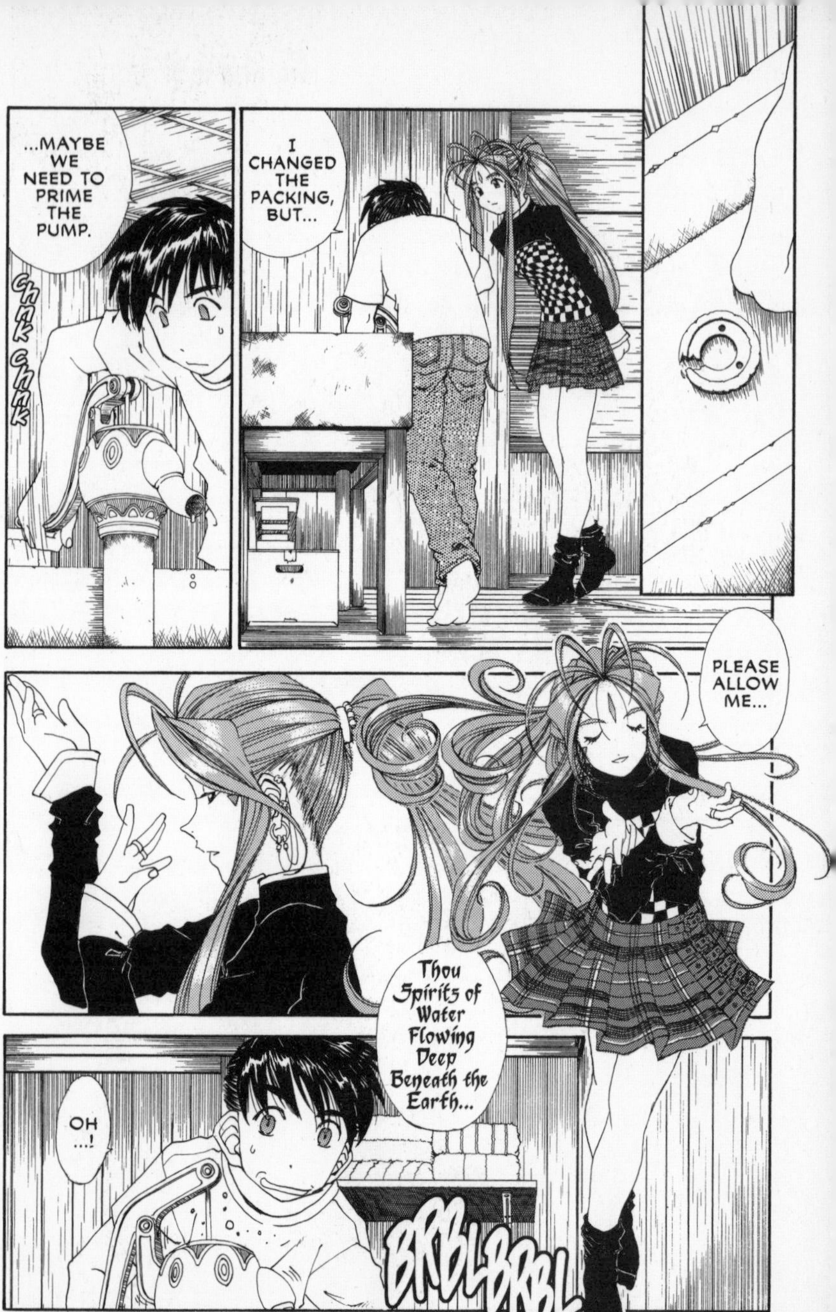
I CHANGED THE PACKING, BUT...
...MAYBE WE NEED TO PRIME THE PUMP.
CHNK CHNK
PLEASE ALLOW ME...
Thou Spirits of Water Flowing Deep Beneath the Earth...
BRBLBRBL
OH ...!

I'LL GET YOU A *TOWEL!*

--!! I'M SORRY!! I OVER-DID IT!!

SPOOSH

'M OKAY.

THANKS.

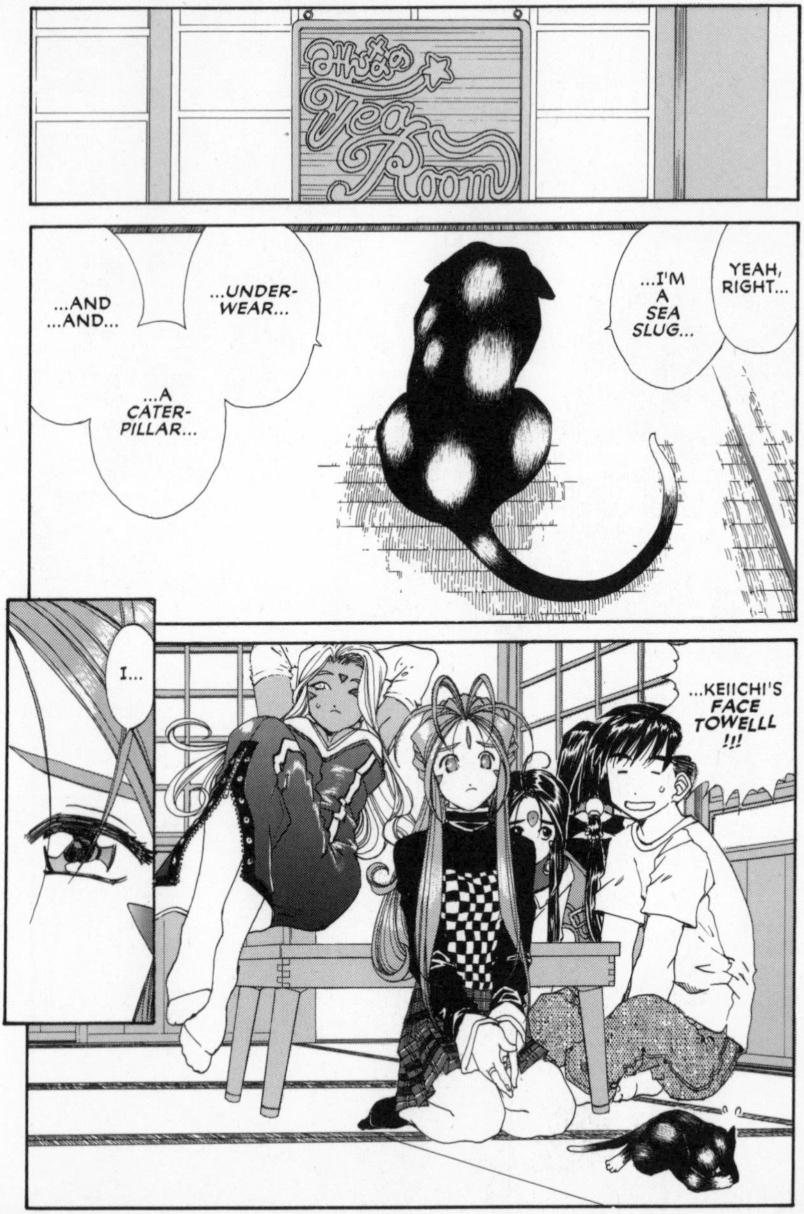
みんなの
Tea Room
YEAH, RIGHT...
...I'M A SEA SLUG...
...UNDER-WEAR...
...AND ...AND...
...A CATER-PILLAR...
...KEIICHI'S FACE TOWELLL !!!
I...

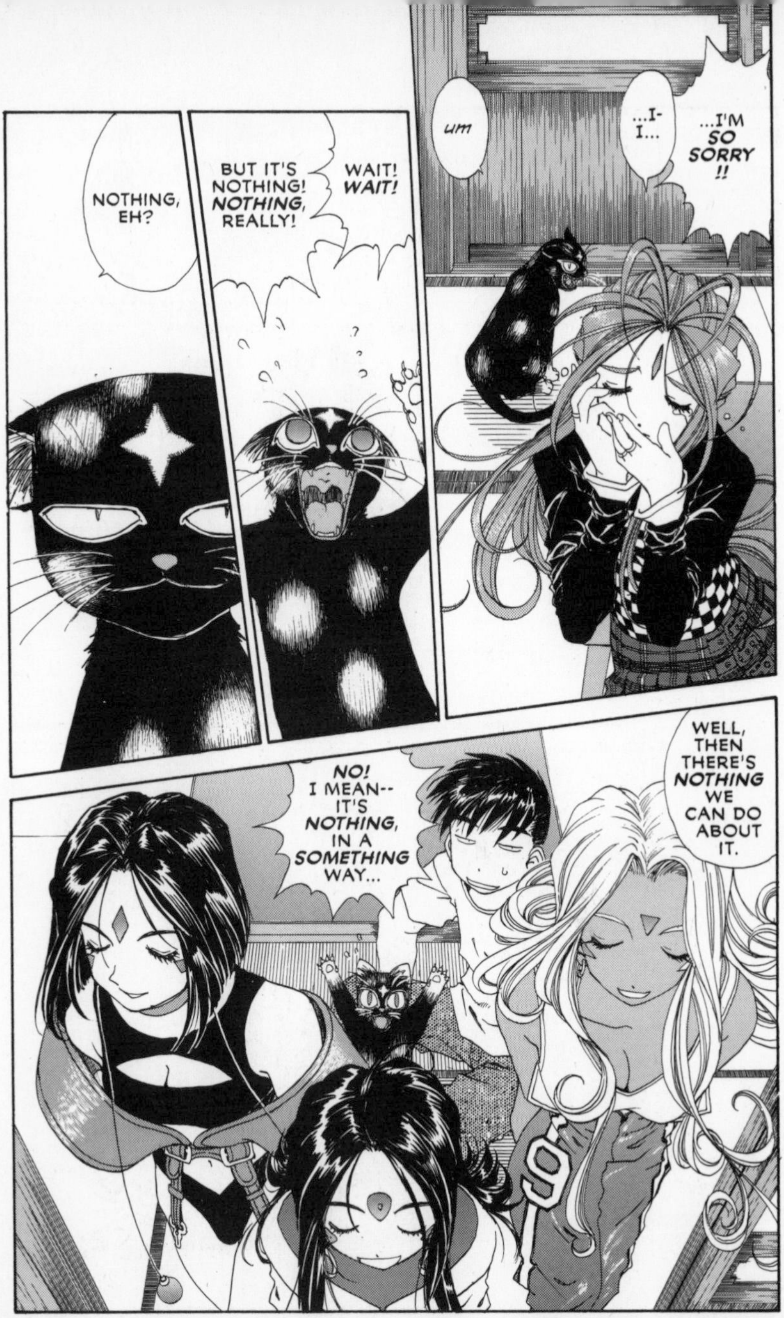
...I'M SO SORRY !!
...I- I...
um
WAIT! WAIT!
BUT IT'S NOTHING! NOTHING, REALLY!
NOTHING, EH?
WELL, THEN THERE'S NOTHING WE CAN DO ABOUT IT.
NO! I MEAN-- IT'S NOTHING, IN A SOMETHING WAY...

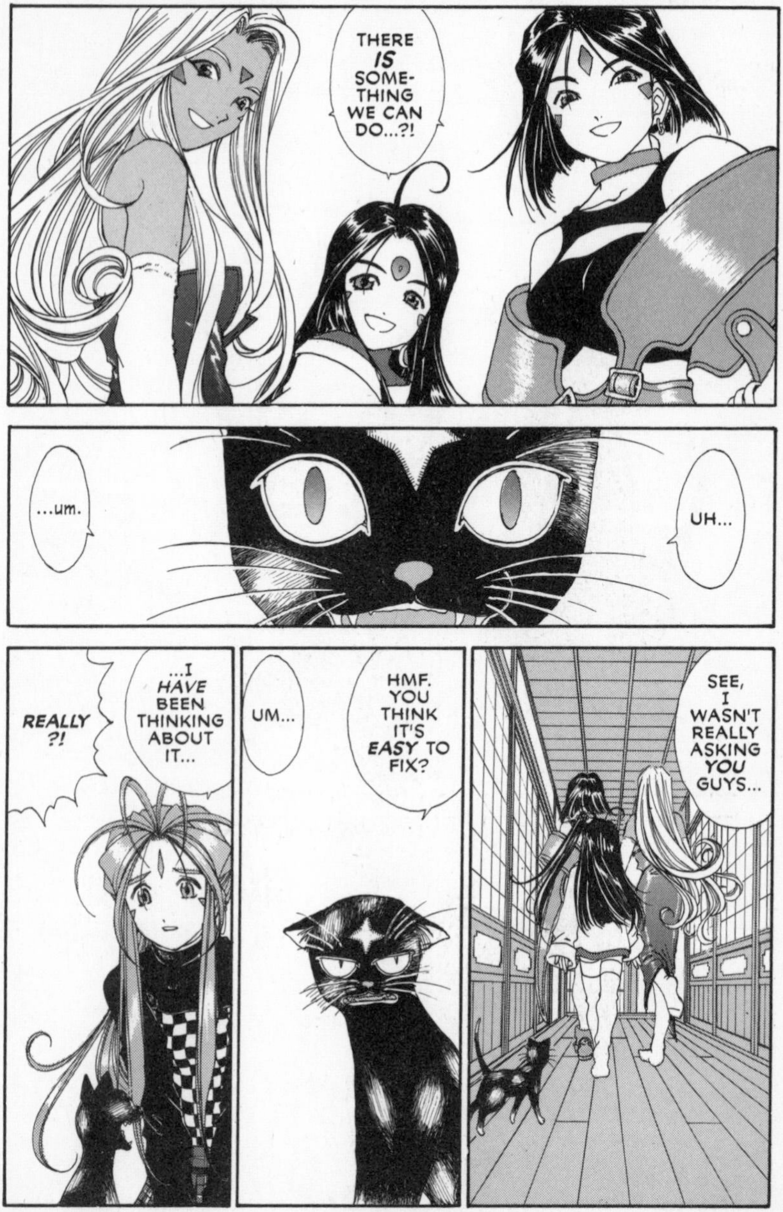
THERE *IS* SOMETHING WE CAN DO...?!
UH...
...um.
SEE, I WASN'T REALLY ASKING *YOU* GUYS...
HMF. YOU THINK IT'S *EASY* TO FIX?
UM...
...I *HAVE* BEEN THINKING ABOUT IT...
REALLY?!

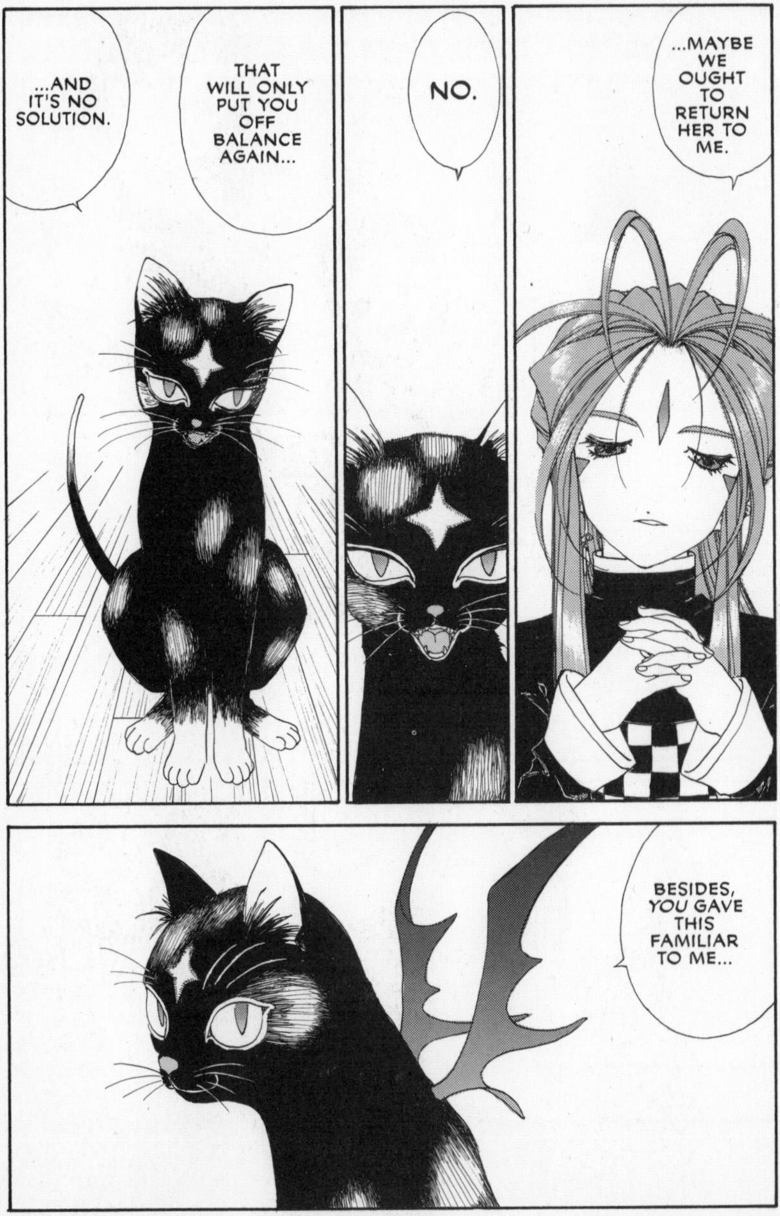
...MAYBE WE OUGHT TO RETURN HER TO ME.
NO.
THAT WILL ONLY PUT YOU OFF BALANCE AGAIN...
...AND IT'S NO SOLUTION.
BESIDES, *YOU* GAVE THIS FAMILIAR TO ME...

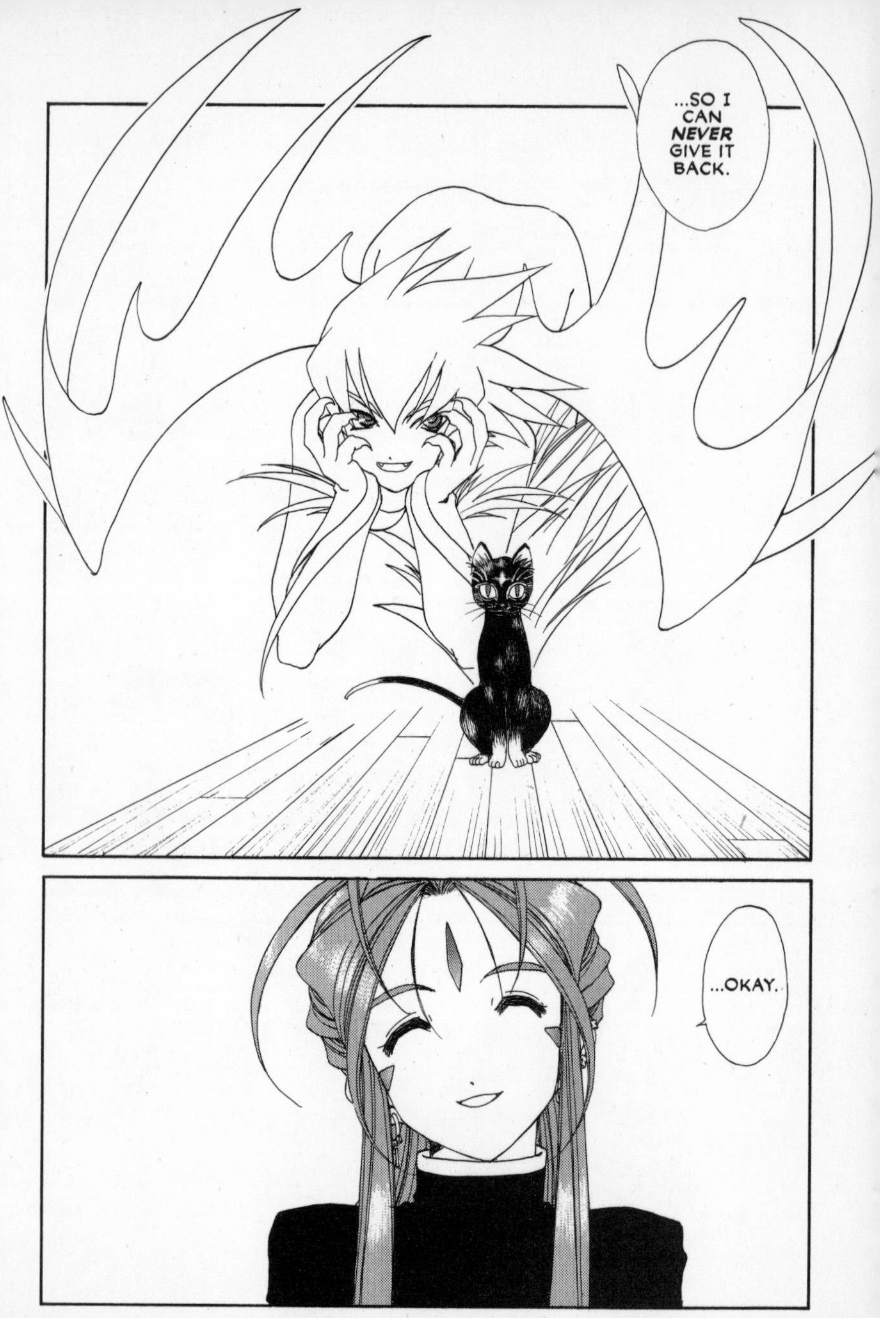
...SO I CAN *NEVER* GIVE IT BACK.
...OKAY.

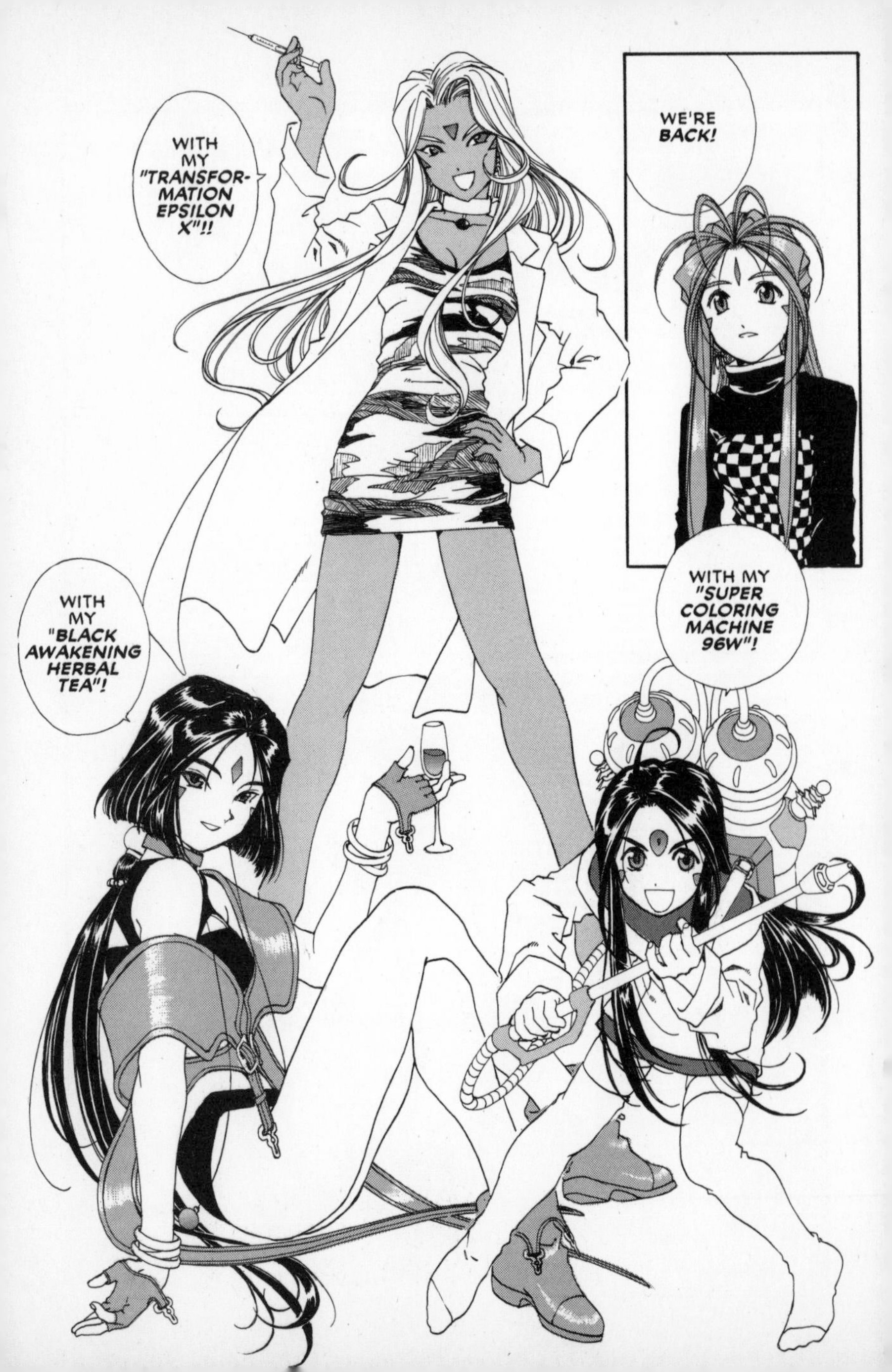
WE'RE BACK!
WITH MY "TRANSFORMATION EPSILON X"!!
WITH MY "SUPER COLORING MACHINE 96W"!
WITH MY "BLACK AWAKENING HERBAL TEA"!

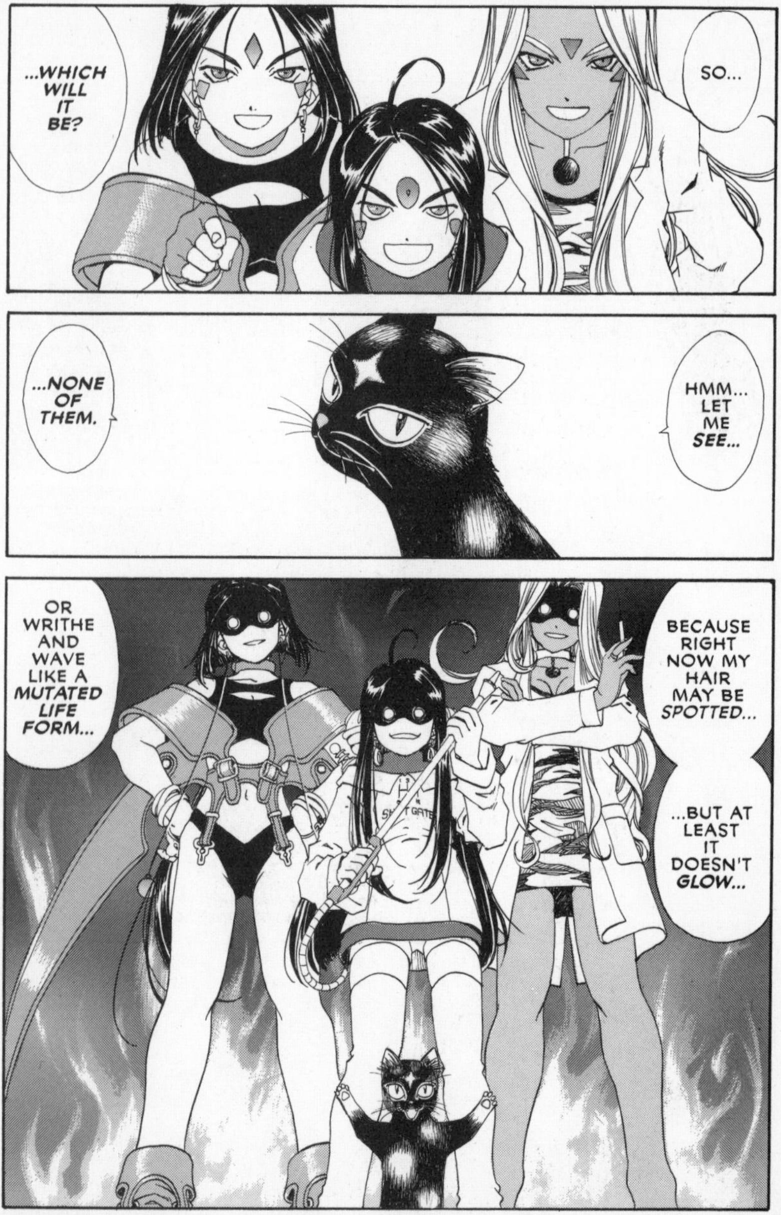
SO...
...WHICH WILL IT BE?
HMM... LET ME SEE...
...NONE OF THEM.
BECAUSE RIGHT NOW MY HAIR MAY BE SPOTTED...
...BUT AT LEAST IT DOESN'T GLOW...
OR WRITHE AND WAVE LIKE A MUTATED LIFE FORM...

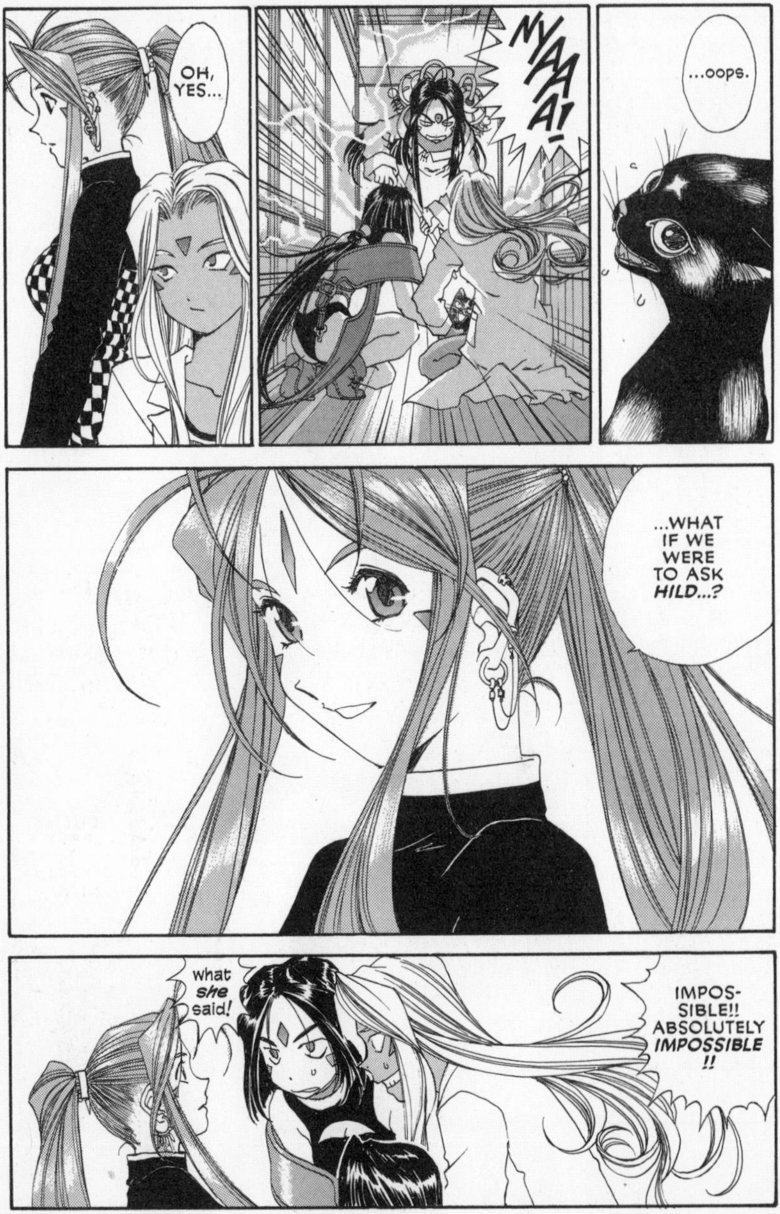
...oops.
NYAAAA!
OH, YES...
...WHAT IF WE WERE TO ASK HILD...?
IMPOS-SIBLE!! ABSOLUTELY IMPOSSIBLE!!
what she said!

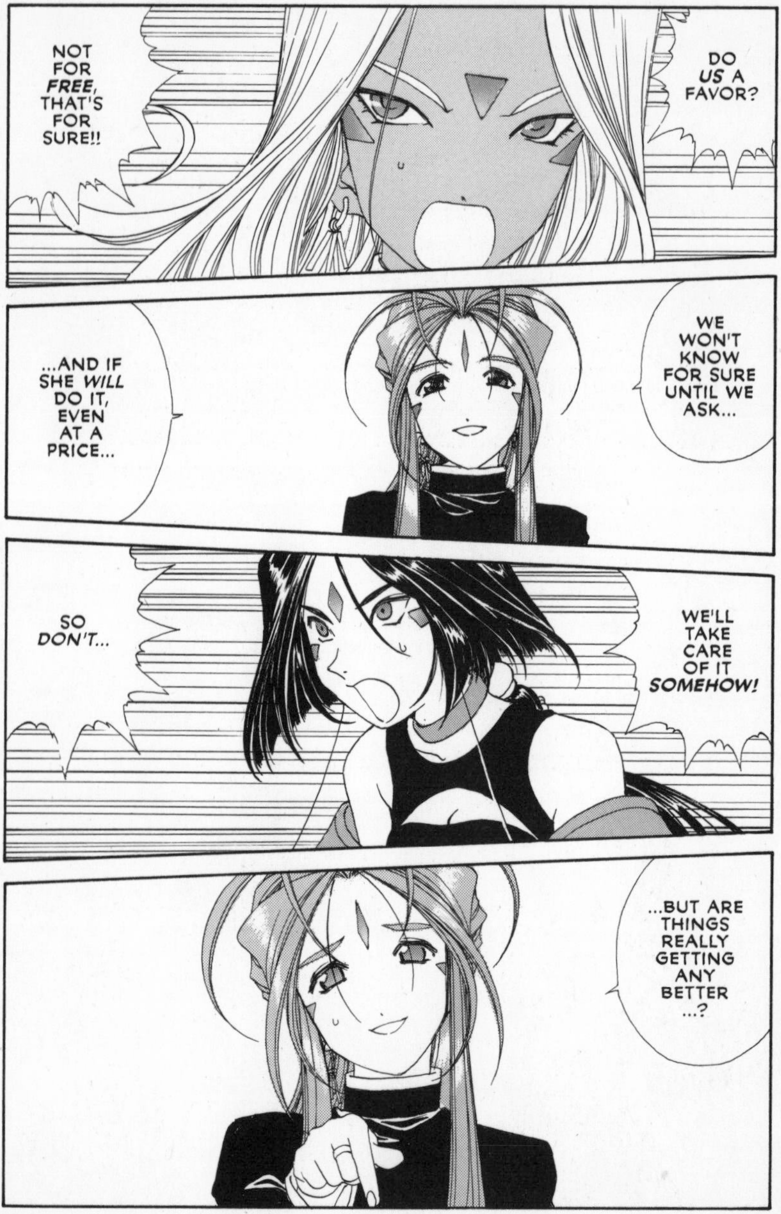
DO *US* A FAVOR?
NOT FOR *FREE*, THAT'S FOR SURE!!
WE WON'T KNOW FOR SURE UNTIL WE ASK...
...AND IF SHE *WILL* DO IT, EVEN AT A PRICE...
WE'LL TAKE CARE OF IT *SOMEHOW!*
SO *DON'T*...
...BUT ARE THINGS REALLY GETTING ANY BETTER ...?

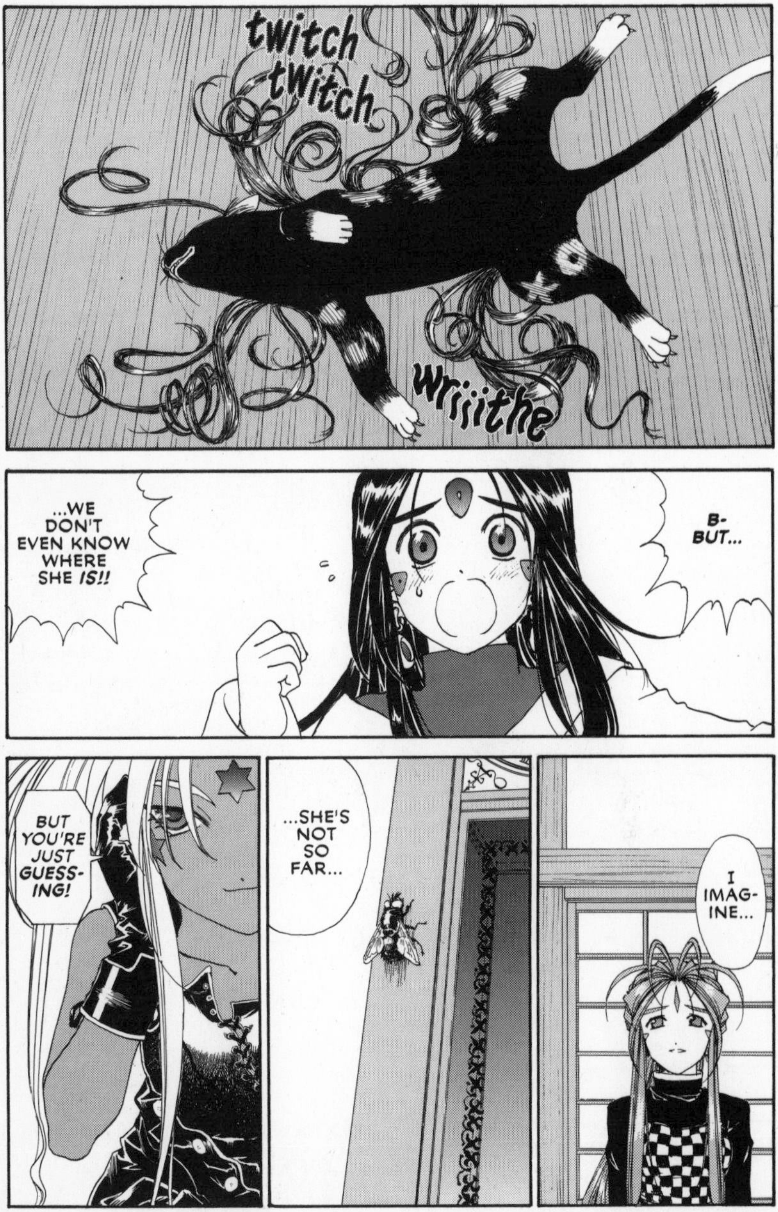
twitch twitch
wriiithe
B- BUT...
...WE DON'T EVEN KNOW WHERE SHE *IS!!*
I IMAGINE...
...SHE'S NOT SO FAR...
BUT YOU'RE JUST **GUESSING!**

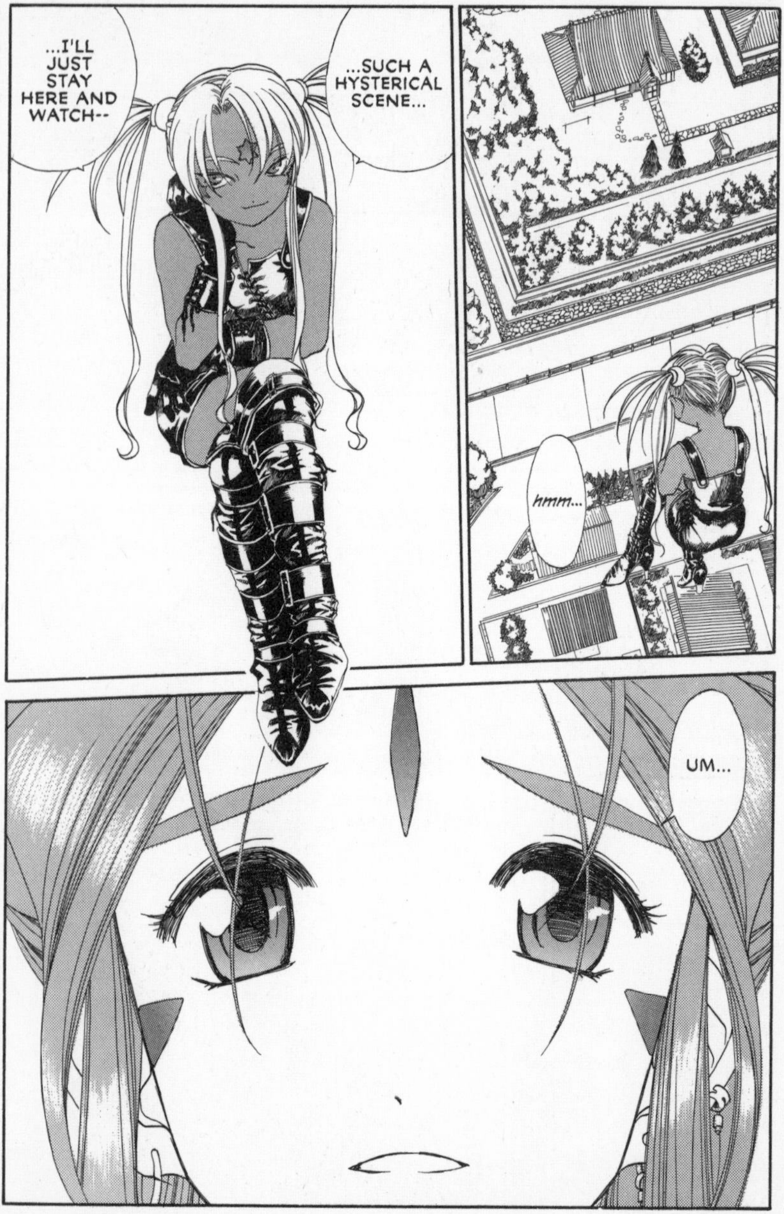
hmm...
...SUCH A HYSTERICAL SCENE...
...I'LL JUST STAY HERE AND WATCH--
UM...

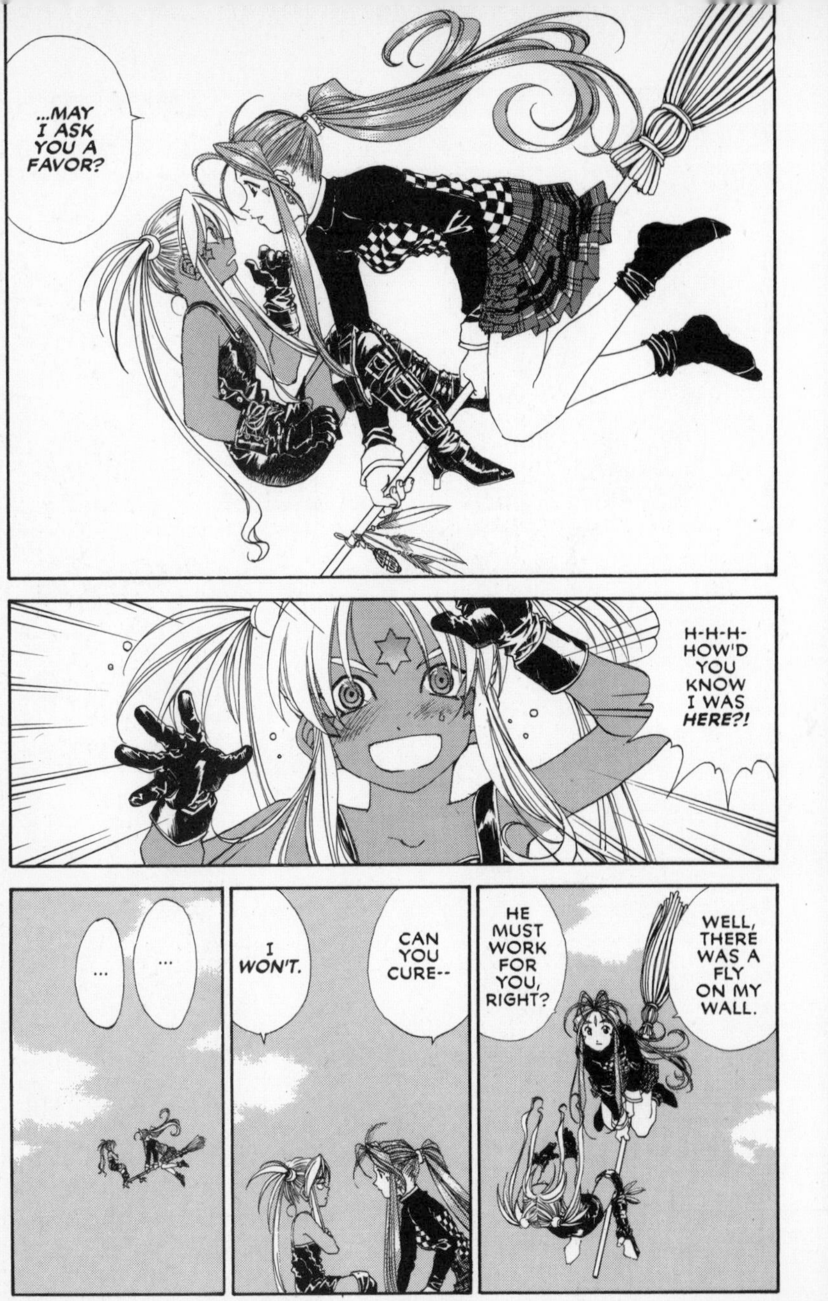
...MAY I ASK YOU A FAVOR?
H-H-H-HOW'D YOU KNOW I WAS *HERE?!*
WELL, THERE WAS A FLY ON MY WALL.
HE MUST WORK FOR YOU, RIGHT?
CAN YOU CURE--
I *WON'T.*
...
...

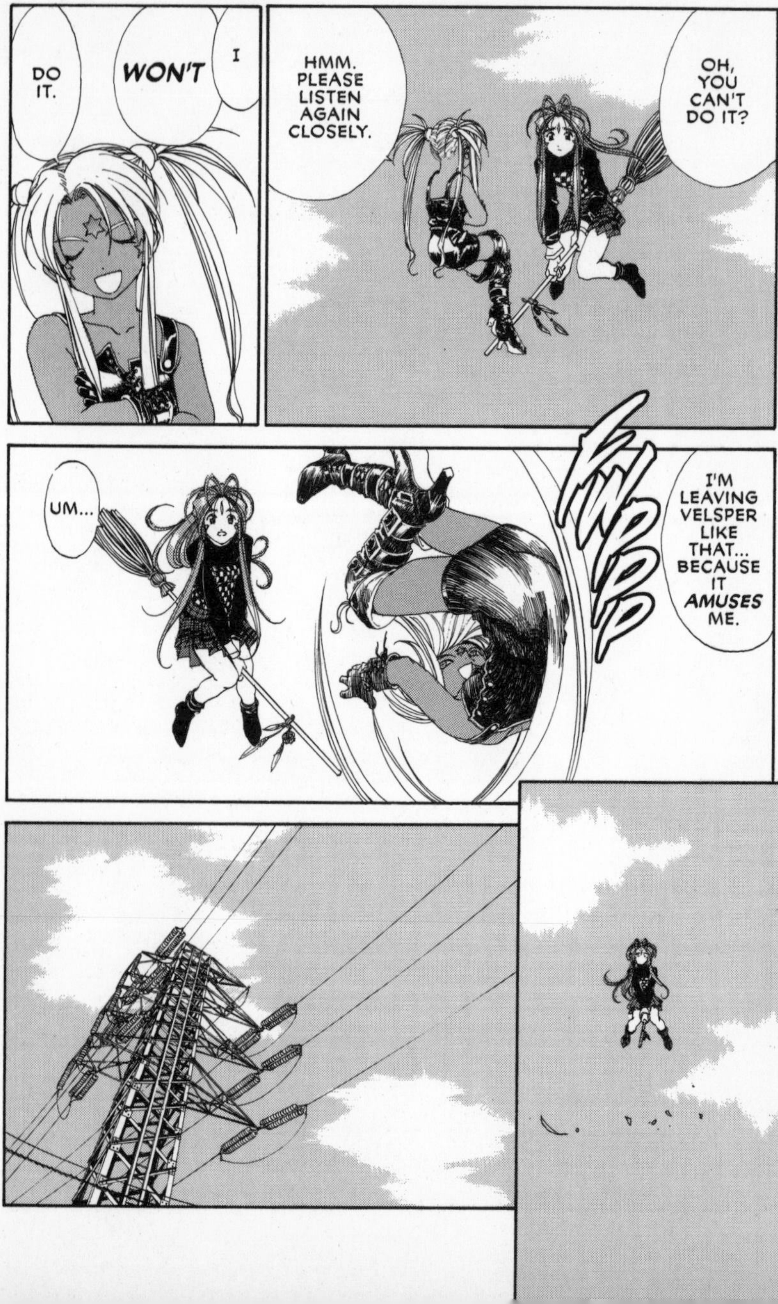
OH, YOU CAN'T DO IT?
HMM. PLEASE LISTEN AGAIN CLOSELY.
I
WON'T
DO IT.
I'M LEAVING VELSPER LIKE THAT... BECAUSE IT *AMUSES* ME.
UM...

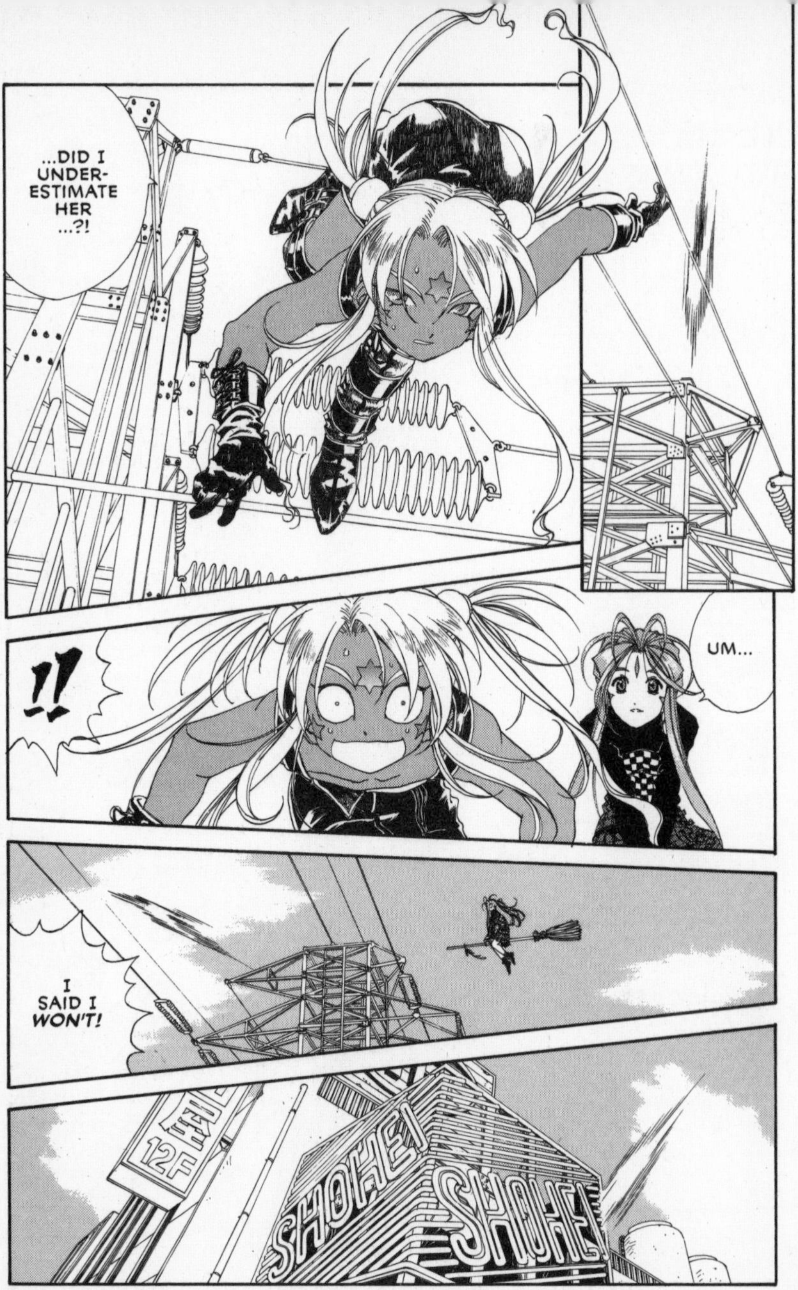
...DID I UNDER-ESTIMATE HER ...?!
UM...
!!
I SAID I *WON'T!*
12F
SHOHEI
SHOHEI

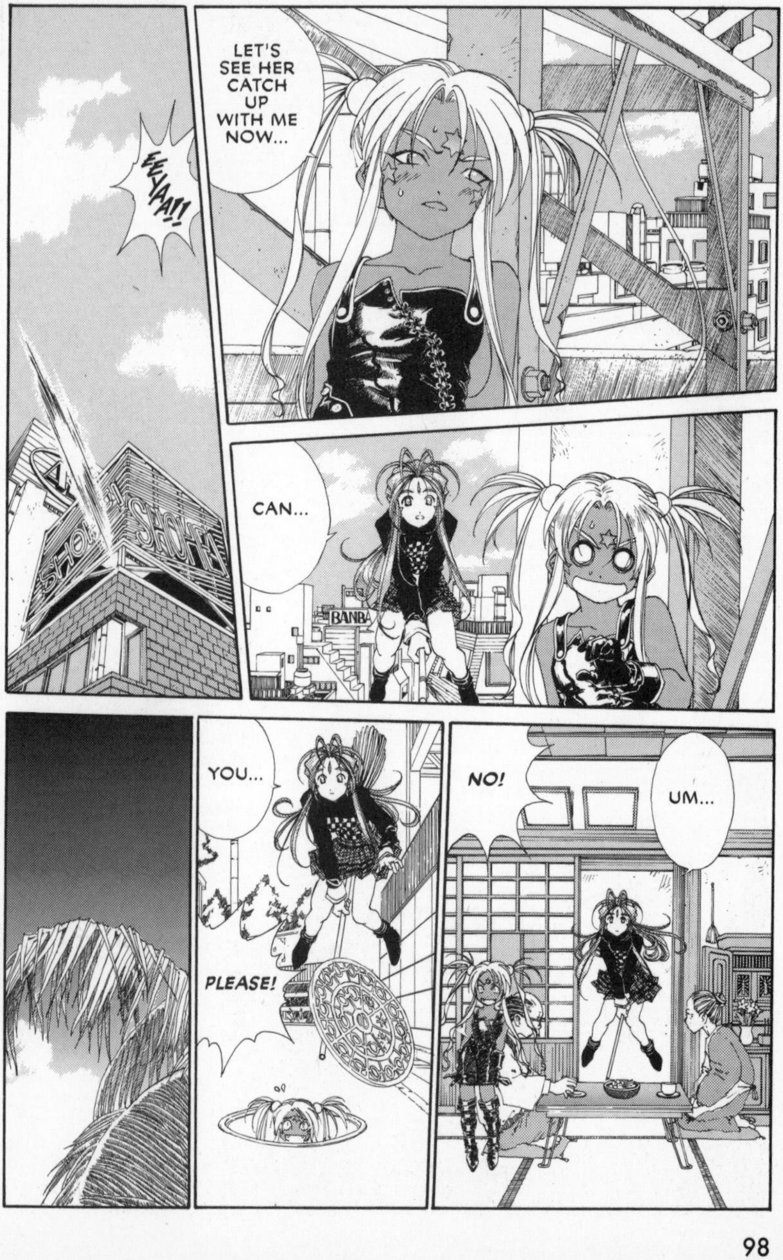

LET'S SEE HER CATCH UP WITH ME NOW...
CAN...
BANBA
EEYAA!!
UM...
NO!
YOU...
PLEASE!

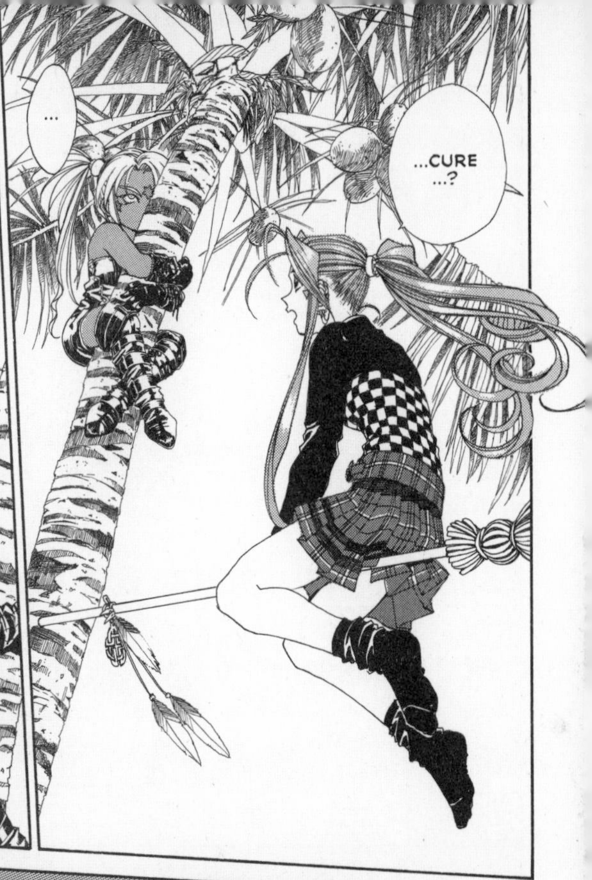
...CURE ...?
...
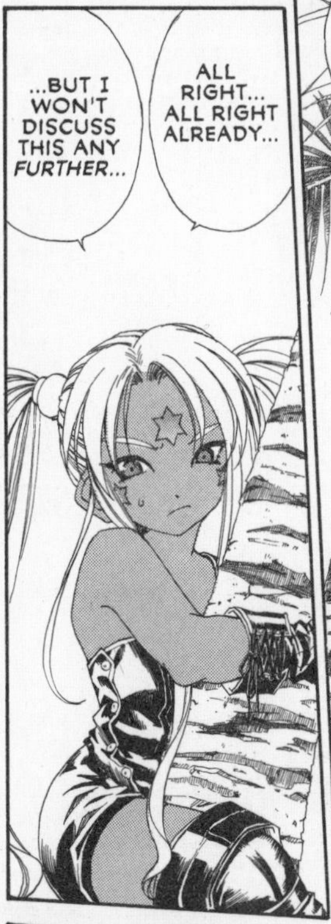
ALL RIGHT... ALL RIGHT ALREADY...
...BUT I WON'T DISCUSS THIS ANY *FURTHER*...
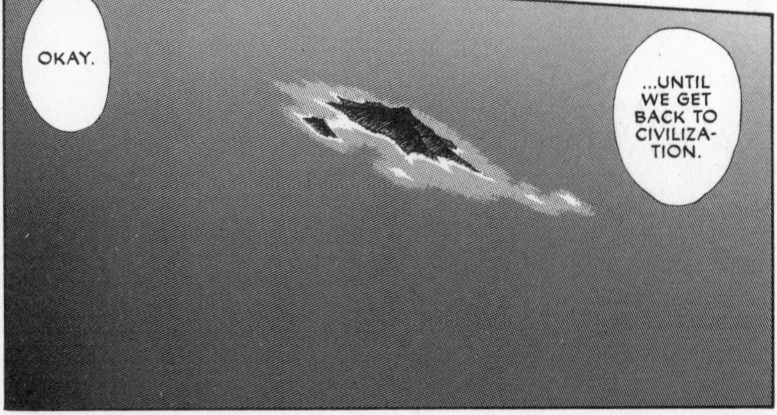
...UNTIL WE GET BACK TO CIVILIZA-TION.
OKAY.

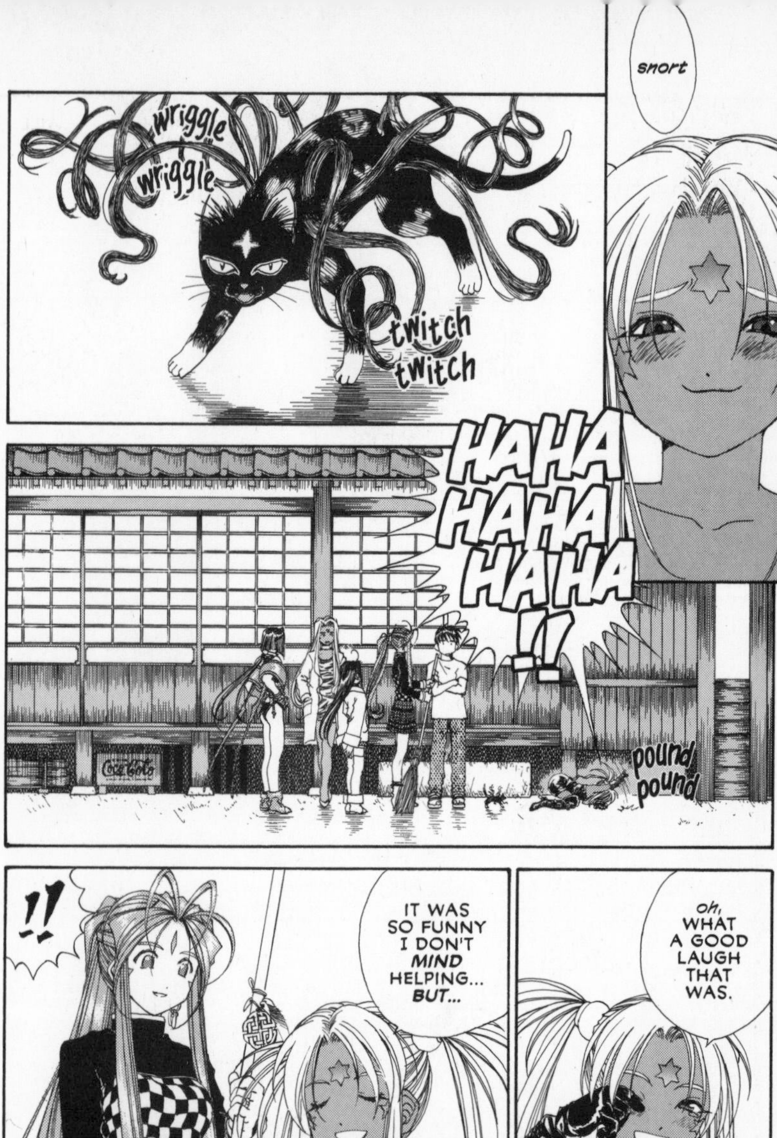
snort
HAHA HAHA HAHA !!
wriggle wriggle
twitch twitch
pound pound
oh, WHAT A GOOD LAUGH THAT WAS.
IT WAS SO FUNNY I DON'T *MIND* HELPING... *BUT*...
!!

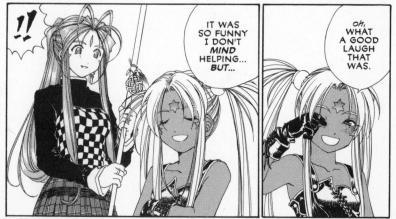

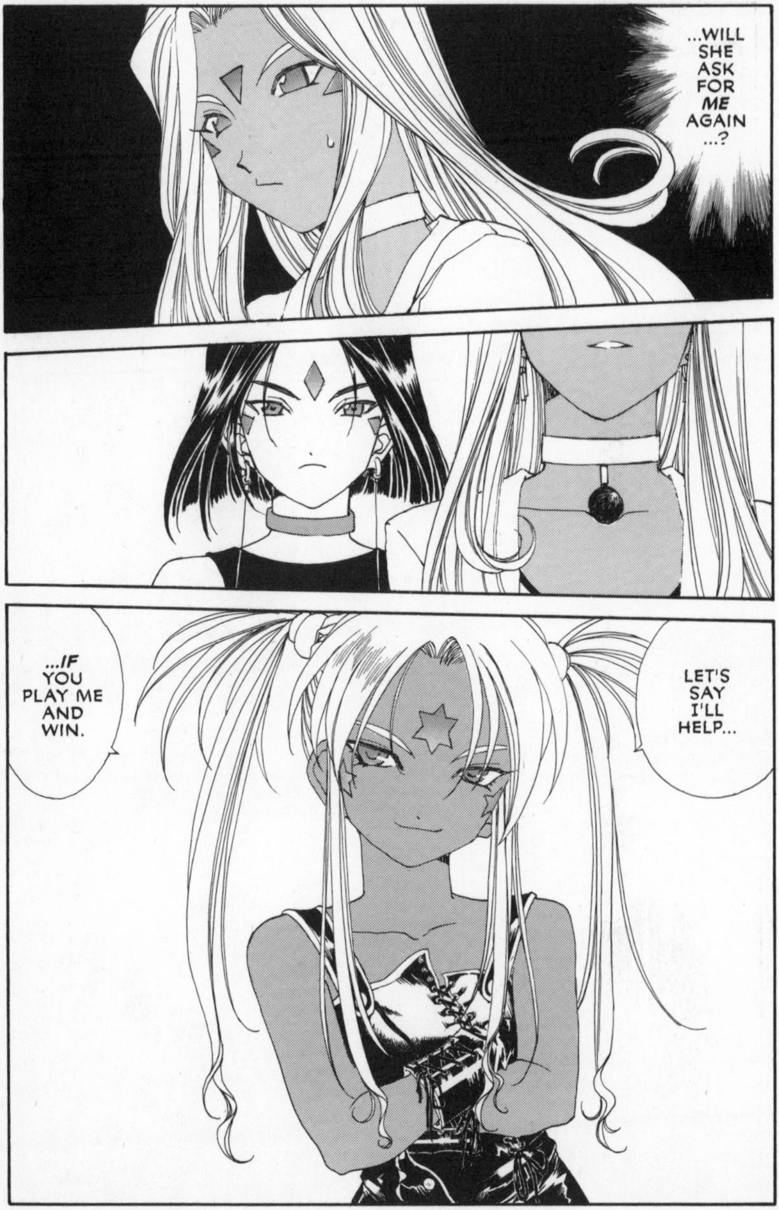
...WILL SHE ASK FOR *ME* AGAIN ...?
LET'S SAY I'LL HELP...
...*IF* YOU PLAY ME AND WIN.

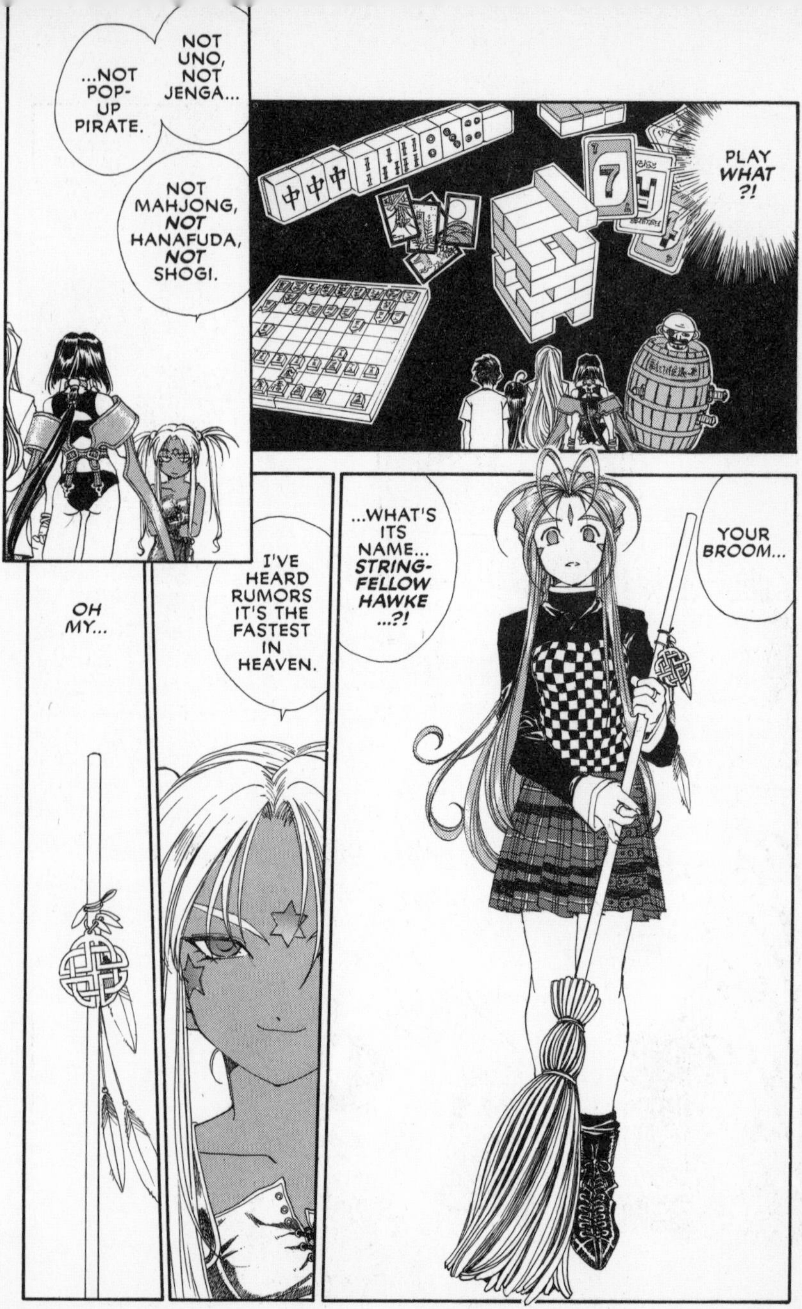
PLAY WHAT?!
NOT UNO, NOT JENGA...
...NOT POP-UP PIRATE.
NOT MAHJONG, NOT HANAFUDA, NOT SHOGI.
YOUR BROOM...
...WHAT'S ITS NAME... STRING-FELLOW HAWKE ...?!
I'VE HEARD RUMORS IT'S THE FASTEST IN HEAVEN.
OH MY...

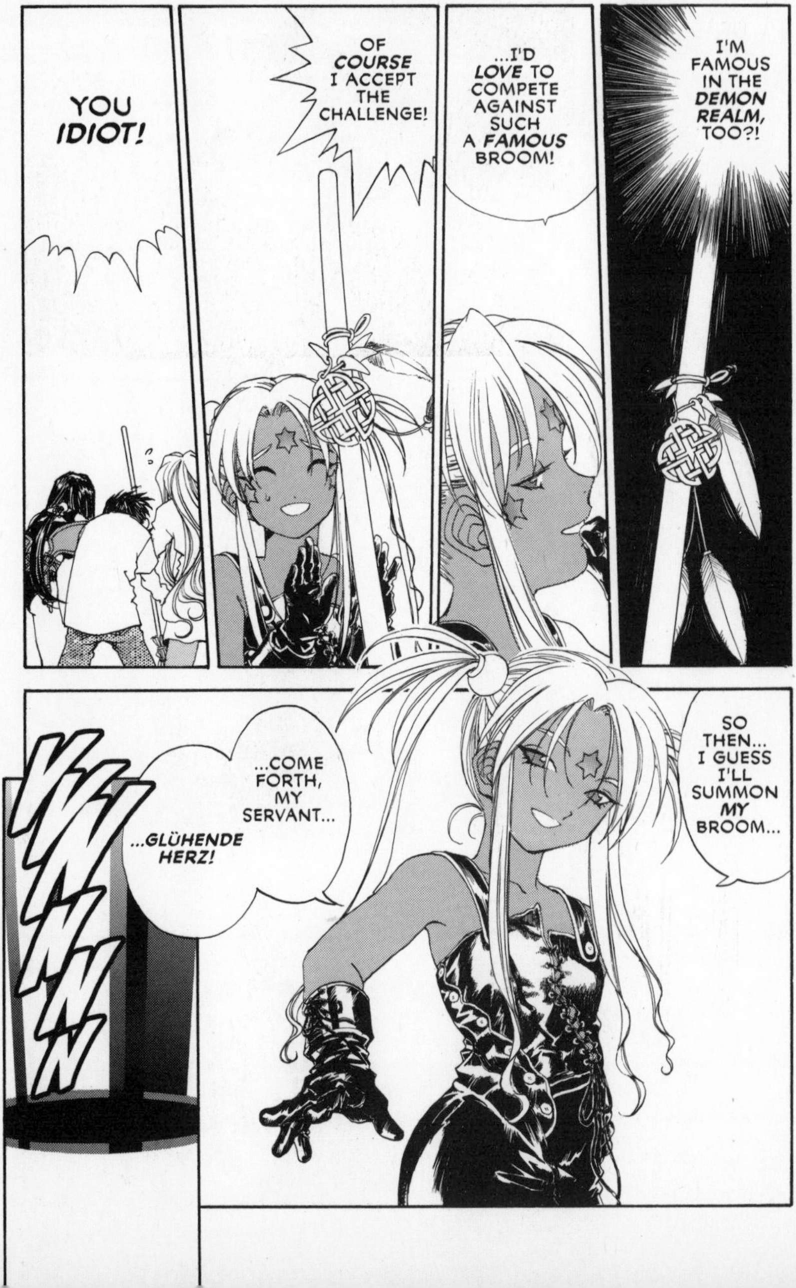
I'M FAMOUS IN THE DEMON REALM, TOO?!
...I'D LOVE TO COMPETE AGAINST SUCH A FAMOUS BROOM!
OF COURSE I ACCEPT THE CHALLENGE!
YOU IDIOT!
SO THEN... I GUESS I'LL SUMMON MY BROOM...
...COME FORTH, MY SERVANT...
...GLÜHENDE HERZ!
VNNNNN

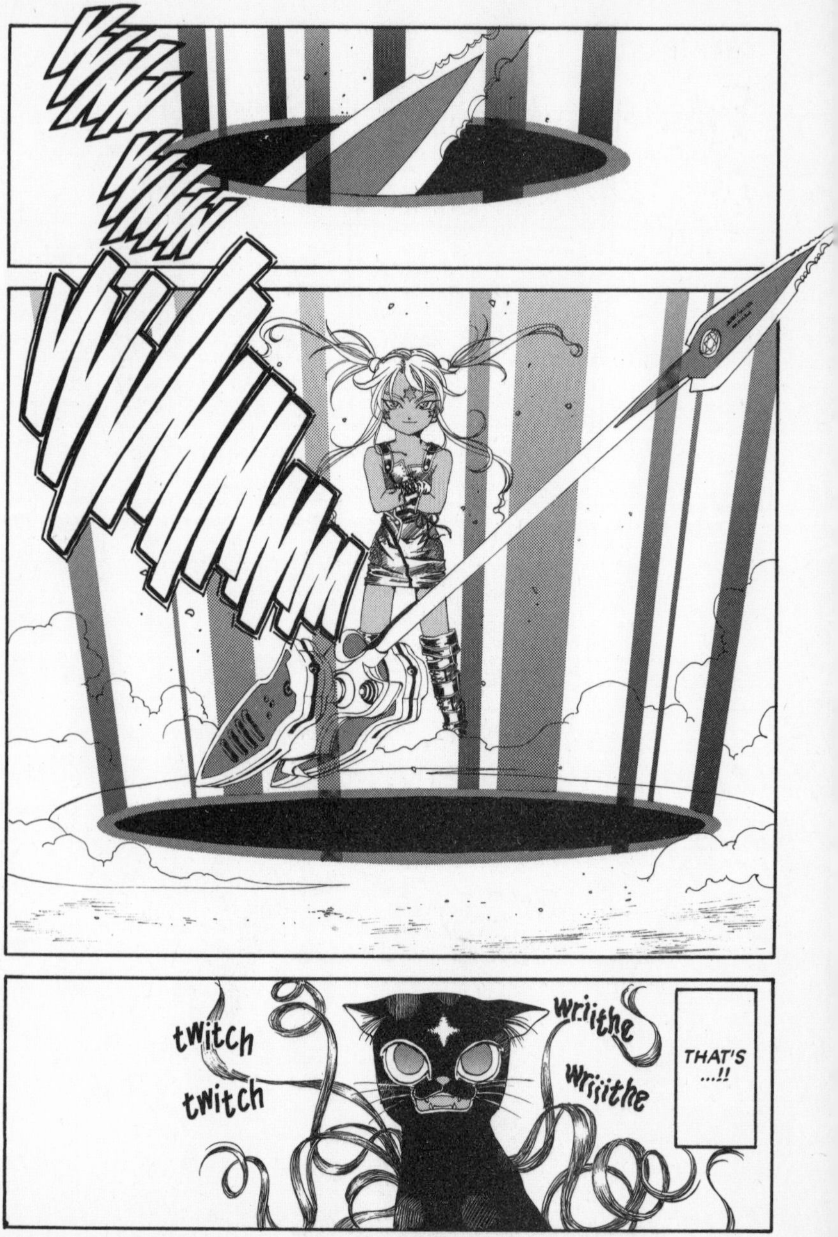
THAT'S ...!!
wriiithe
wriiithe
twitch
twitch

CHAPTER 181

Fastest Broom, Greatest Race!

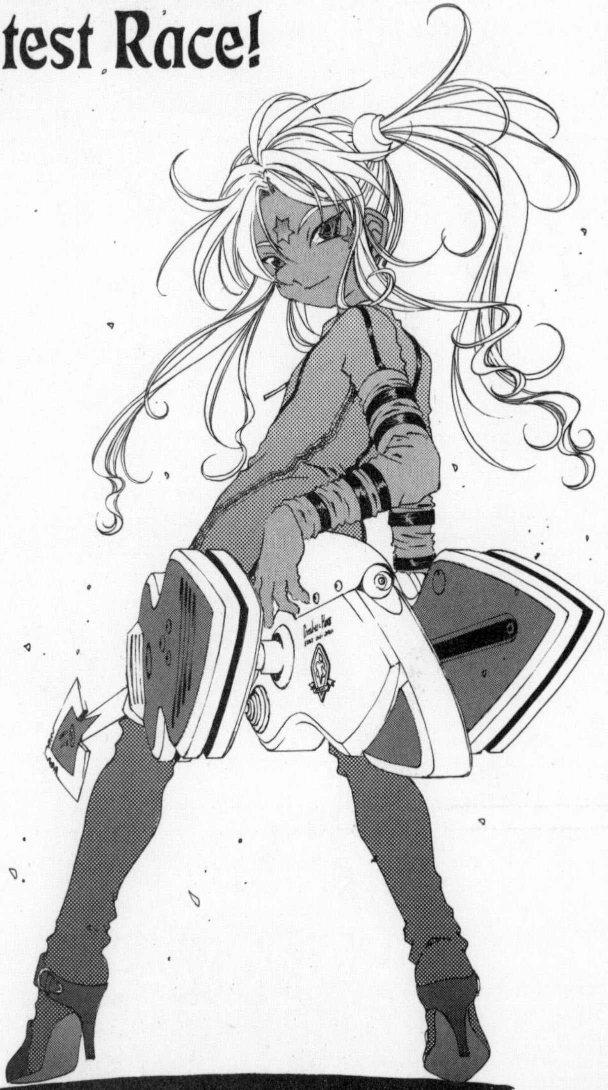

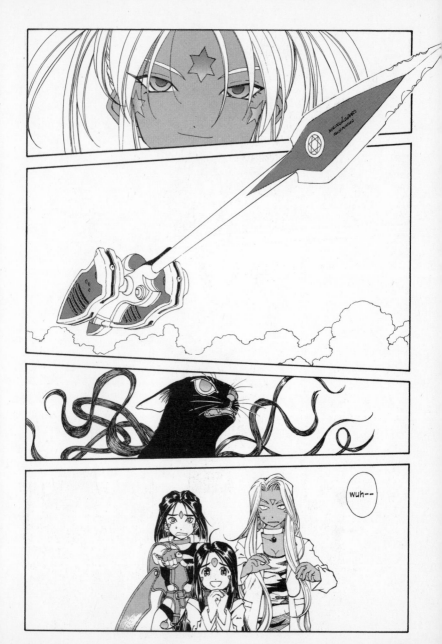

wuh--

106

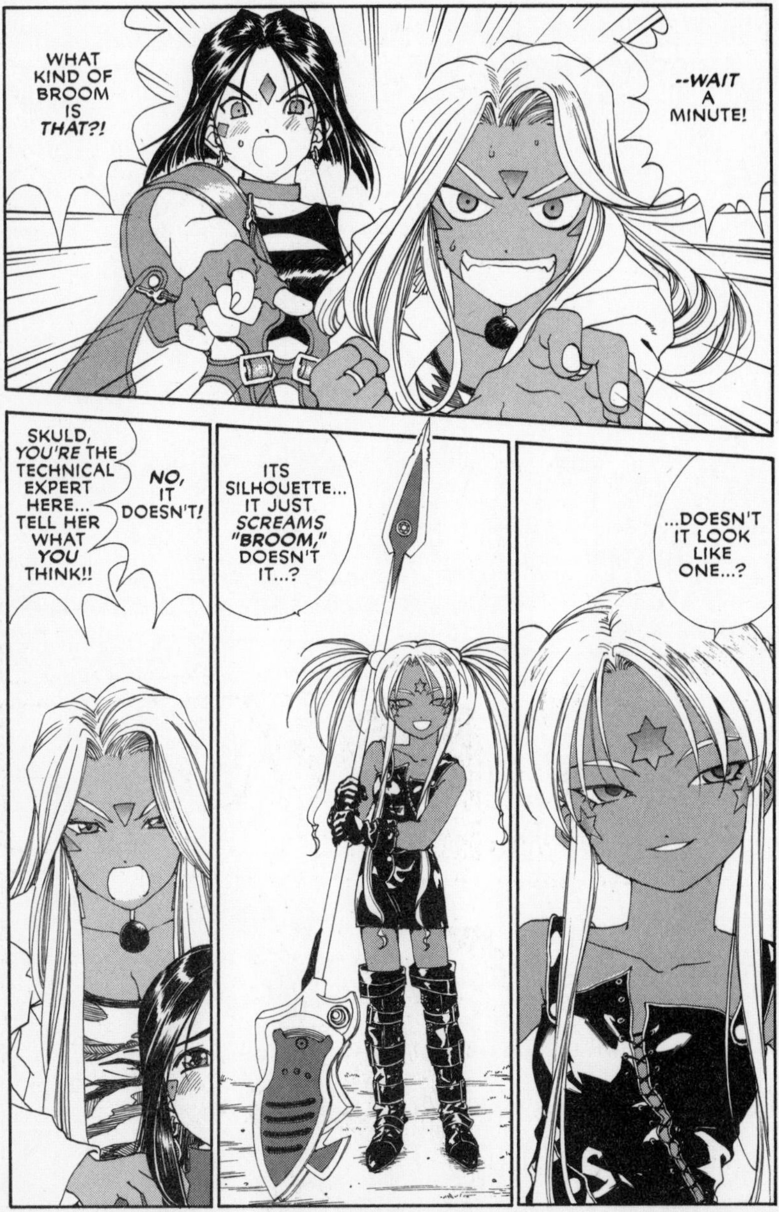
--*WAIT* A MINUTE!
WHAT KIND OF BROOM IS *THAT?!*
...DOESN'T IT LOOK LIKE ONE...?
ITS SILHOUETTE... IT JUST *SCREAMS* *"BROOM,"* DOESN'T IT...?
NO, IT DOESN'T!
SKULD, *YOU'RE* THE TECHNICAL EXPERT HERE... TELL HER WHAT *YOU* THINK!!

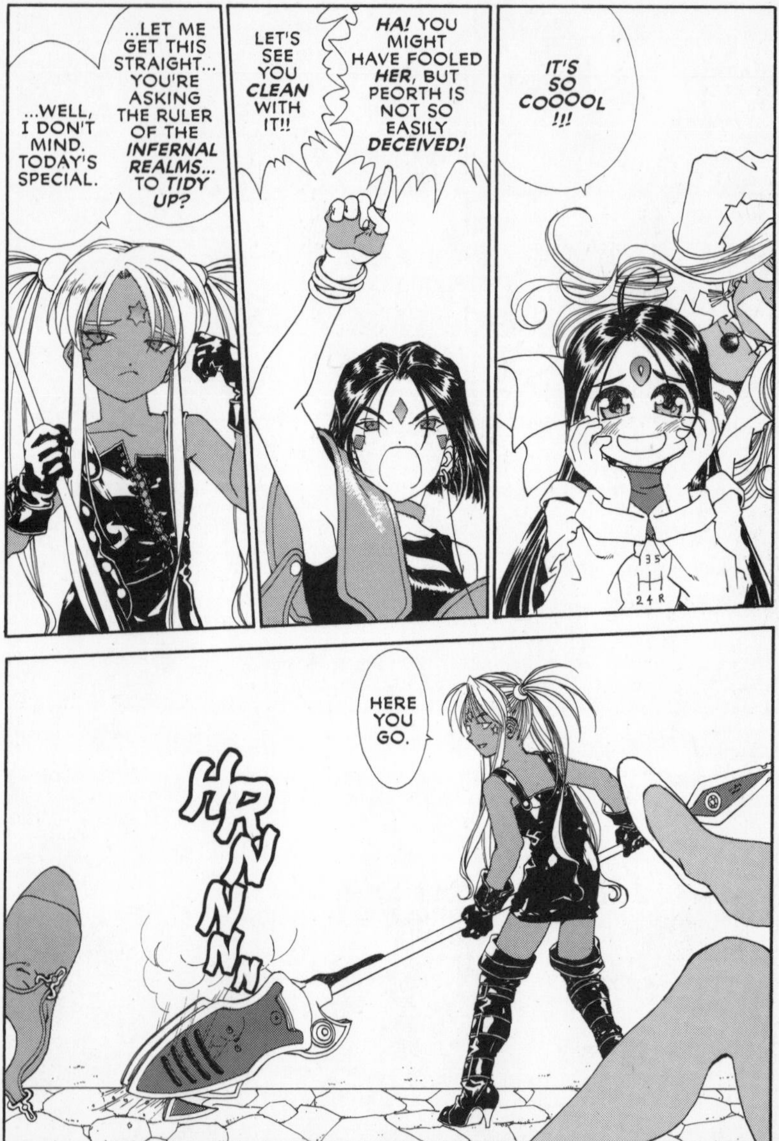
IT'S SO COOOOL!!!
HA! YOU MIGHT HAVE FOOLED HER, BUT PEORTH IS NOT SO EASILY DECEIVED!
LET'S SEE YOU CLEAN WITH IT!!
...LET ME GET THIS STRAIGHT... YOU'RE ASKING THE RULER OF THE INFERNAL REALMS... TO TIDY UP?
...WELL, I DON'T MIND. TODAY'S SPECIAL.
HERE YOU GO.
HRNNNN

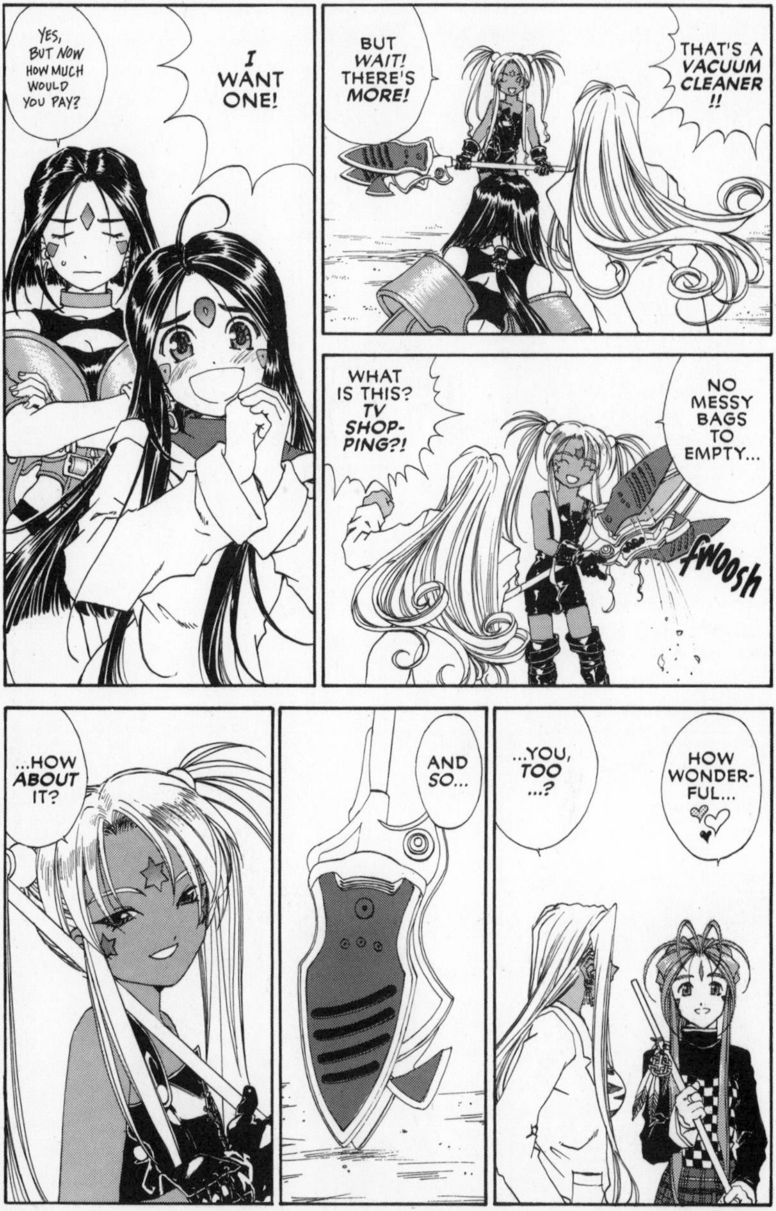
THAT'S A VACUUM CLEANER!!
BUT WAIT! THERE'S MORE!
NO MESSY BAGS TO EMPTY...
WHAT IS THIS? TV SHOP-PING?!
FWOOSH
I WANT ONE!
YES, BUT NOW HOW MUCH WOULD YOU PAY?
HOW WONDER-FUL...
...YOU, TOO ...?
AND SO...
...HOW ABOUT IT?

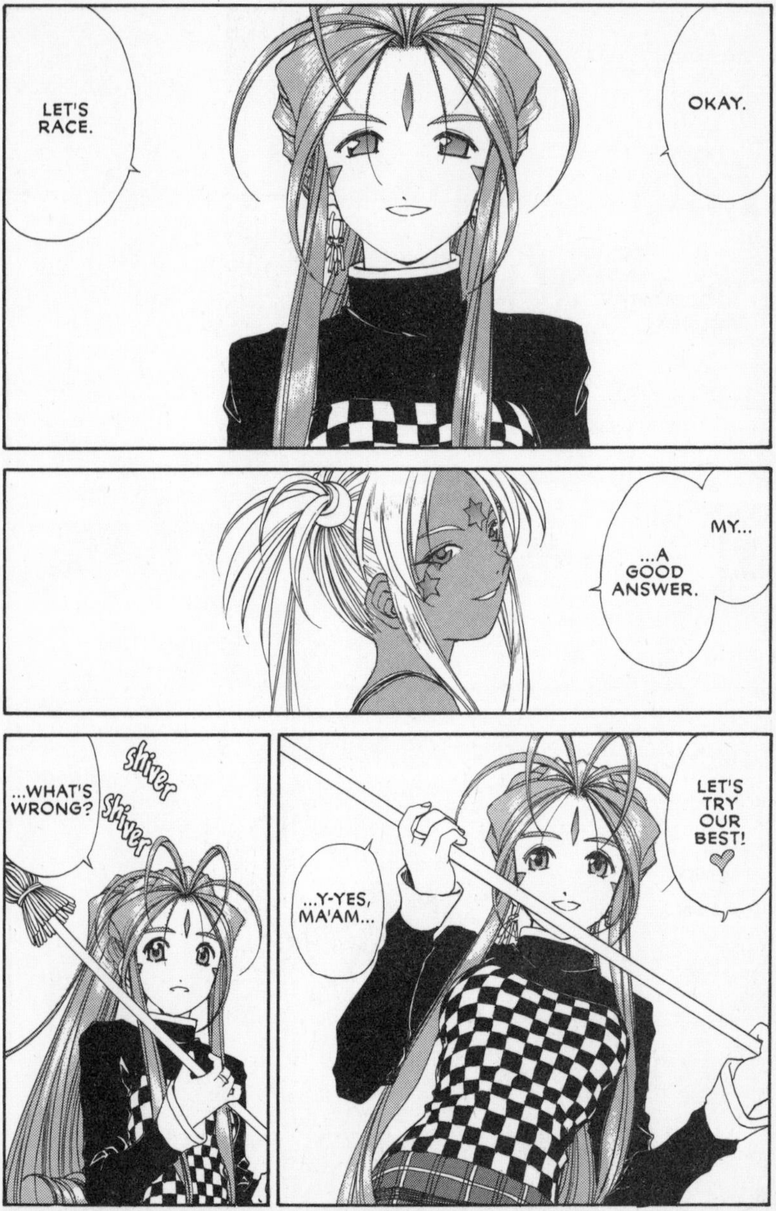
OKAY.
LET'S RACE.
MY...
...A GOOD ANSWER.
LET'S TRY OUR BEST! ♥
...Y-YES, MA'AM...
shiver
shiver
...WHAT'S WRONG?

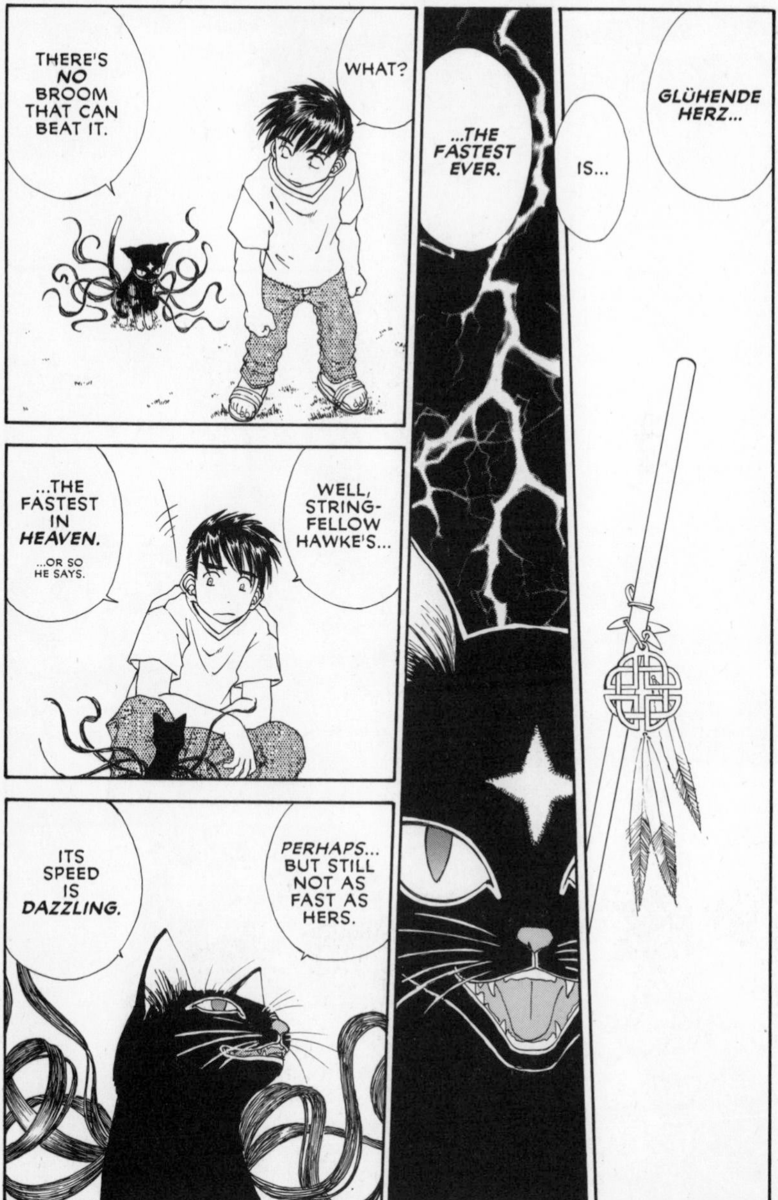
GLÜHENDE HERZ...
IS...
...THE FASTEST EVER.
WHAT?
THERE'S NO BROOM THAT CAN BEAT IT.
WELL, STRING-FELLOW HAWKE'S...
...THE FASTEST IN HEAVEN.
...OR SO HE SAYS.
PERHAPS... BUT STILL NOT AS FAST AS HERS.
ITS SPEED IS DAZZLING.

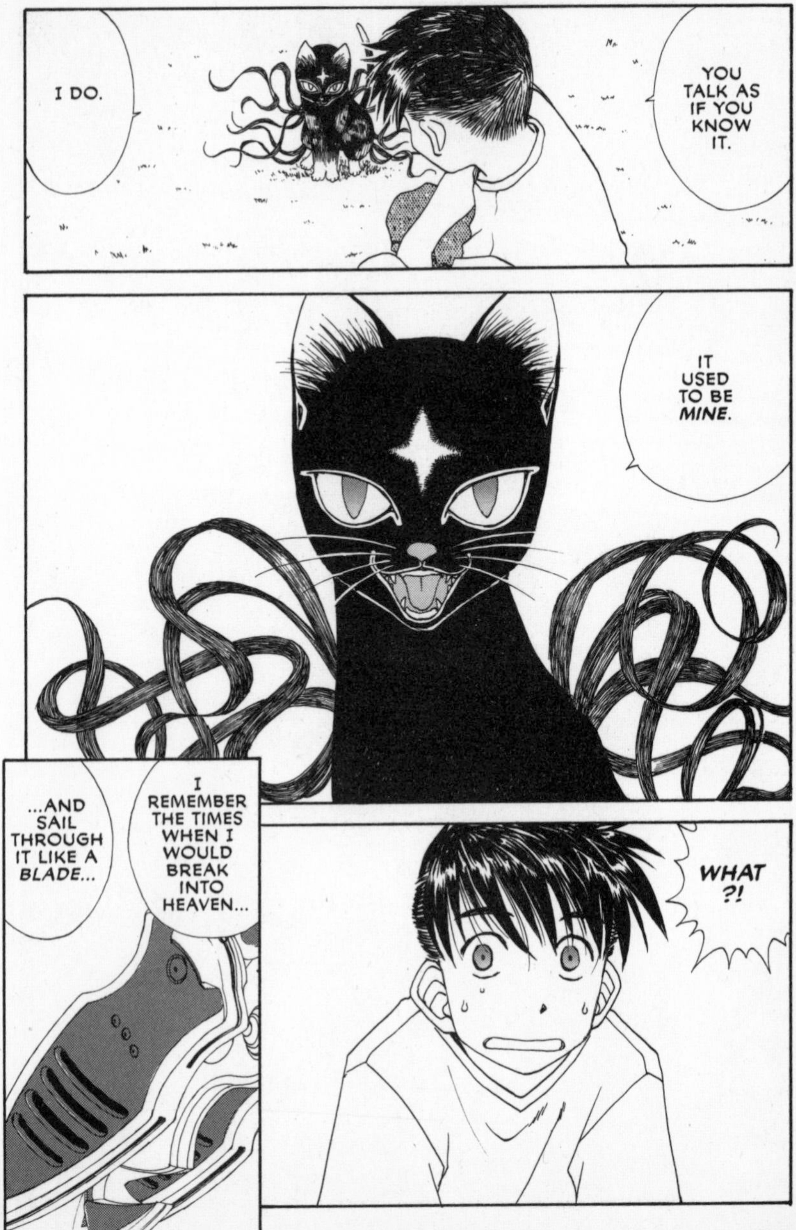
YOU TALK AS IF YOU KNOW IT.
I DO.
IT USED TO BE *MINE*.
WHAT ?!
I REMEMBER THE TIMES WHEN I WOULD BREAK INTO HEAVEN...
...AND SAIL THROUGH IT LIKE A *BLADE*...

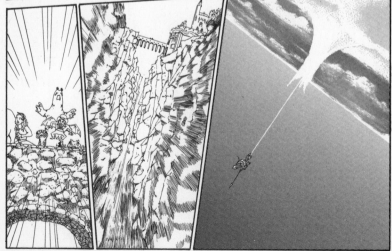

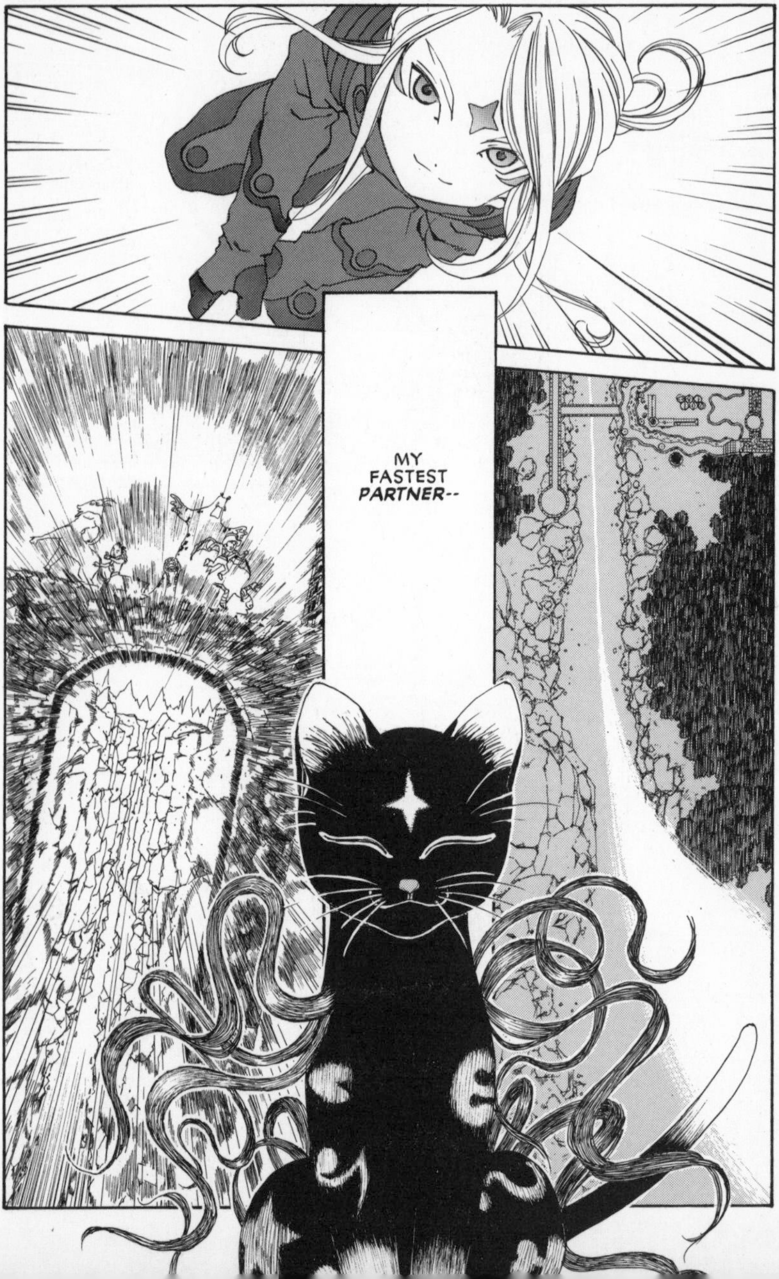
MY FASTEST PARTNER--

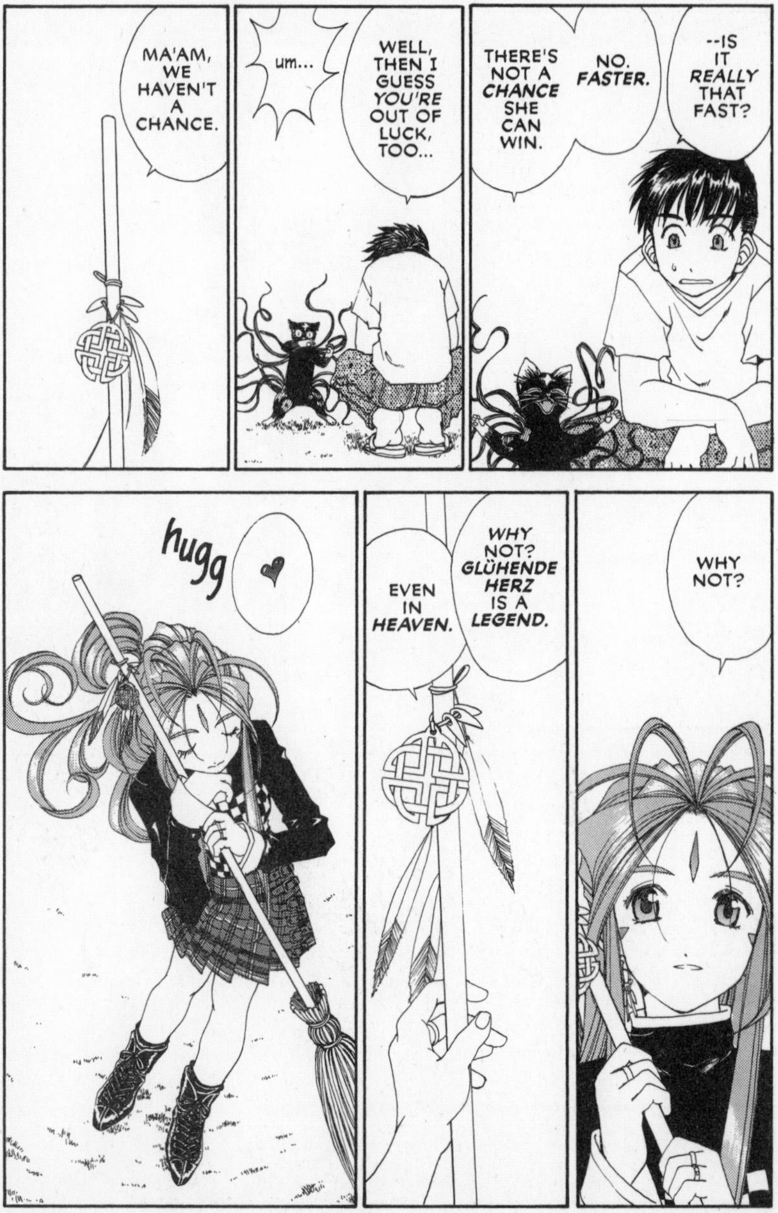
--IS IT REALLY THAT FAST?
NO. FASTER.
THERE'S NOT A CHANCE SHE CAN WIN.
WELL, THEN I GUESS YOU'RE OUT OF LUCK, TOO...
um...
MA'AM, WE HAVEN'T A CHANCE.
WHY NOT?
WHY NOT? GLÜHENDE HERZ IS A LEGEND.
EVEN IN HEAVEN.
hugg

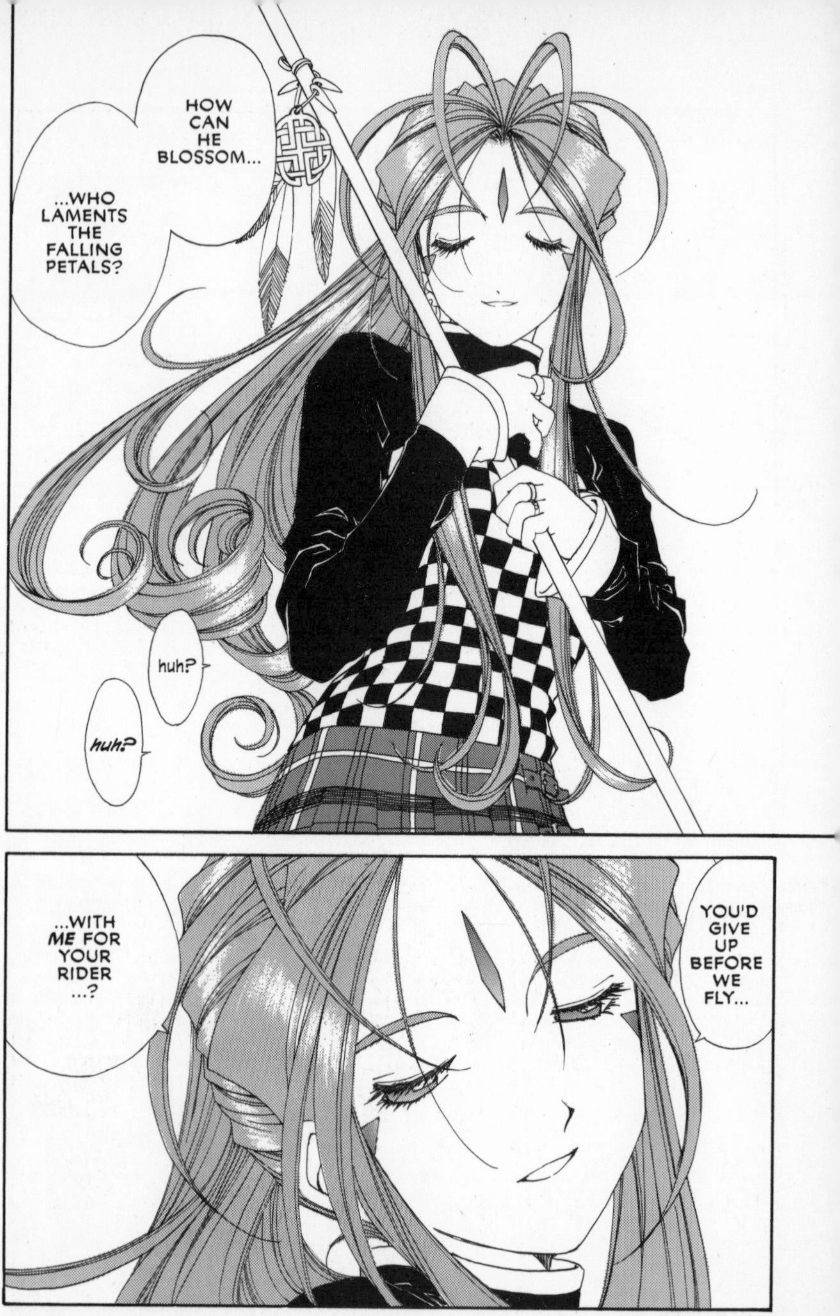
HOW CAN HE BLOSSOM... ...WHO LAMENTS THE FALLING PETALS?
huh?
huh?
YOU'D GIVE UP BEFORE WE FLY...
...WITH *ME* FOR YOUR RIDER ...?

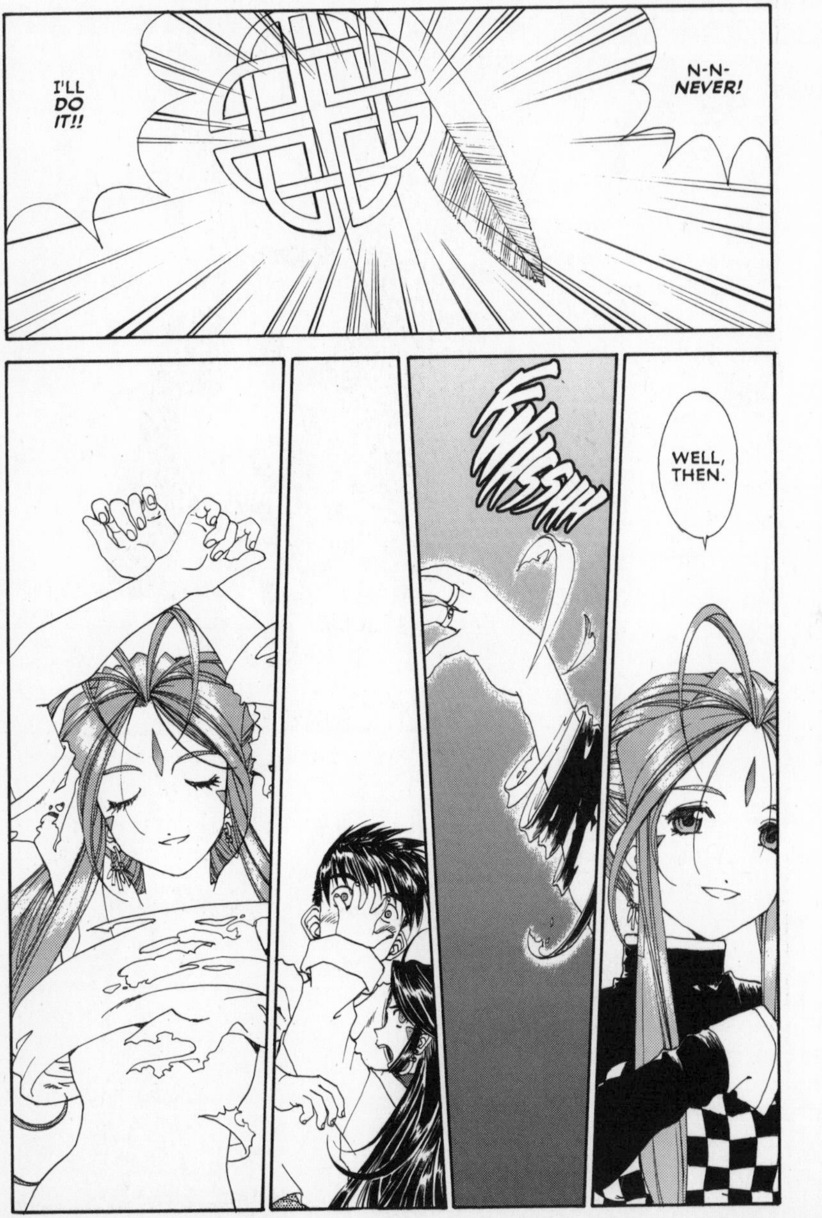
N-N-
NEVER!
I'LL
DO
IT!!
WELL,
THEN.

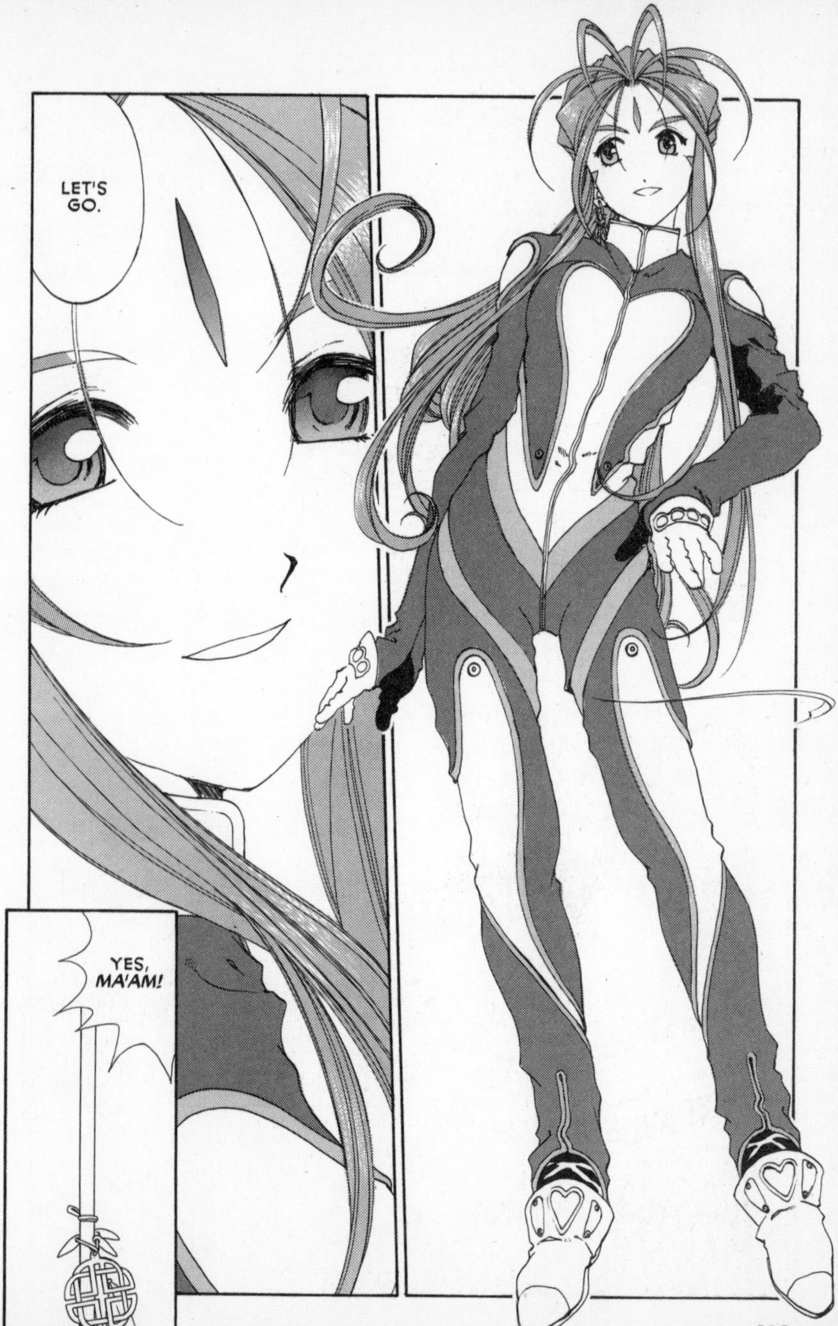
LET'S GO.
YES, MA'AM!

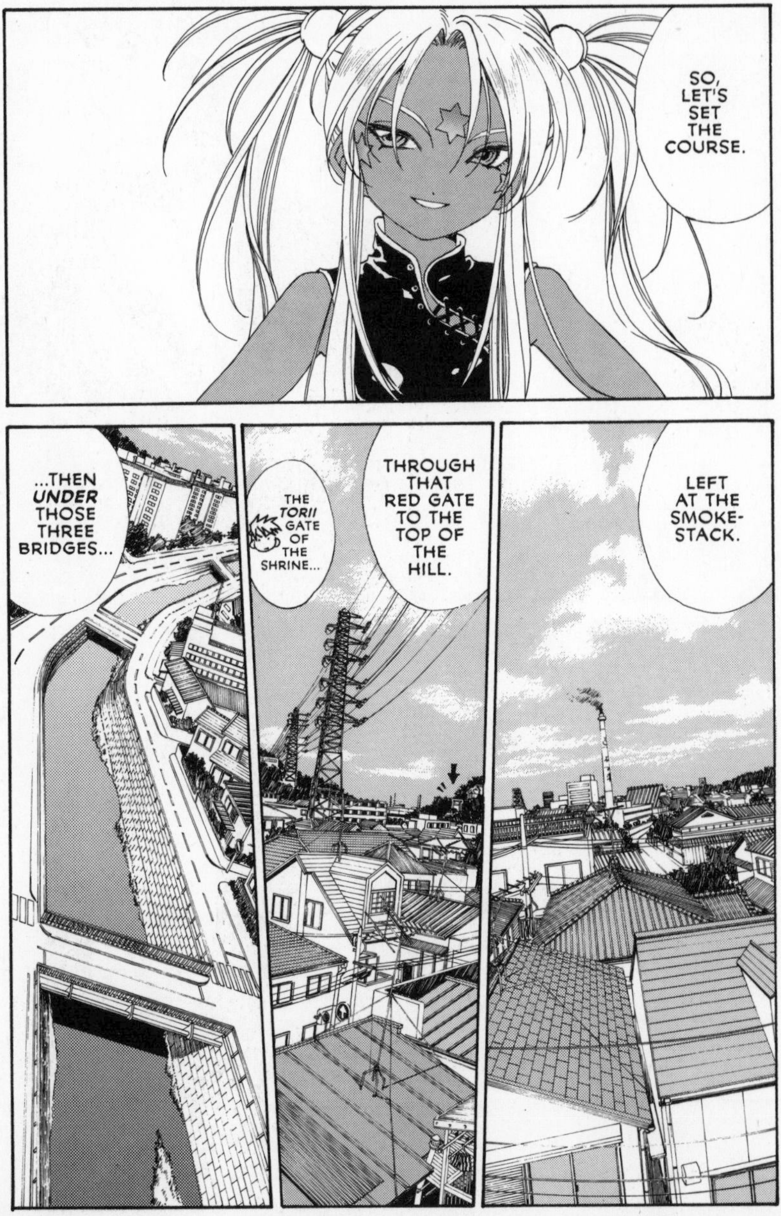
SO, LET'S SET THE COURSE.
LEFT AT THE SMOKE-STACK.
THROUGH THAT RED GATE TO THE TOP OF THE HILL.
THE *TORII* GATE OF THE SHRINE...
...THEN *UNDER* THOSE THREE BRIDGES...

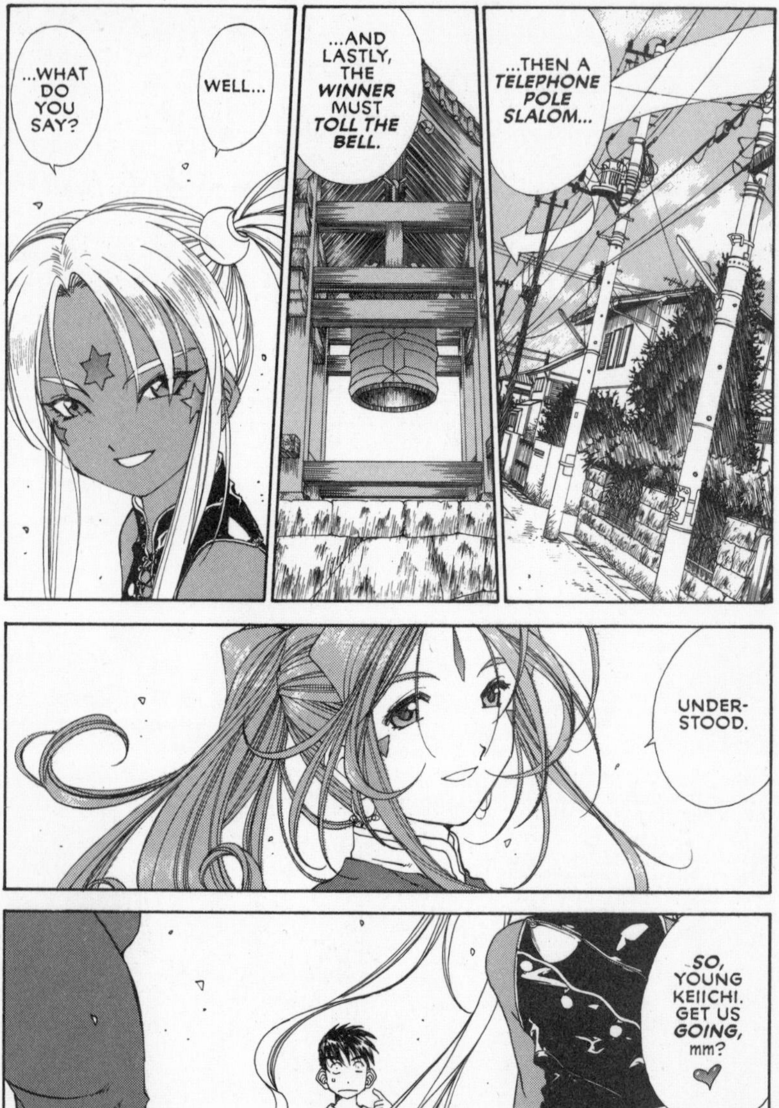
...THEN A TELEPHONE POLE SLALOM...
...AND LASTLY, THE WINNER MUST TOLL THE BELL.
WELL...
...WHAT DO YOU SAY?
UNDER-STOOD.
SO, YOUNG KEIICHI. GET US GOING, mm? ❤

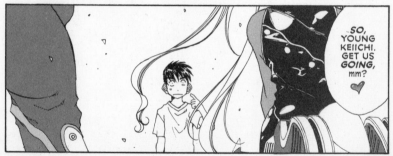

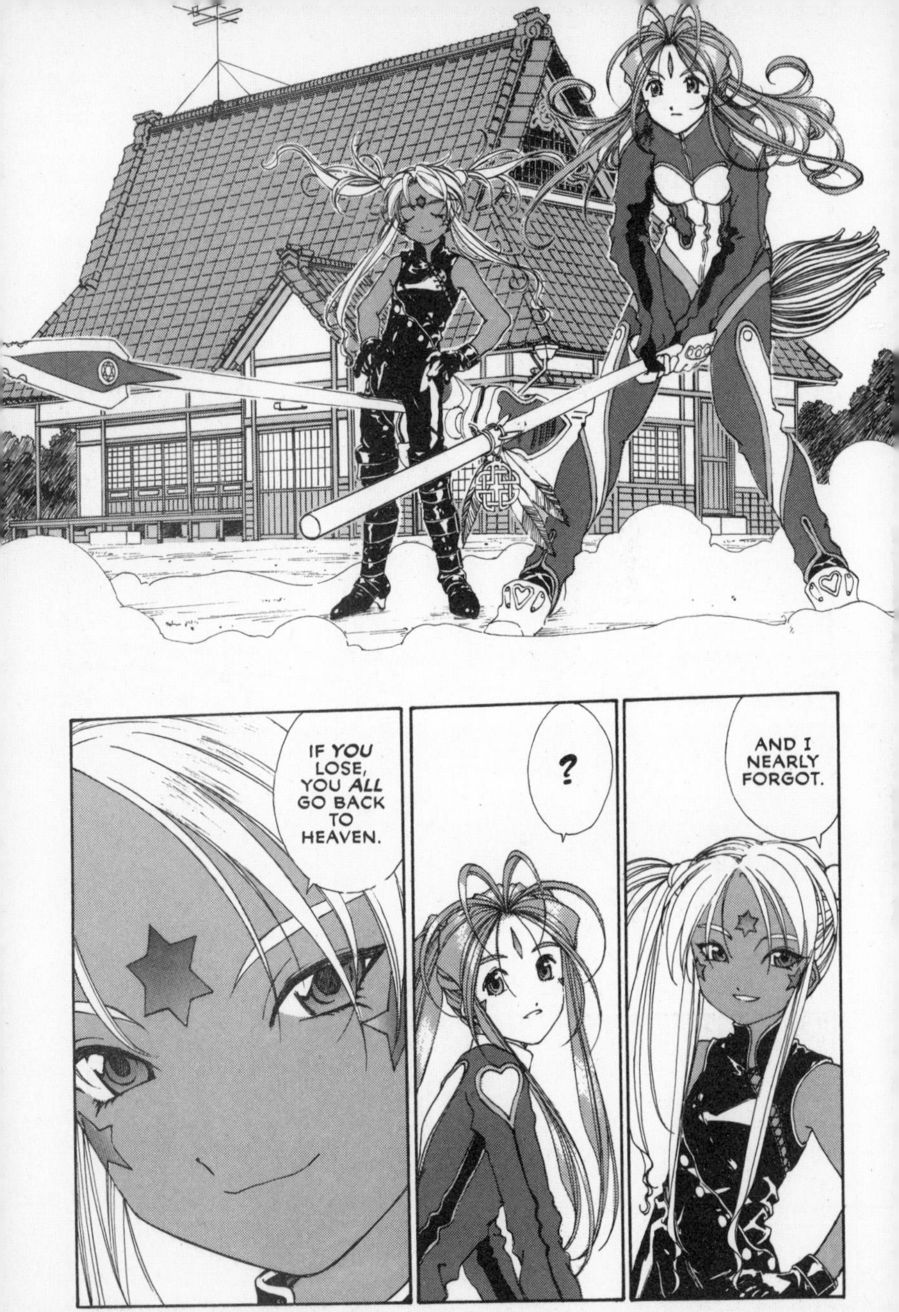
AND I NEARLY FORGOT.
?
IF *YOU* LOSE, YOU *ALL* GO BACK TO HEAVEN.

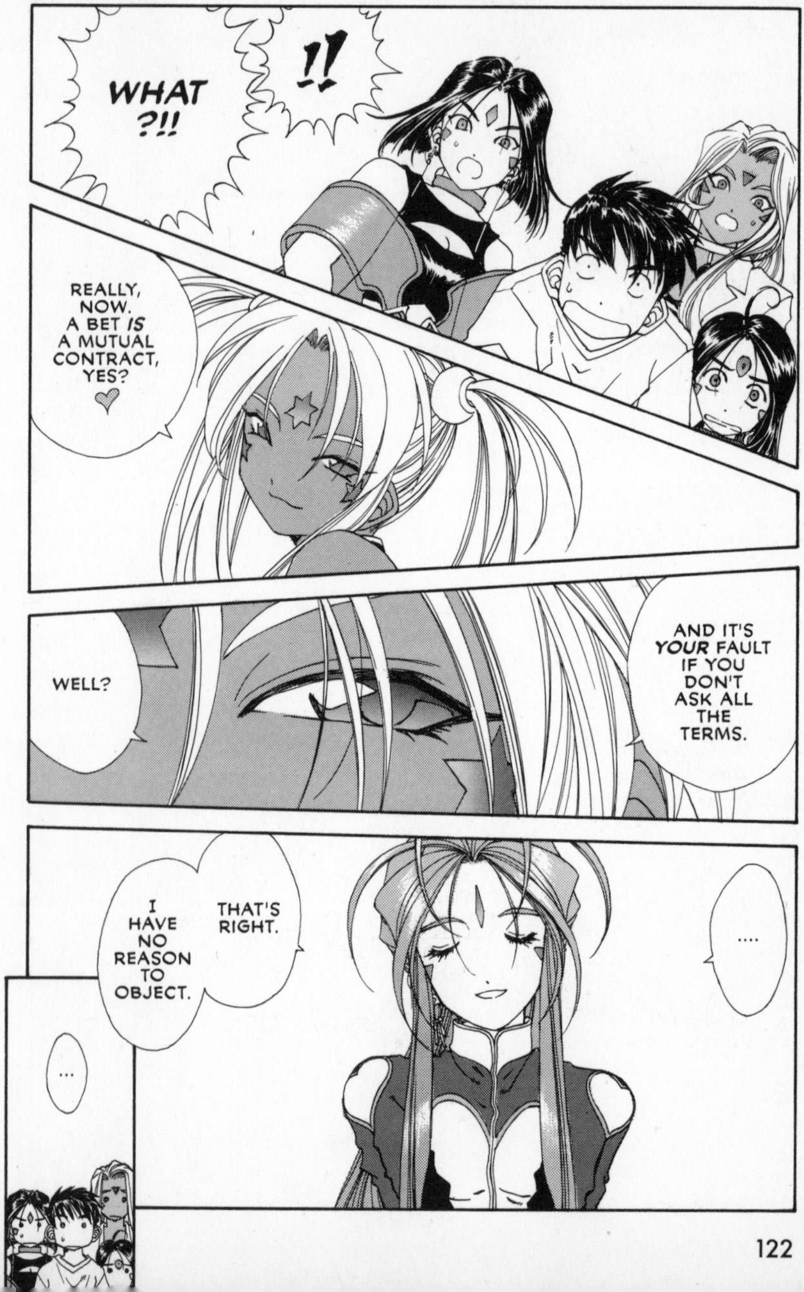
!!
WHAT ?!!
REALLY, NOW. A BET *IS* A MUTUAL CONTRACT, YES? ♥
AND IT'S *YOUR* FAULT IF YOU DON'T ASK ALL THE TERMS.
WELL?
....
THAT'S RIGHT.
I HAVE NO REASON TO OBJECT.
...

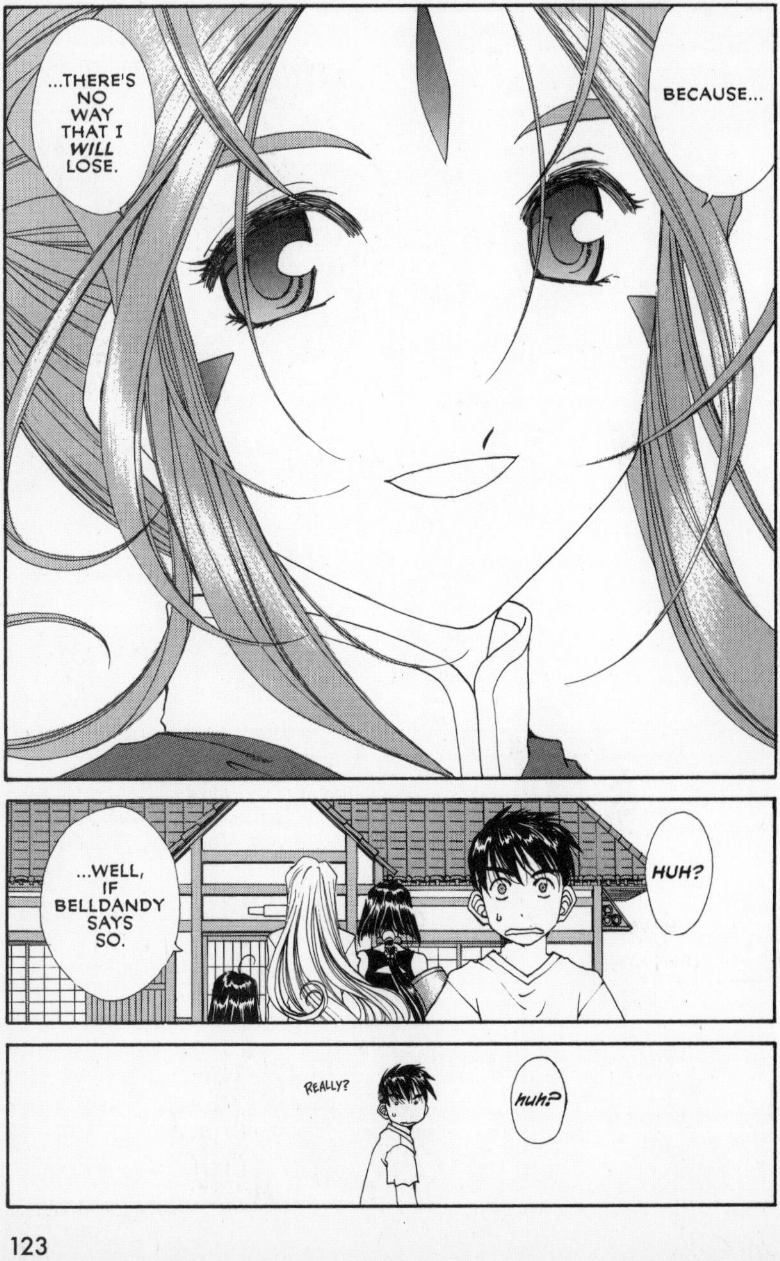
BECAUSE...
...THERE'S NO WAY THAT I *WILL* LOSE.
HUH?
...WELL, IF BELLDANDY SAYS SO.
huh?
REALLY?

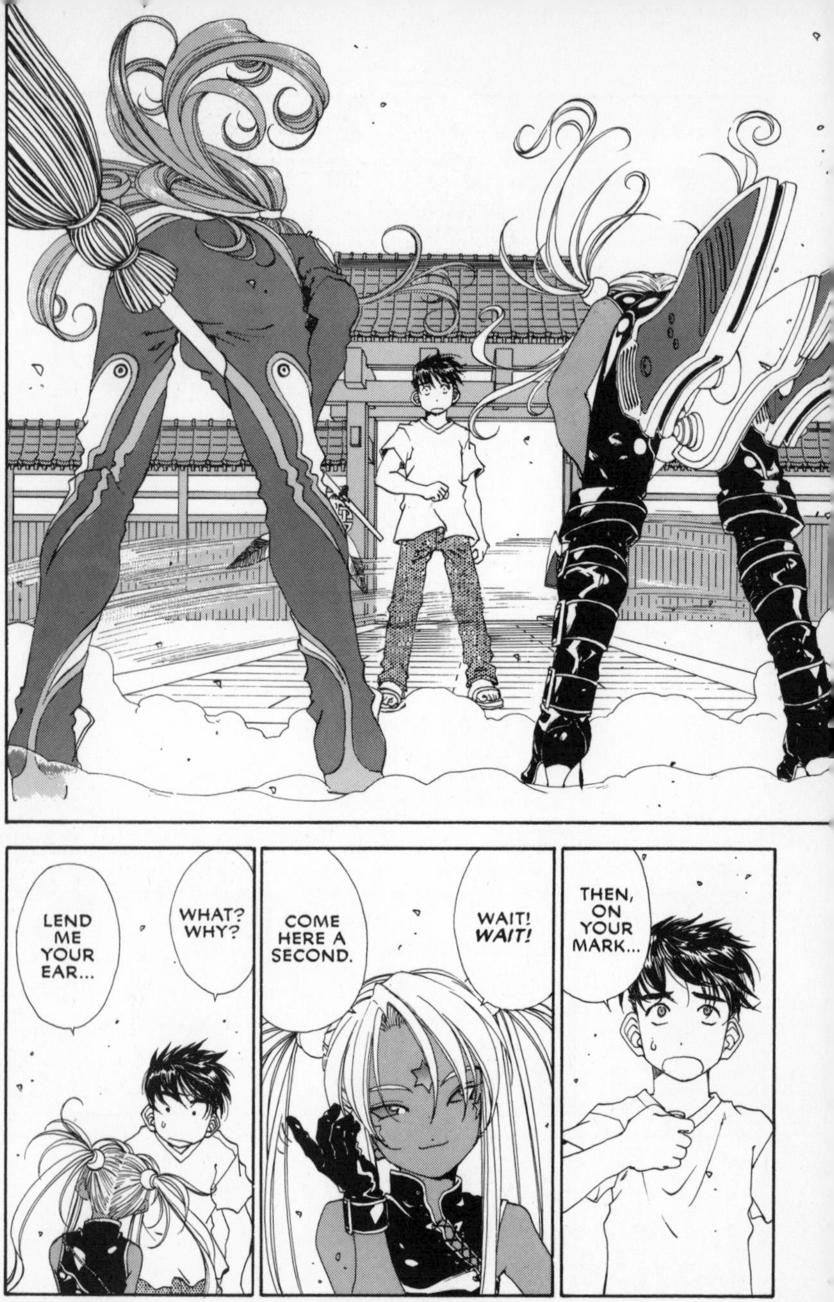
THEN, ON YOUR MARK...
WAIT! *WAIT!*
COME HERE A SECOND.
WHAT? WHY?
LEND ME YOUR EAR...

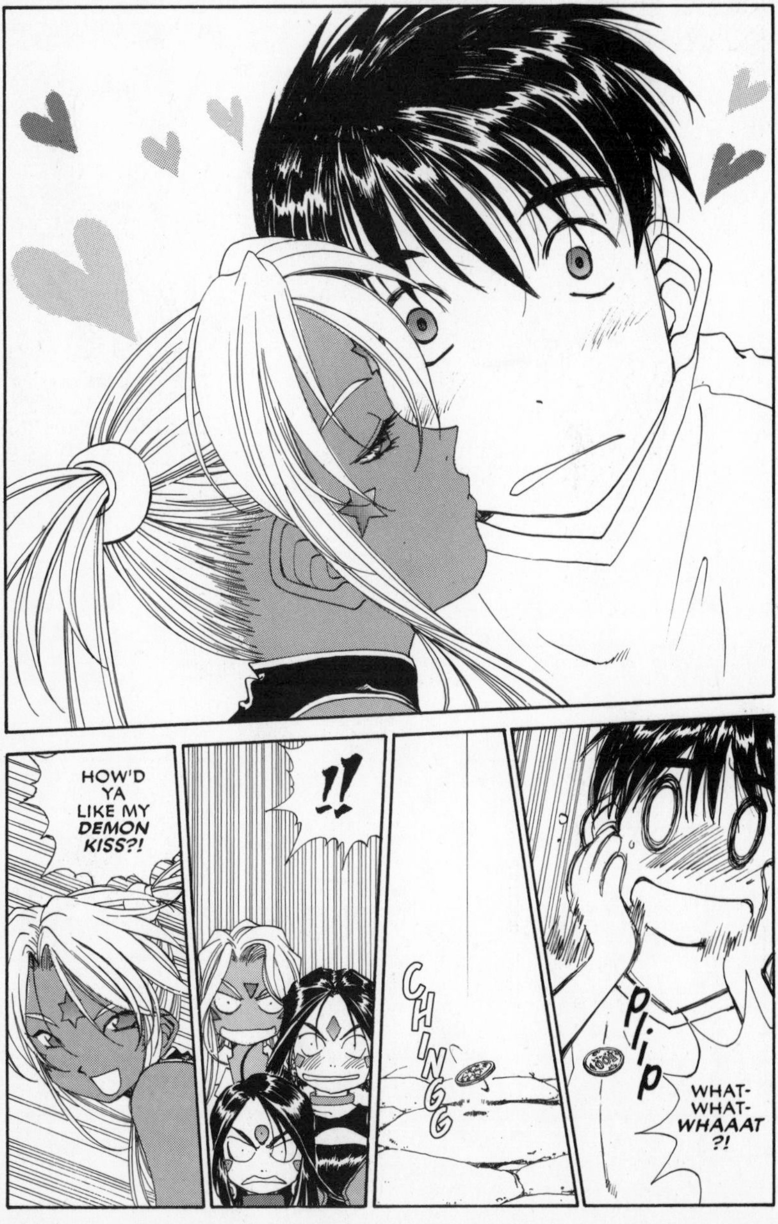
PLIP
WHAT-WHAT-WHAAAT?!
CHINGG
!!
HOW'D YA LIKE MY DEMON KISS?!

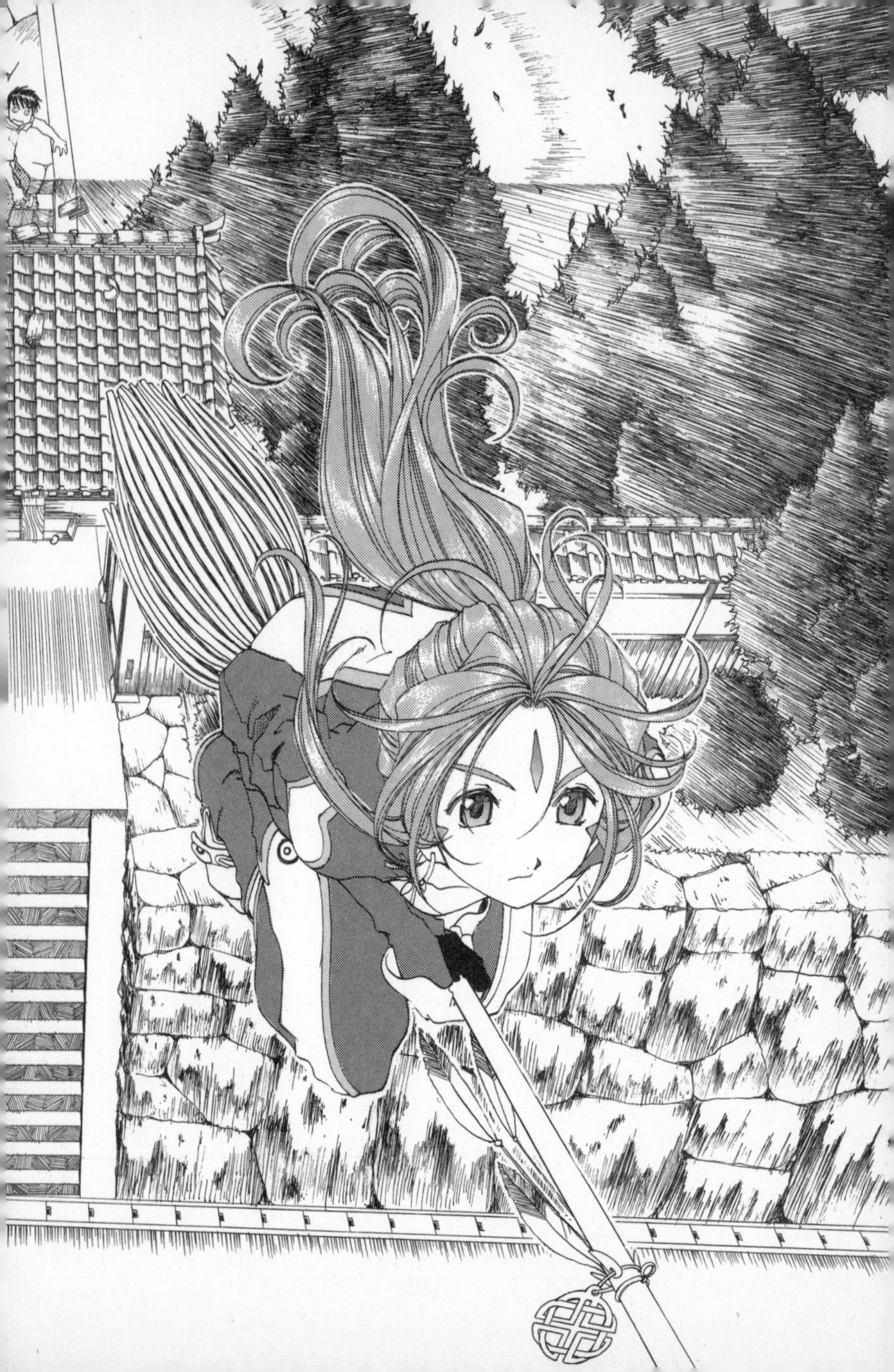

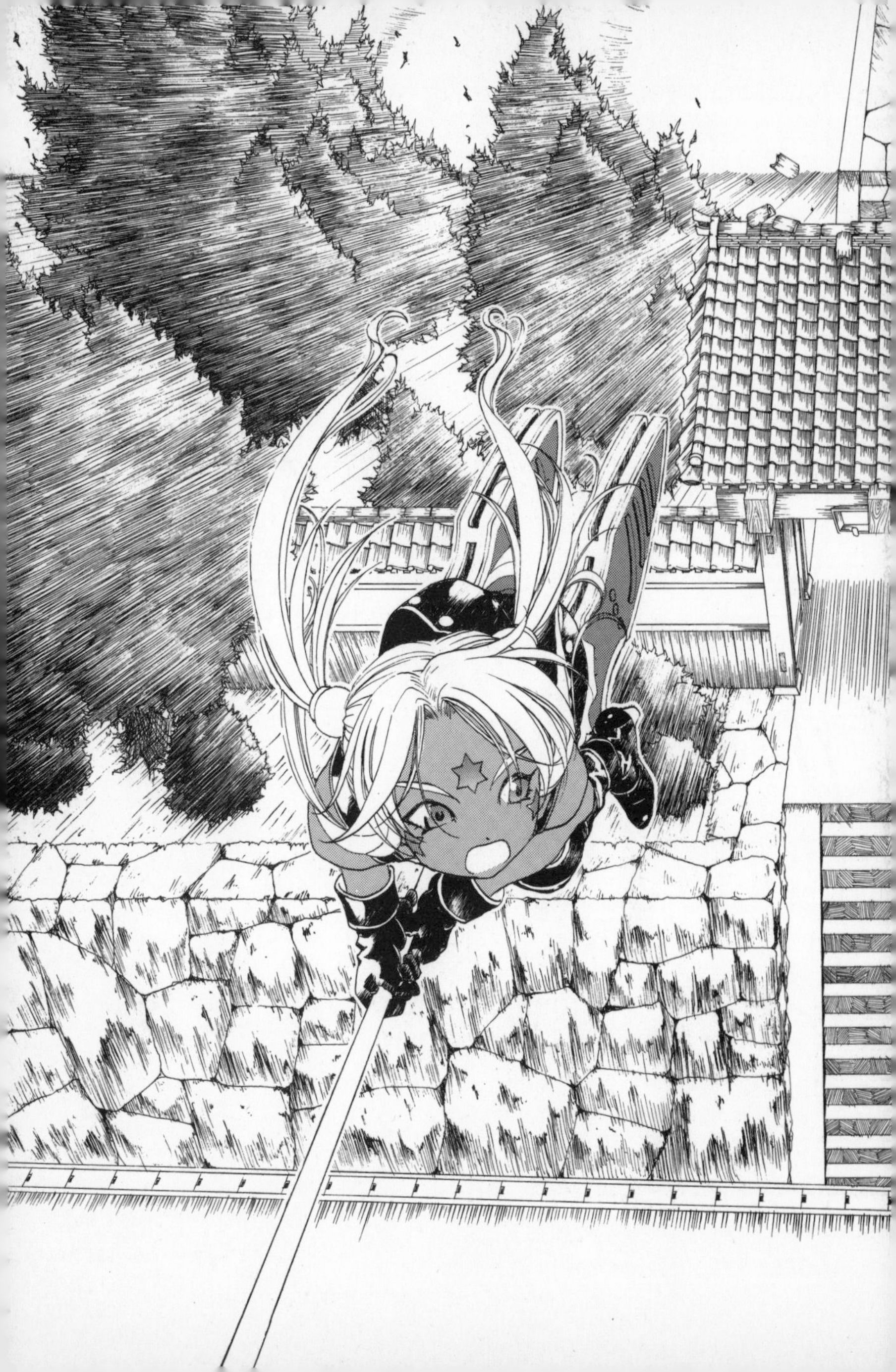

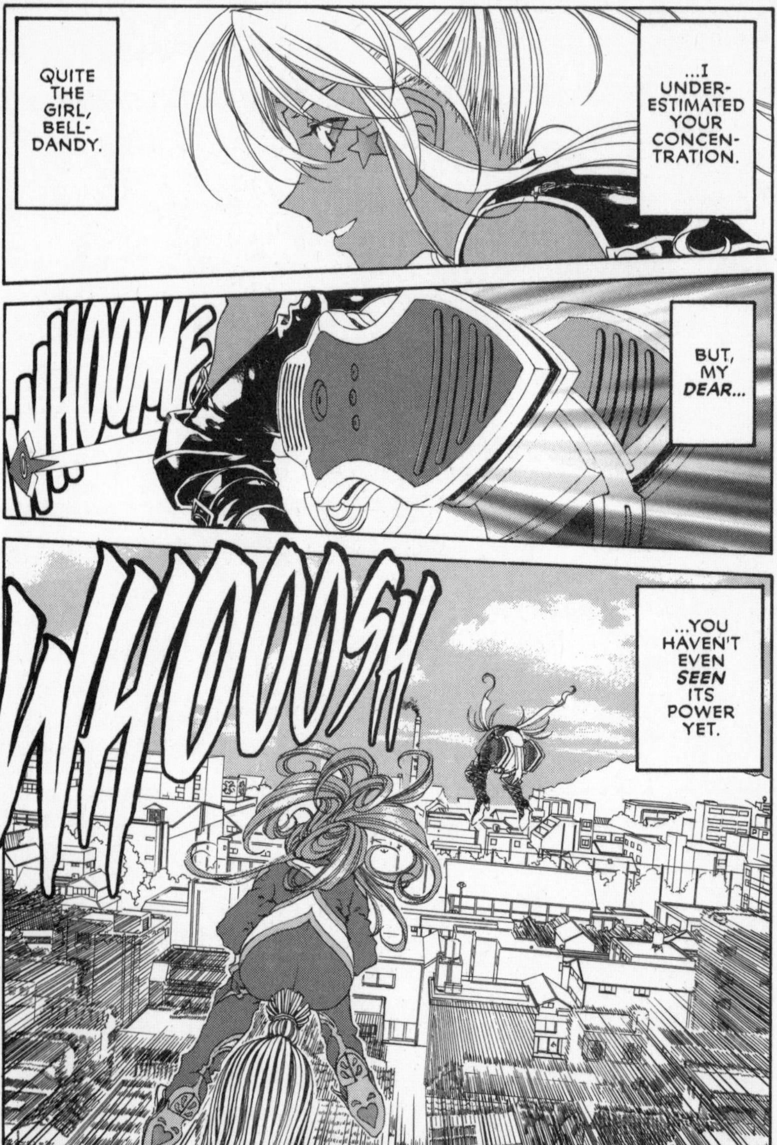
...I UNDER-ESTIMATED YOUR CONCEN-TRATION.
QUITE THE GIRL, BELL-DANDY.
BUT, MY *DEAR*...
WHOOMF
...YOU HAVEN'T EVEN *SEEN* ITS POWER YET.
WHOOOSH

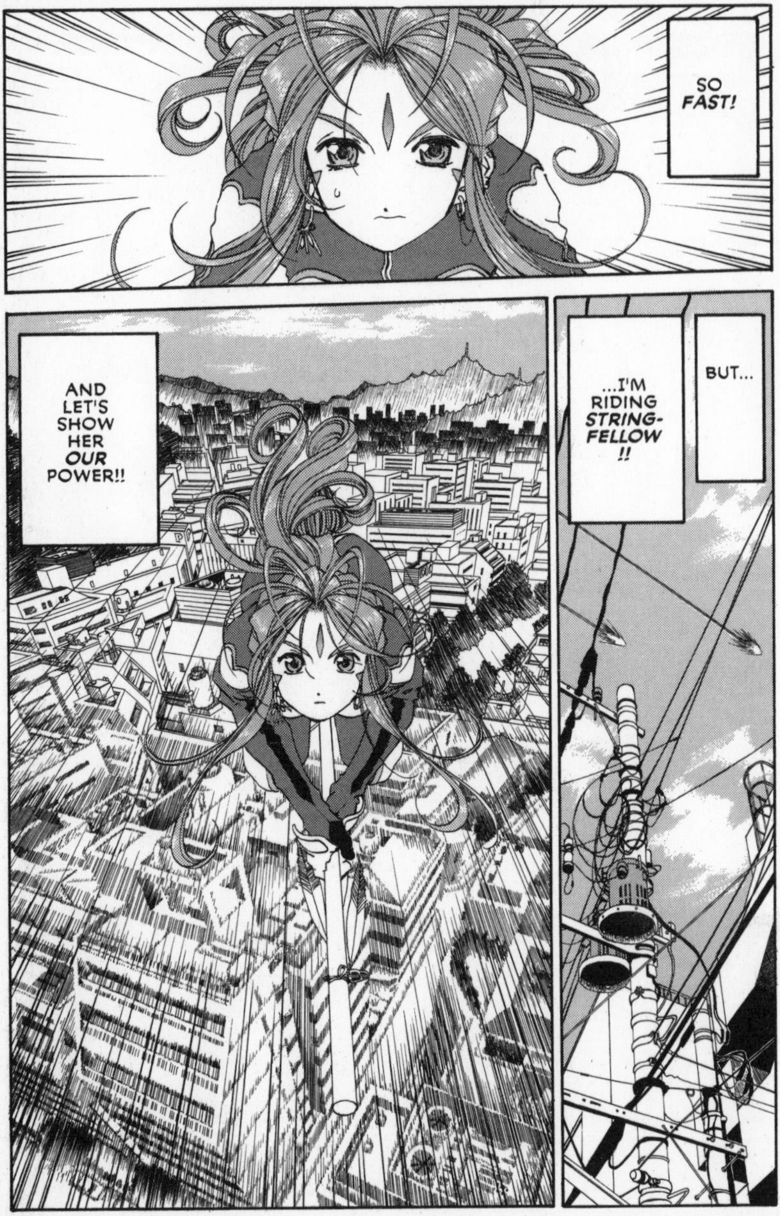
SO FAST!
BUT...
...I'M RIDING STRING-FELLOW!!
AND LET'S SHOW HER OUR POWER!!

OH MY GODDESS!

BELLDANDY

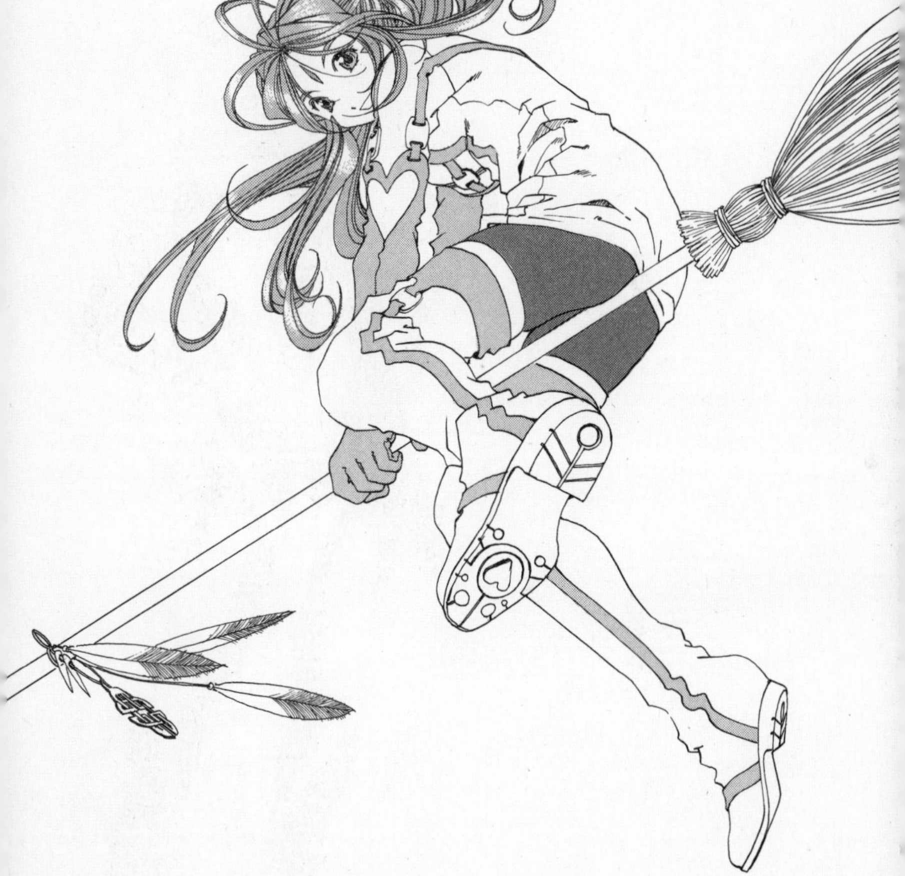

CHAPTER 182

Courage and Trial

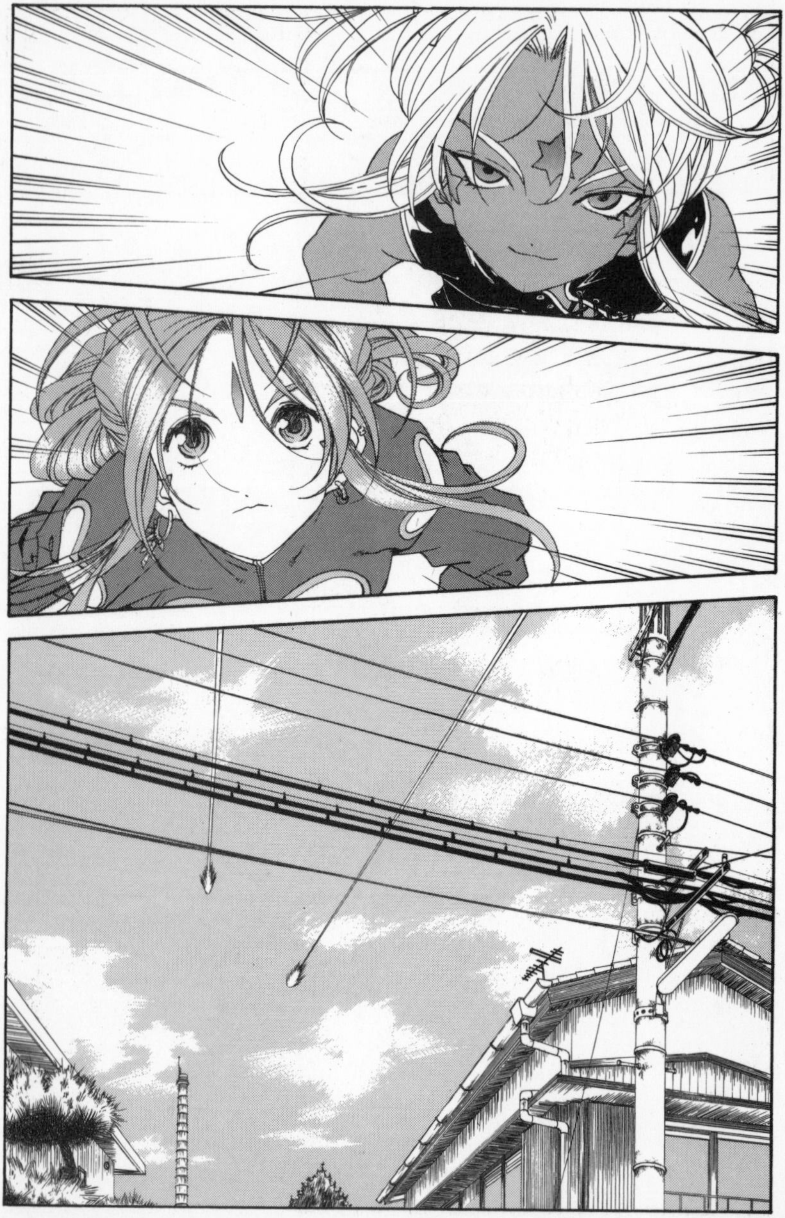

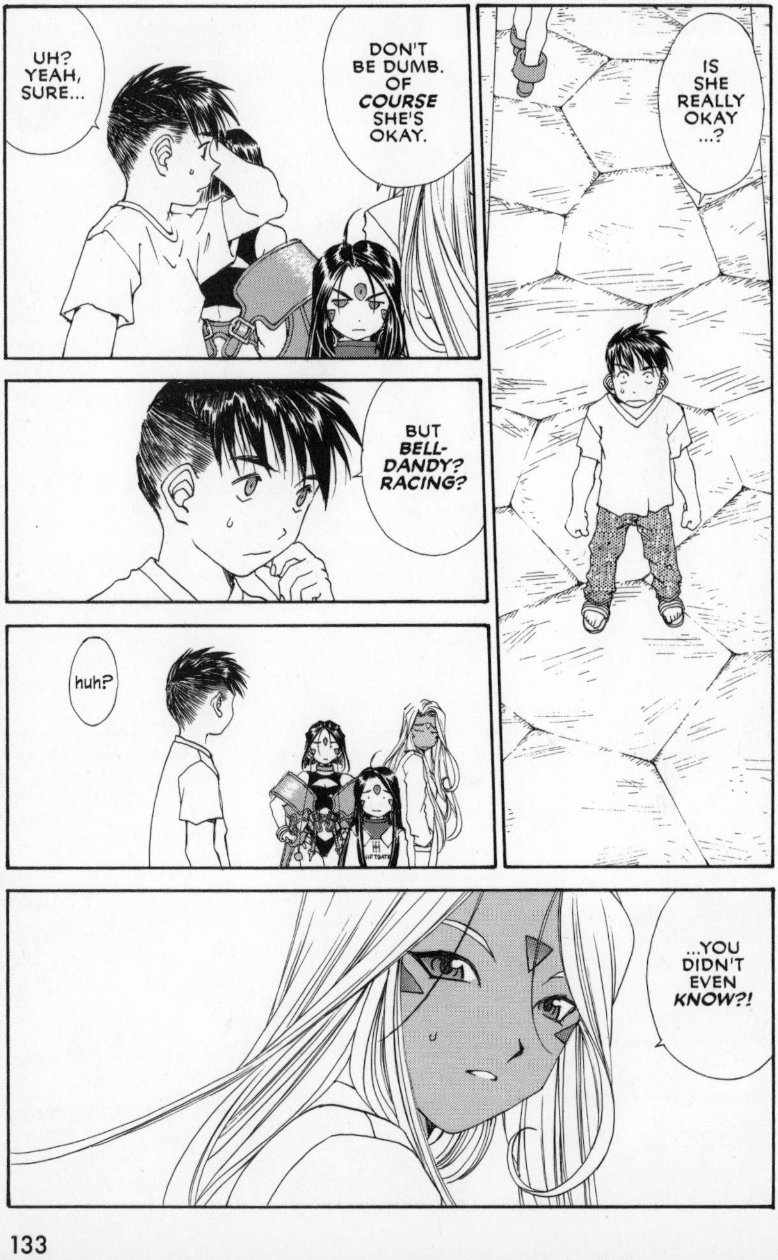
IS SHE REALLY OKAY ...?
DON'T BE DUMB. OF *COURSE* SHE'S OKAY.
UH? YEAH, SURE...
BUT *BELL-DANDY? RACING?*
huh?
...YOU DIDN'T EVEN *KNOW?!*

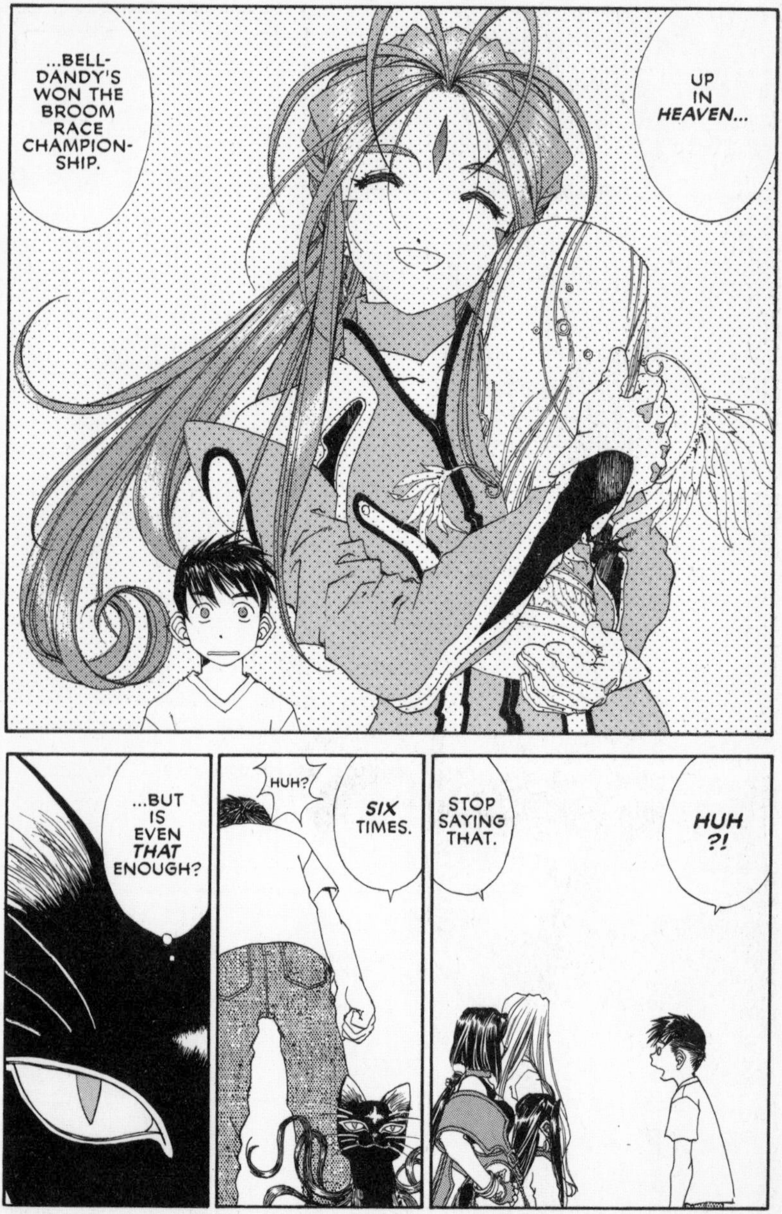
UP IN *HEAVEN...*
...BELL-DANDY'S WON THE BROOM RACE CHAMPION-SHIP.
HUH ?!
STOP SAYING THAT.
SIX TIMES.
HUH?
...BUT IS EVEN *THAT* ENOUGH?

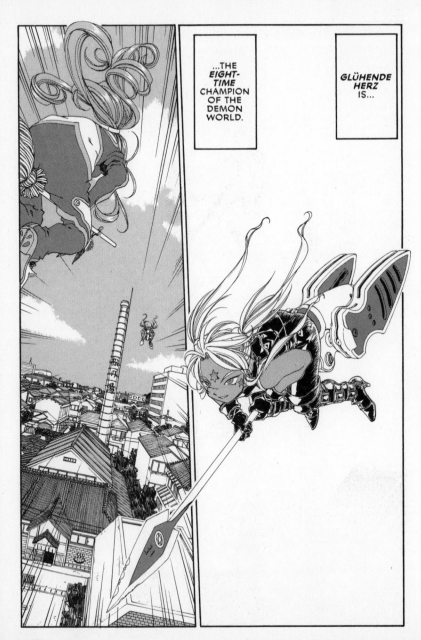

GLÜHENDE HERZ IS...
...THE *EIGHT-TIME* CHAMPION OF THE DEMON WORLD.

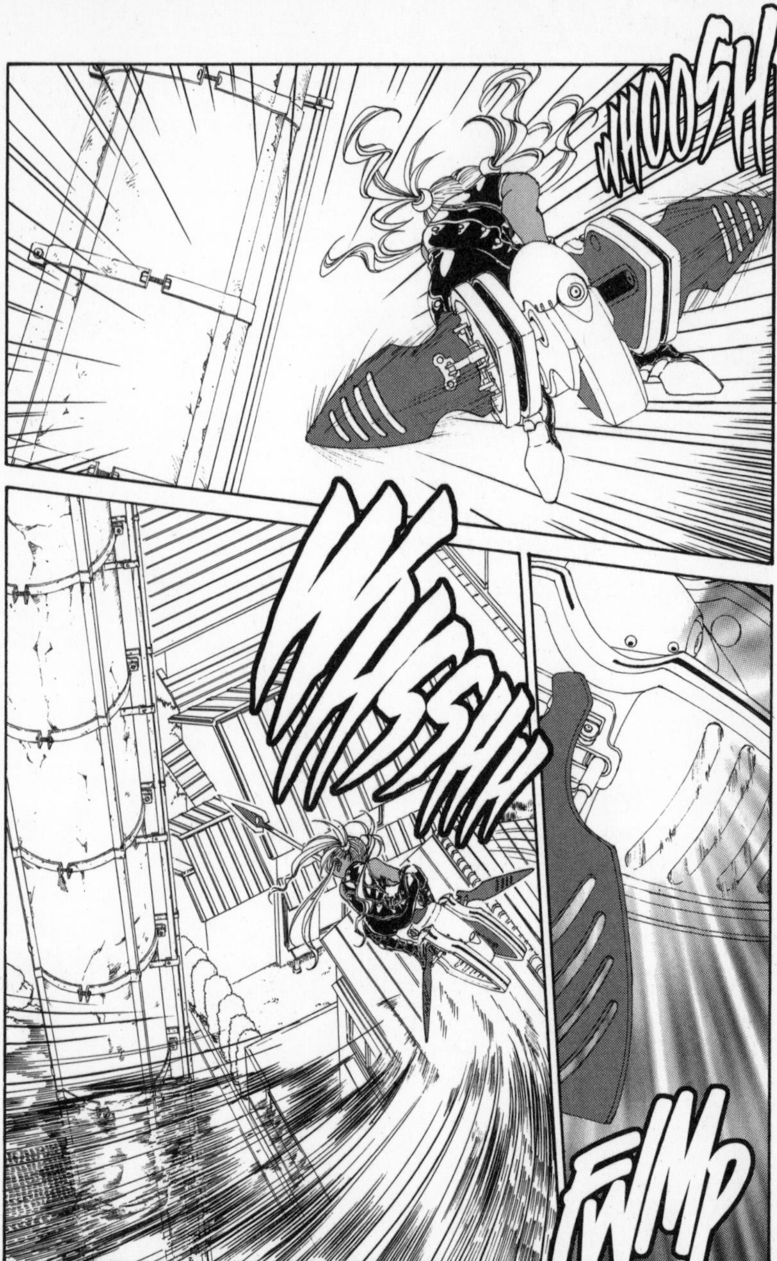
WHOOSH
FWMP
WHSHH

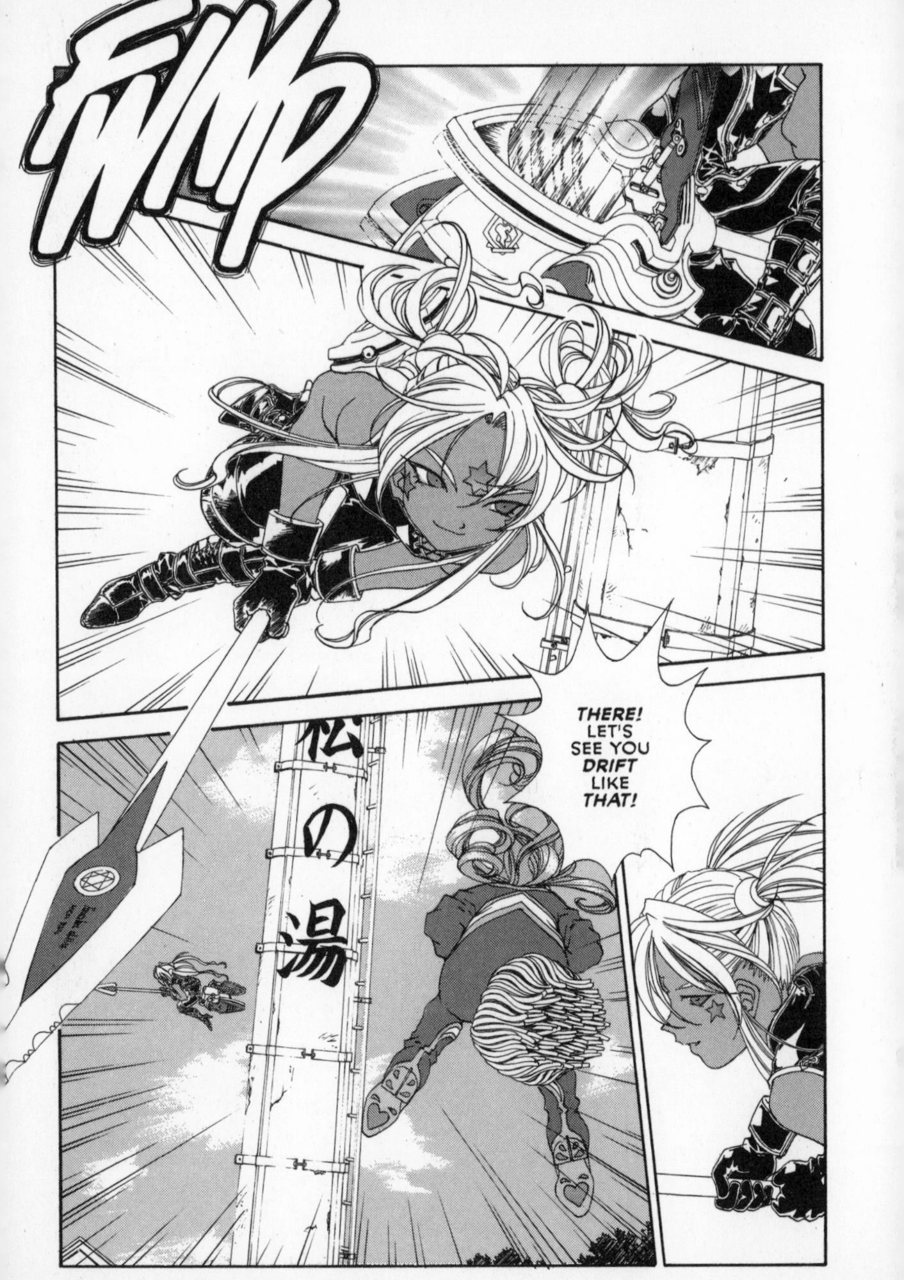
FWIP
松の湯
THERE! LET'S SEE YOU DRIFT LIKE THAT!

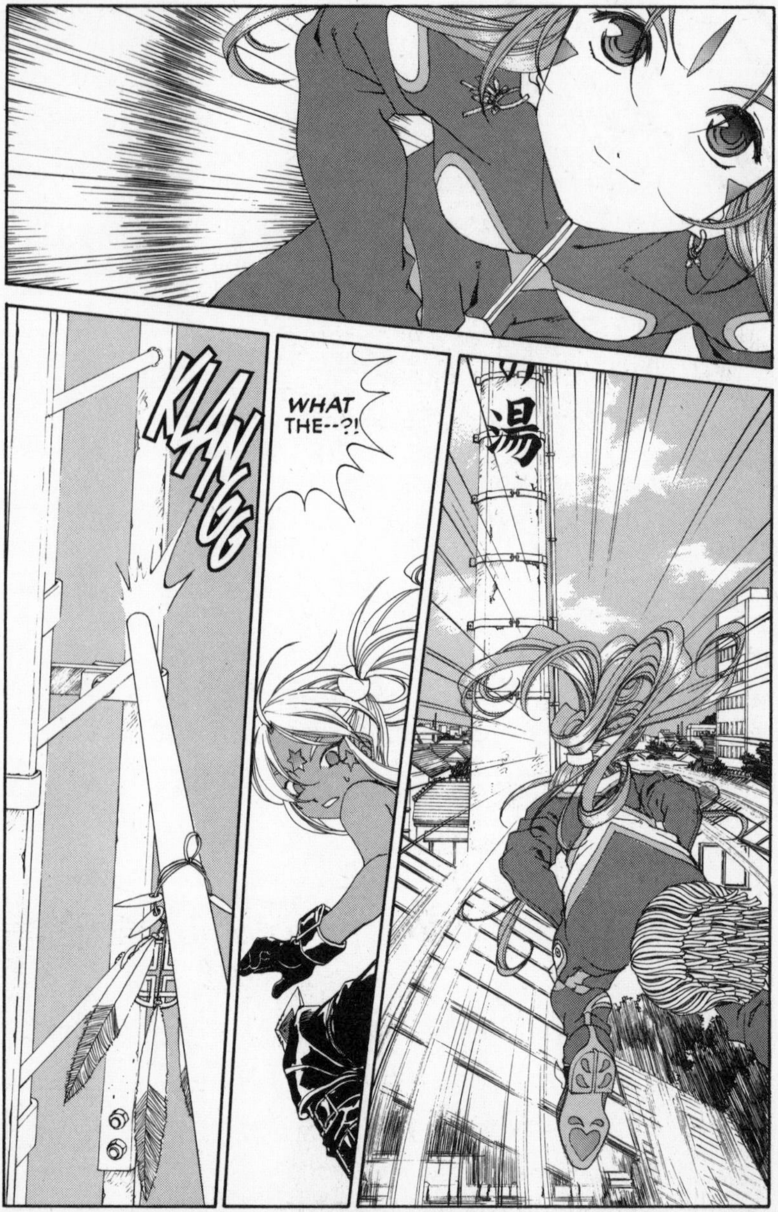
湯
WHAT THE--?!
KLANGG

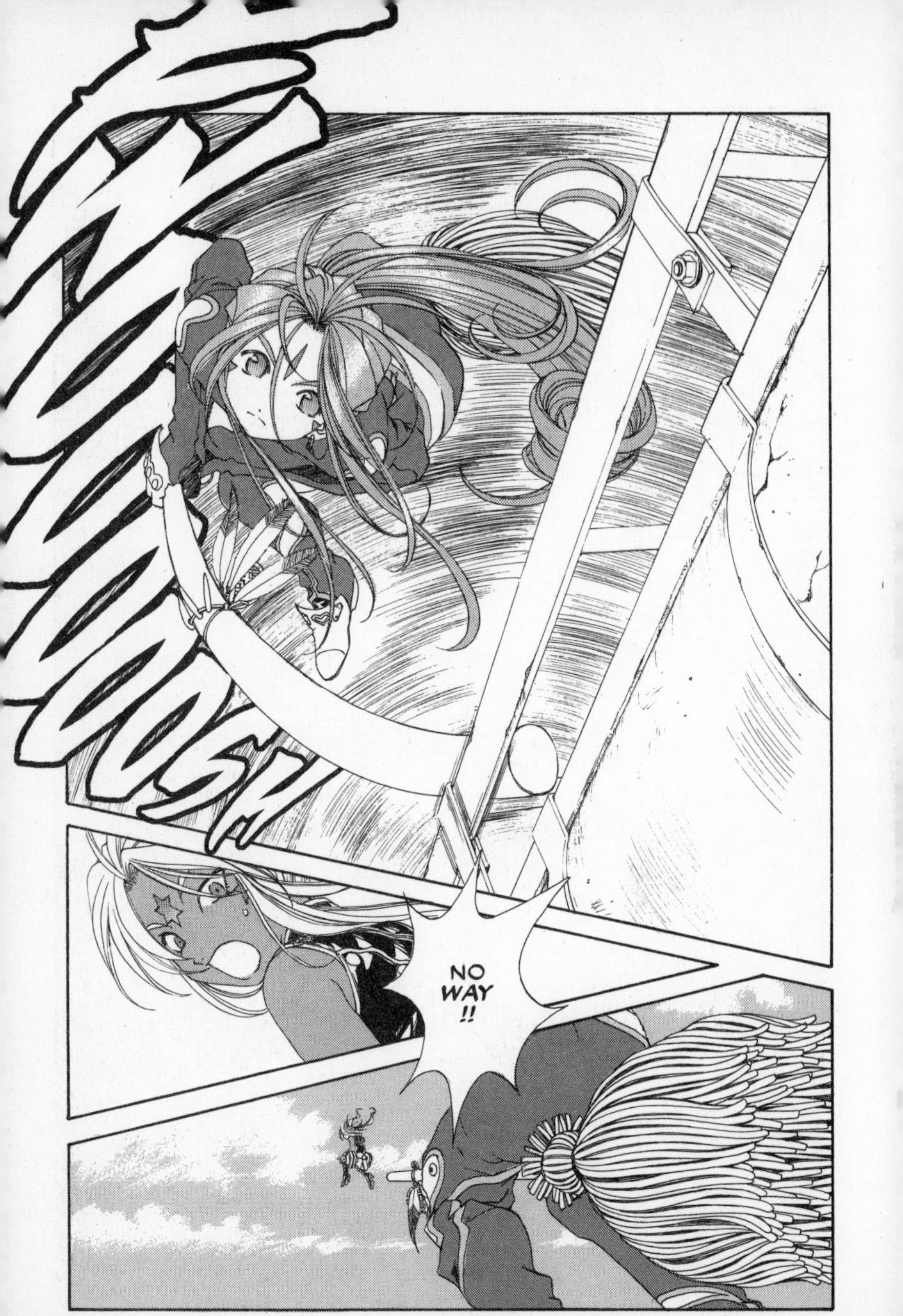
NO WAY !!

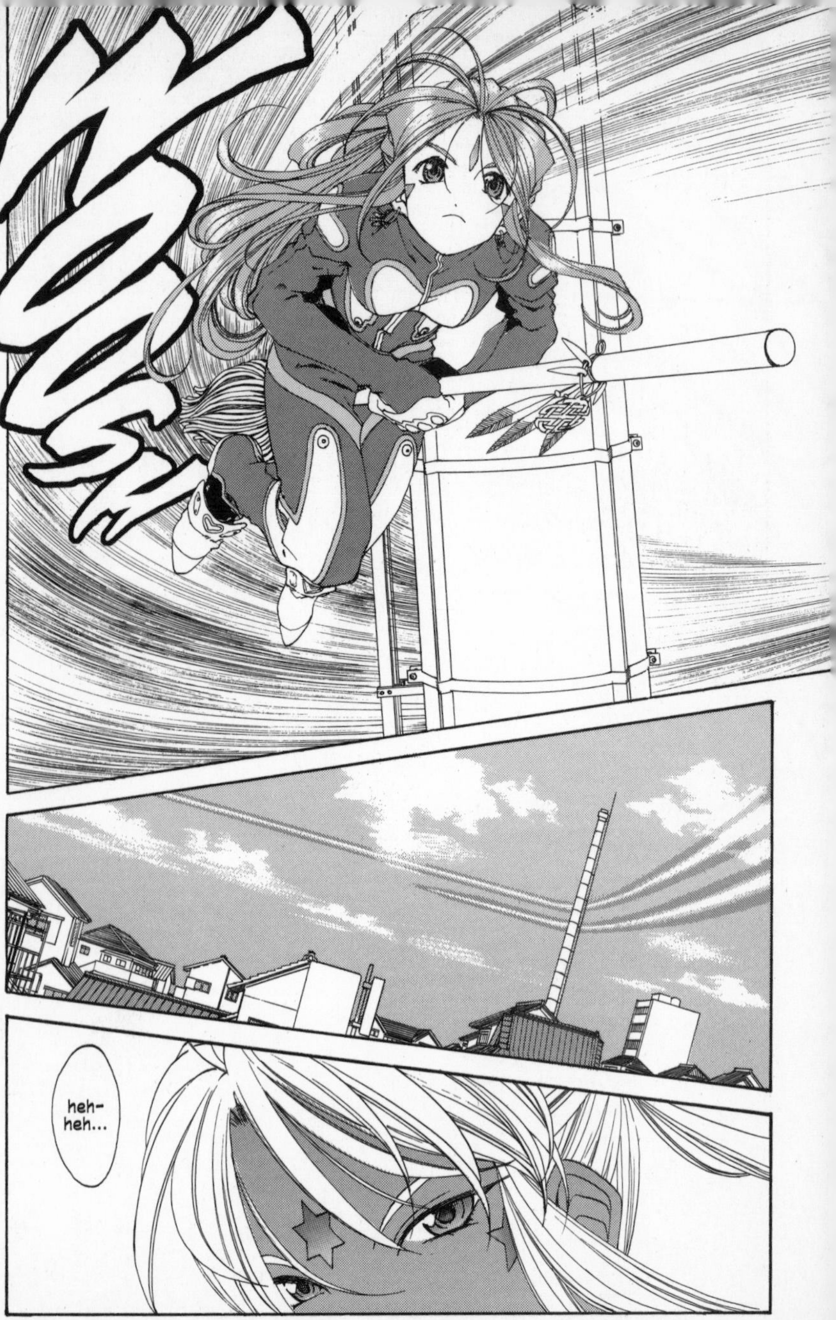
ZOOM
heh-heh...

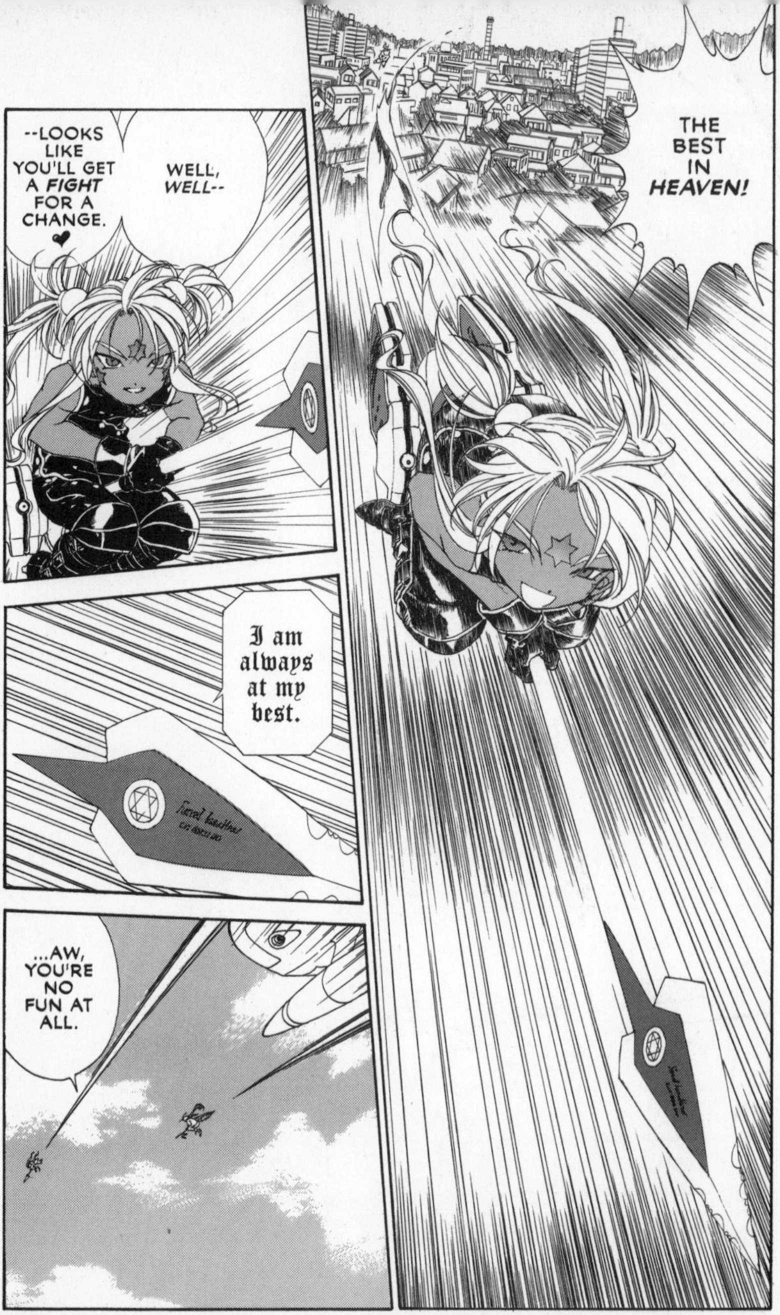
THE BEST IN *HEAVEN!*
WELL, *WELL*--
--LOOKS LIKE YOU'LL GET A *FIGHT* FOR A CHANGE. ♥
I am always at my best.
...AW, YOU'RE NO FUN AT ALL.

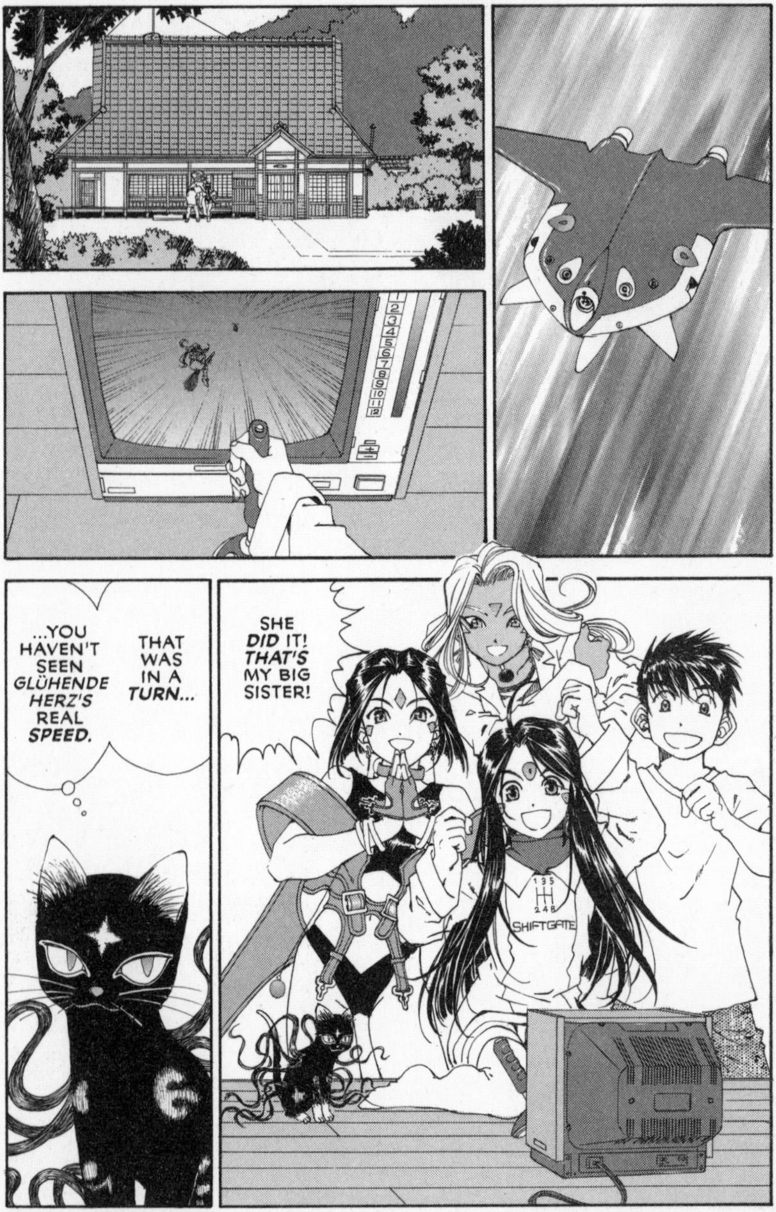
SHE DID IT! THAT'S MY BIG SISTER!
SHIFTGATE
THAT WAS IN A TURN...
...YOU HAVEN'T SEEN GLÜHENDE HERZ'S REAL SPEED.

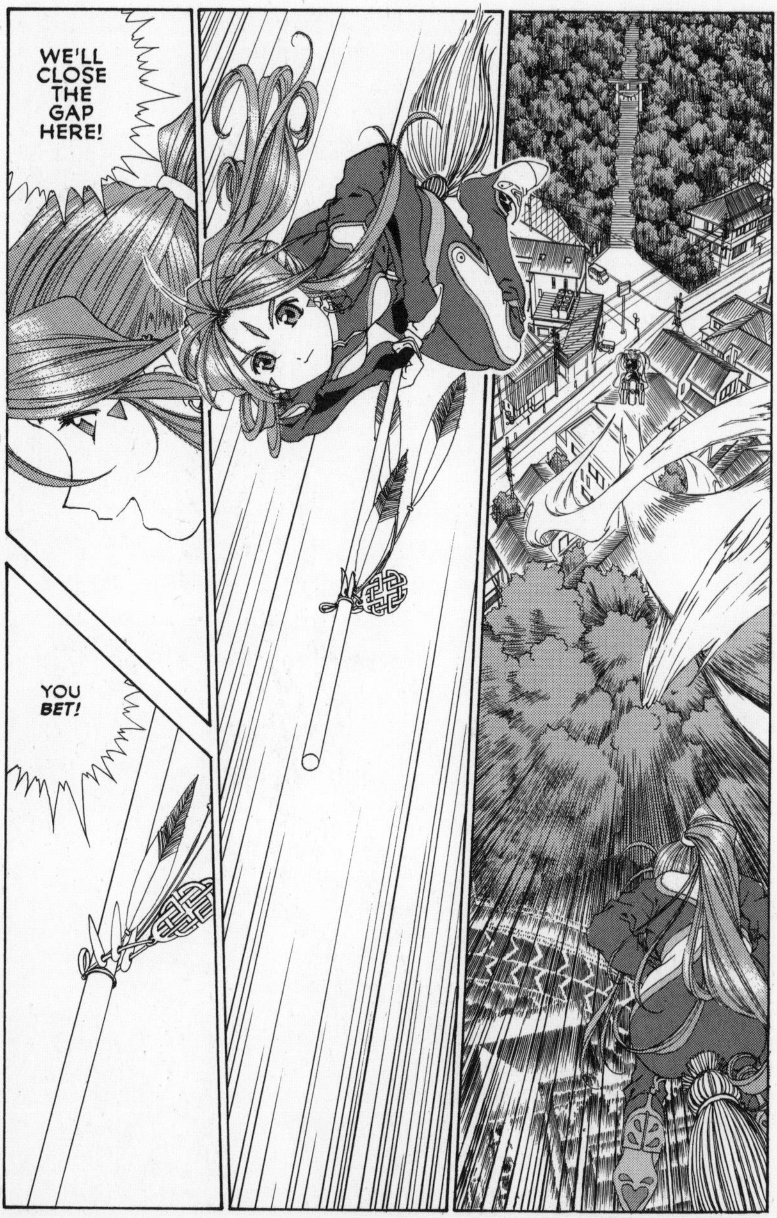
WE'LL CLOSE THE GAP HERE!
YOU *BET!*

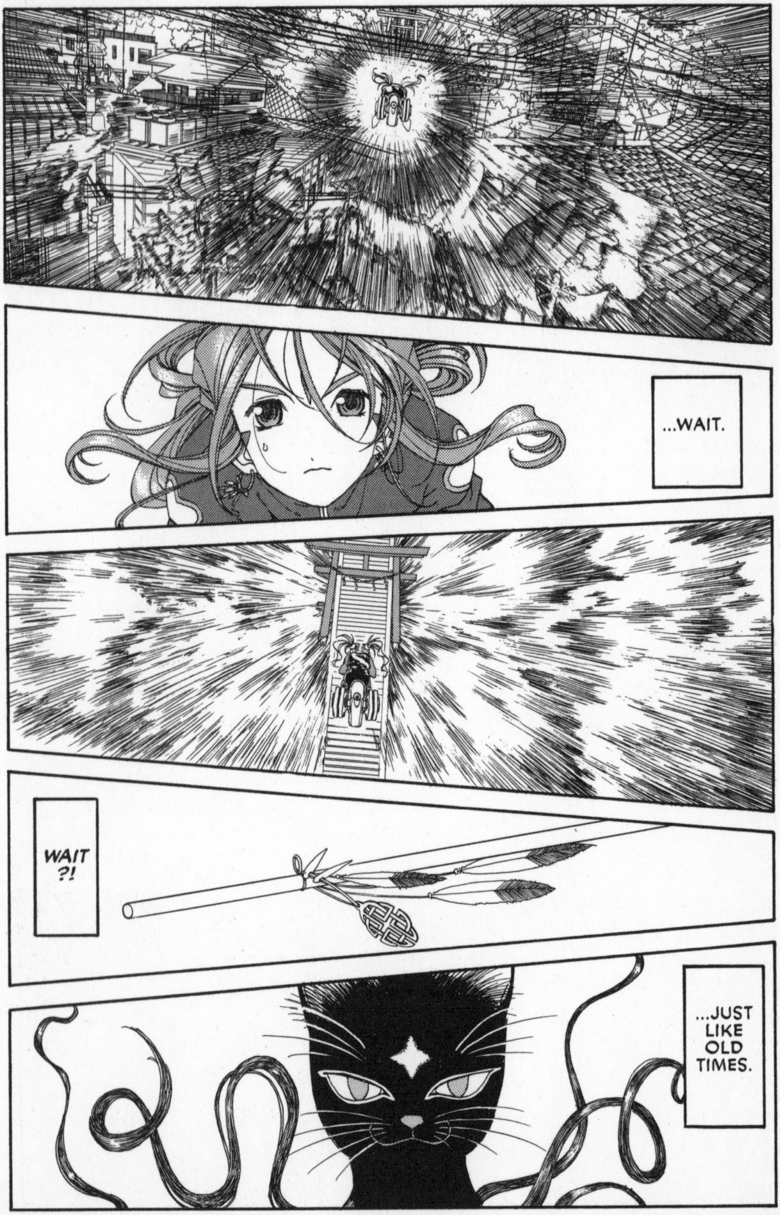
...WAIT.
WAIT ?!
...JUST LIKE OLD TIMES.

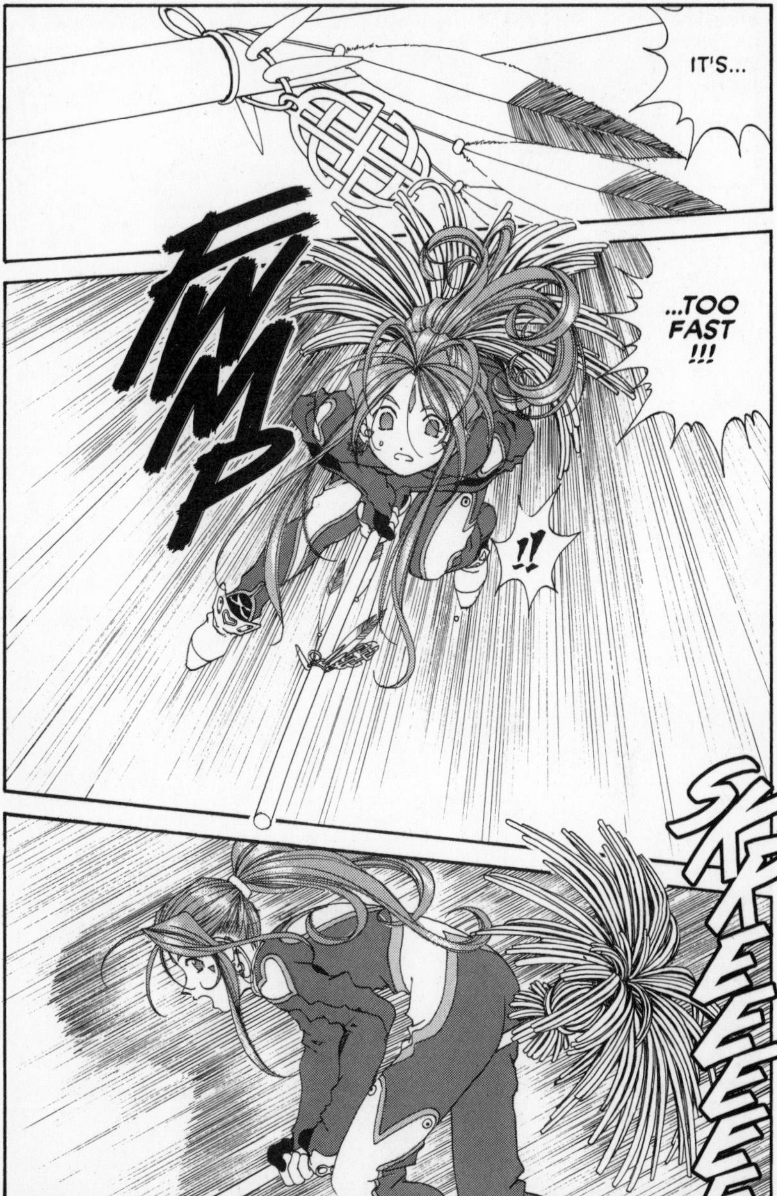
IT'S...
...TOO FAST !!!
FMP
!!
SKREEEEEE

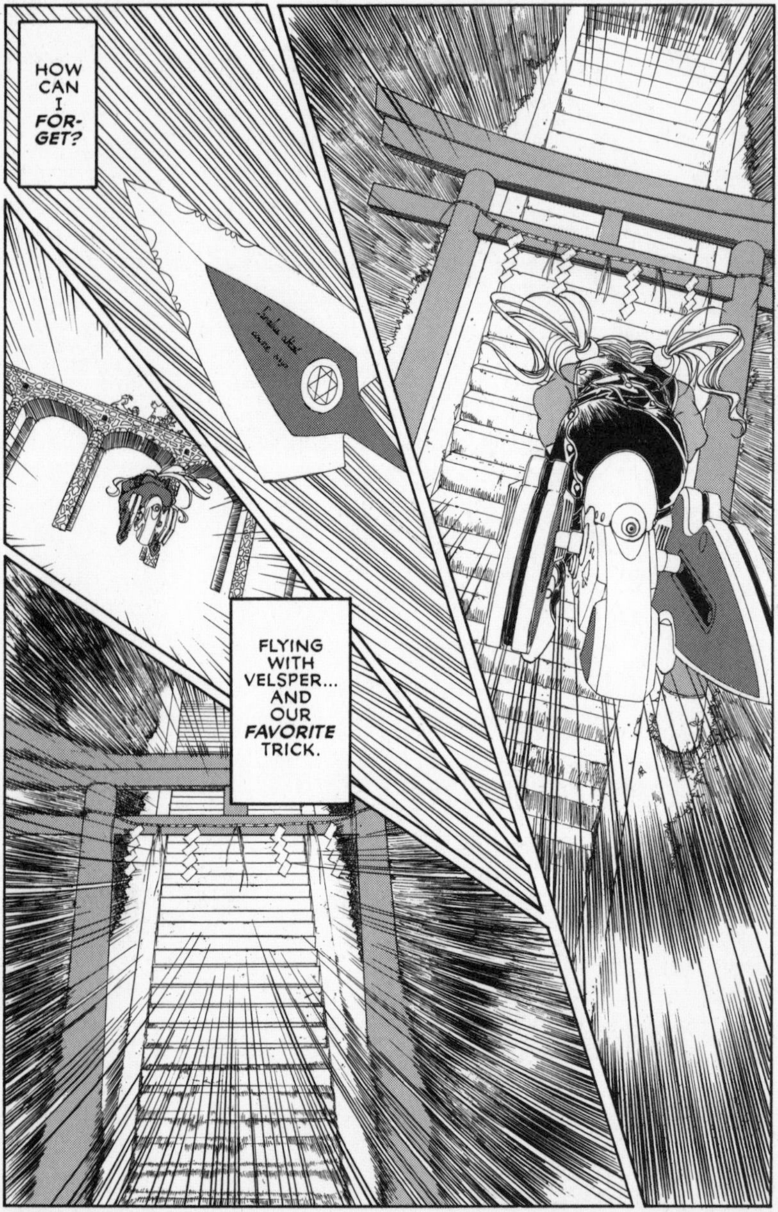
HOW CAN I FORGET?
FLYING WITH VELSPER... AND OUR FAVORITE TRICK.

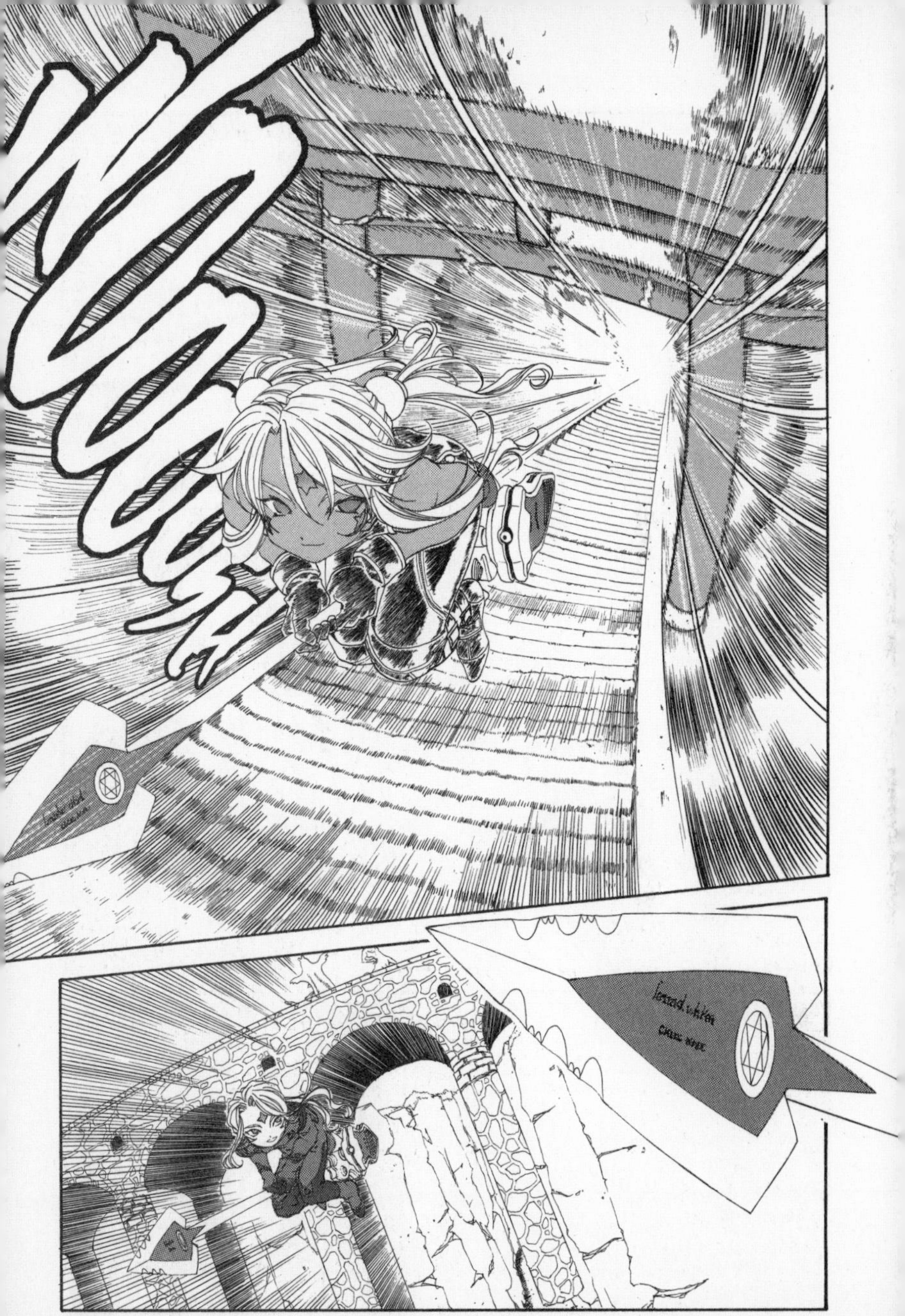
ZOOOOSH

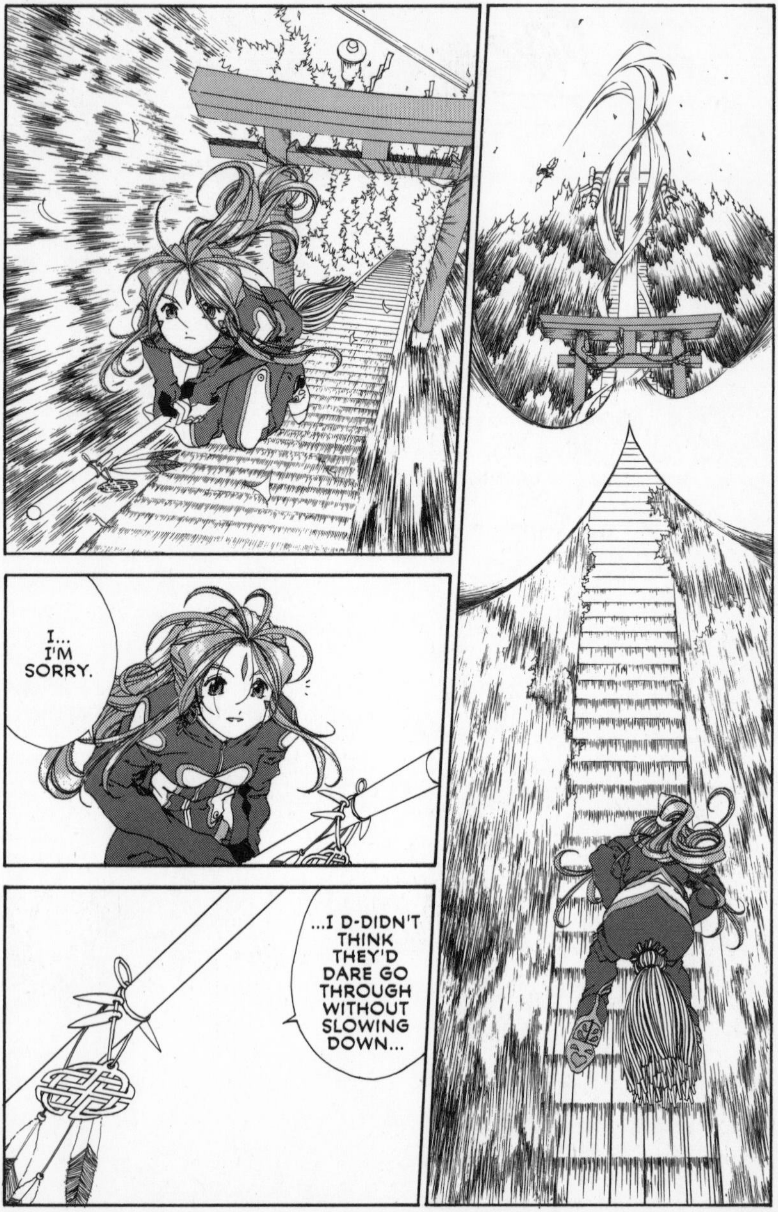
I... I'M SORRY.
...I D-DIDN'T THINK THEY'D DARE GO THROUGH WITHOUT SLOWING DOWN...

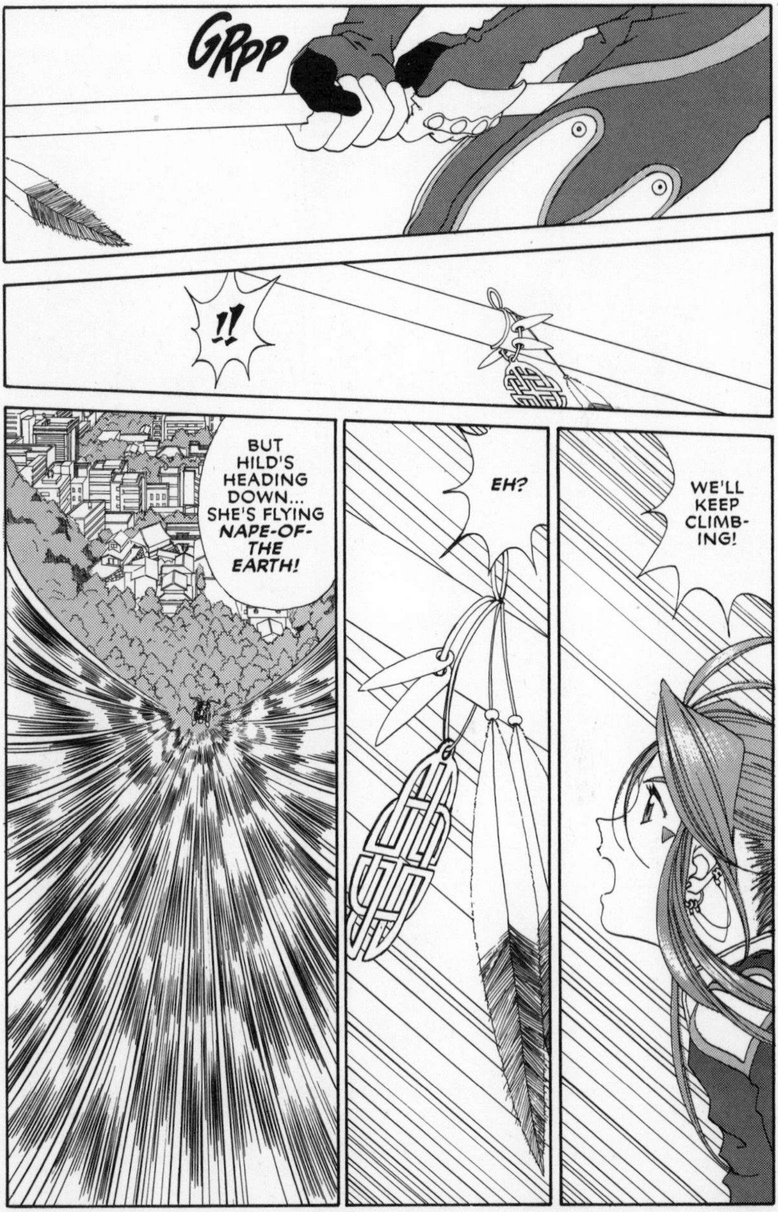
GRPP
!!
WE'LL KEEP CLIMBING!
EH?
BUT HILD'S HEADING DOWN... SHE'S FLYING NAPE-OF-THE EARTH!

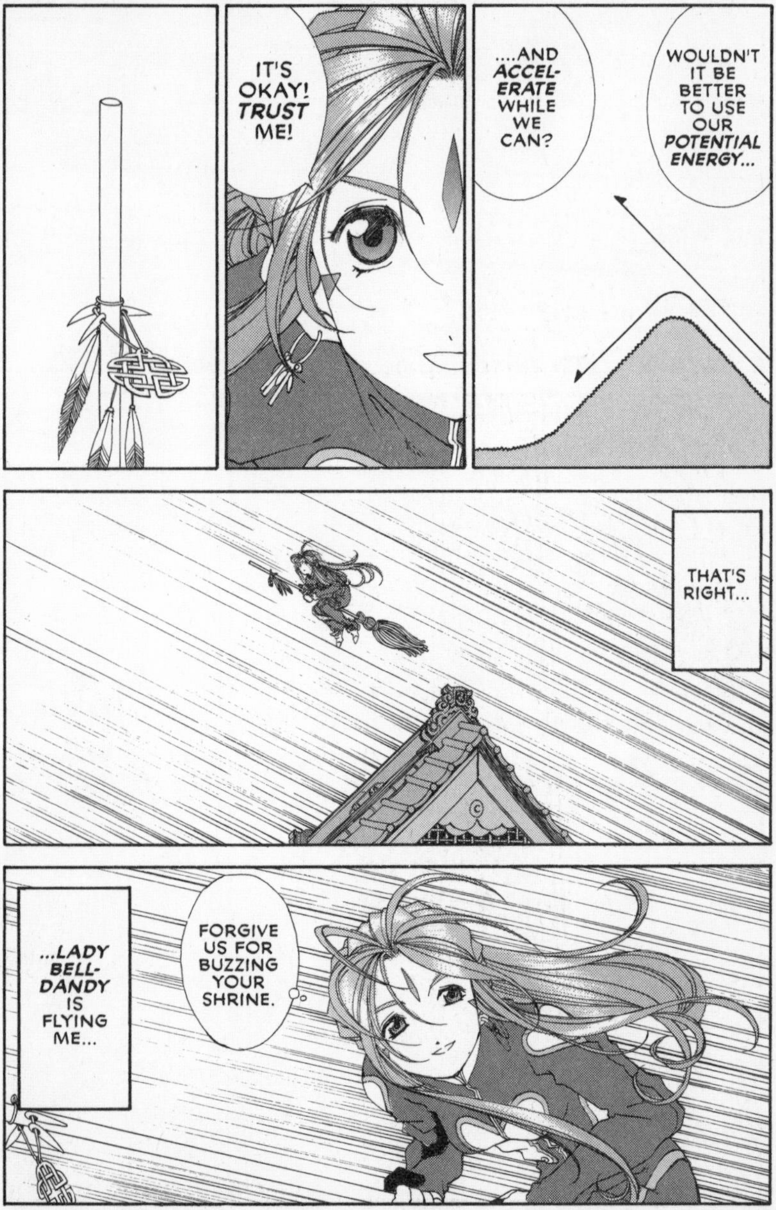
WOULDN'T IT BE BETTER TO USE OUR POTENTIAL ENERGY...
....AND ACCEL-ERATE WHILE WE CAN?
IT'S OKAY! TRUST ME!
THAT'S RIGHT...
FORGIVE US FOR BUZZING YOUR SHRINE.
...LADY BELL-DANDY IS FLYING ME...

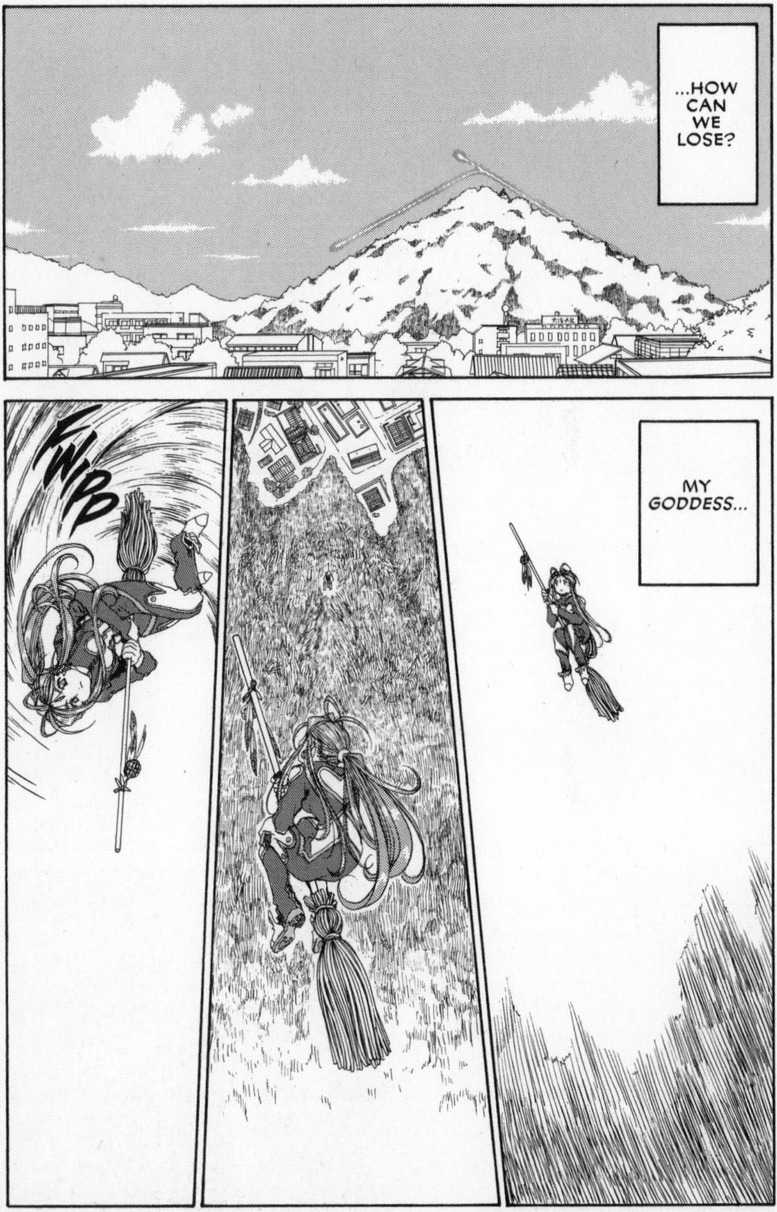
...HOW CAN WE LOSE?
MY GODDESS...
KWIPP

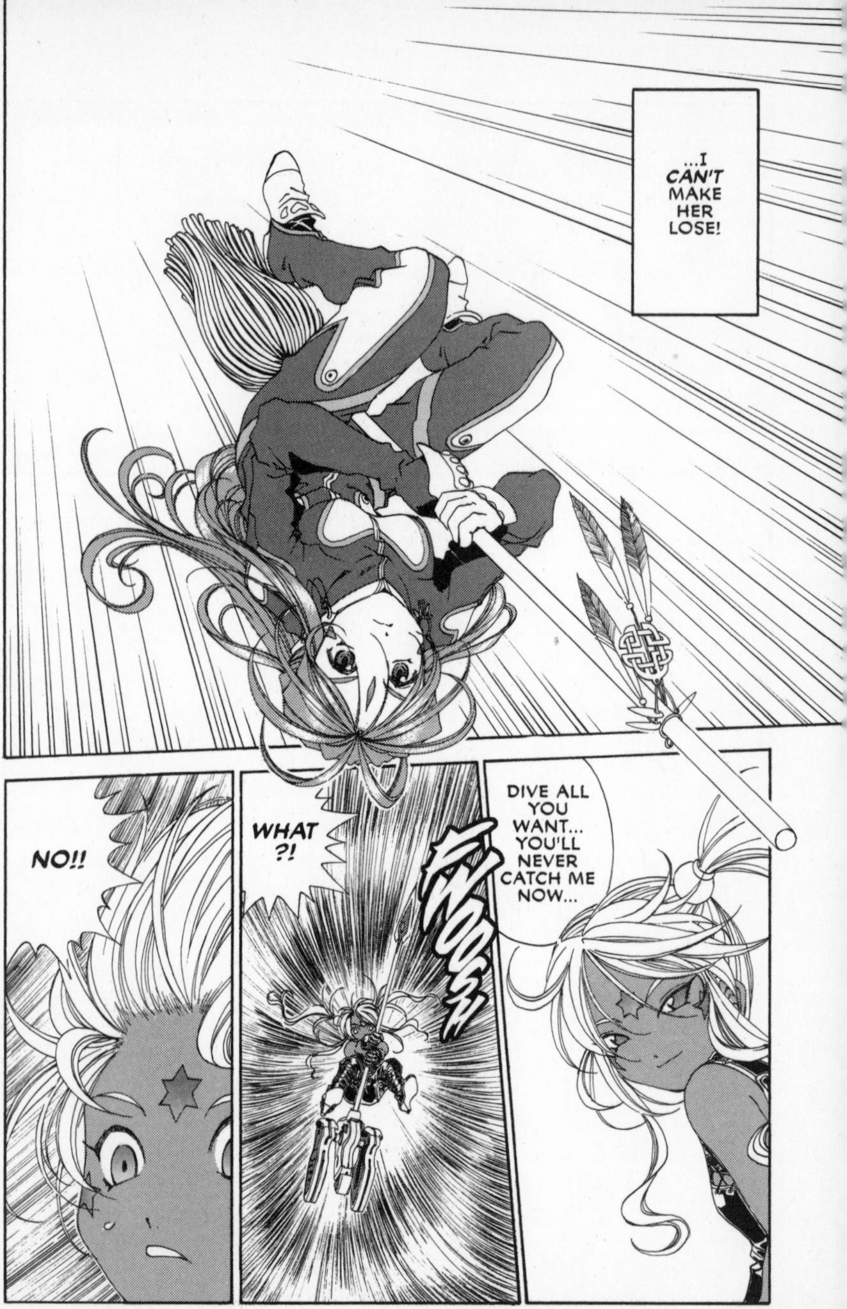
...I CAN'T MAKE HER LOSE!
DIVE ALL YOU WANT... YOU'LL NEVER CATCH ME NOW...
WHAT ?!
NO!!

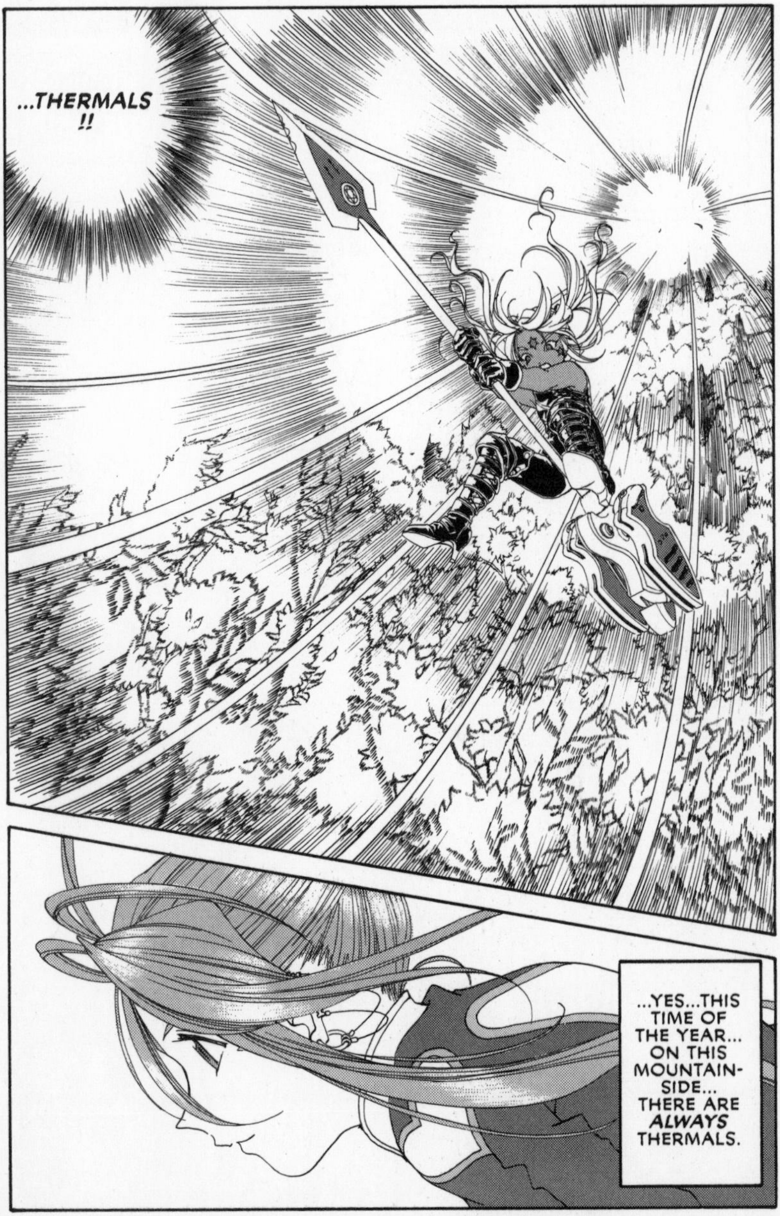
...THERMALS !!
...YES...THIS TIME OF THE YEAR... ON THIS MOUNTAIN-SIDE... THERE ARE *ALWAYS* THERMALS.

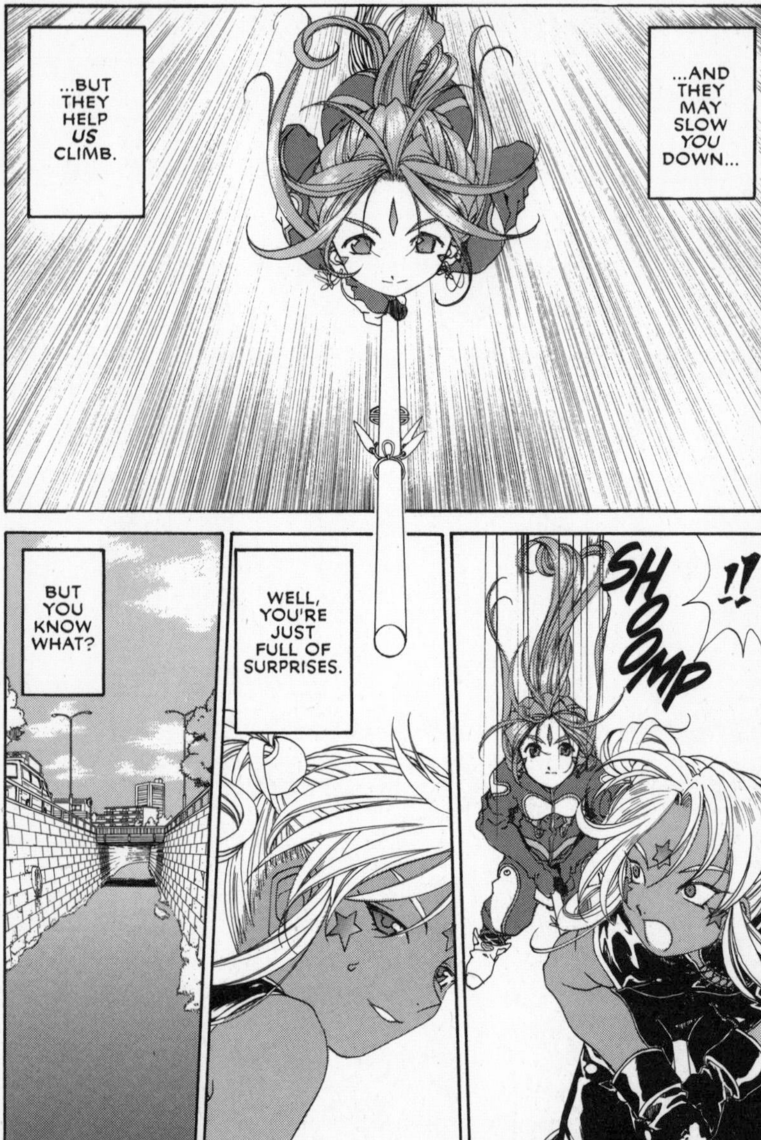
...AND THEY MAY SLOW *YOU* DOWN...
...BUT THEY HELP *US* CLIMB.
!!
SHOOMP
WELL, YOU'RE JUST FULL OF SURPRISES.
BUT YOU KNOW WHAT?

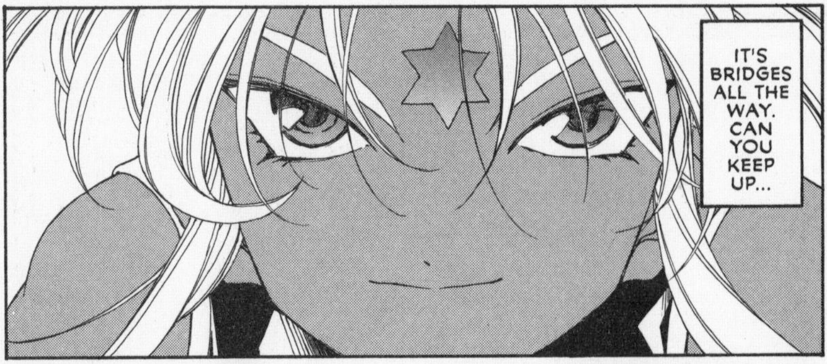
IT'S BRIDGES ALL THE WAY. CAN YOU KEEP UP...

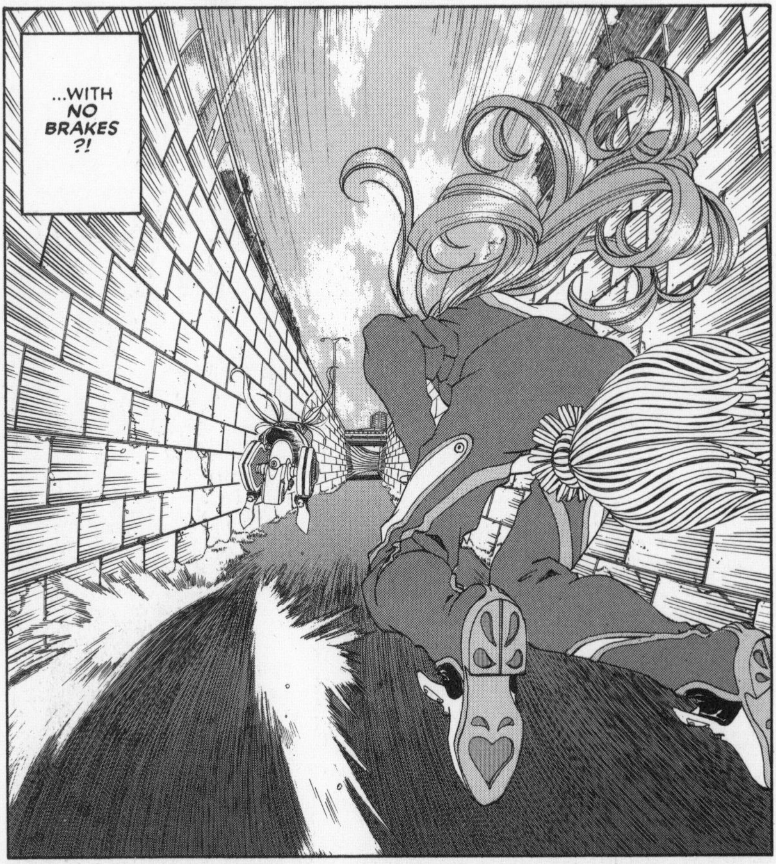
...WITH NO BRAKES ?!

EDITOR
Carl Gustav Horn

DESIGNER
Scott Cook

ART DIRECTOR
Lia Ribacchi

PUBLISHER
Mike Richardson

English-language version
produced by Dark Horse Comics

Published by Dark Horse Manga
a division of Dark Horse Comics, Inc.
10956 SE Main Street
Milwaukie, OR 97222
www.darkhorse.com

To find a comics shop in your area,
call the Comic Shop Locator Service
toll-free at 1-888-266-4226

First edition: December 2007
ISBN: 978-1-59307-857-7

1 3 5 7 9 10 8 6 4 2

Printed in Canada

letters to the
ENCHANTRESS

10956 SE Main Street, Milwaukie, Oregon 97222
omg@darkhorse.com • www.darkhorse.com

NOTE: Full addresses and e-mail addresses will not be printed, unless you ask! All fan artwork, letters, and e-mails submitted become the property of Dark Horse Comics.

We'll start this installment of *Letters to the Enchantress* with something I'm well experienced with—saying sorry. Of course, we didn't run letters and fan art last time because of the sneak preview for Yumi Tohma's *Oh My Goddess!—First End* novel. But recently we found some correspondence from Chris Smigliano and Doris Kwan that was actually sent to us by e-mail way back in *February!* Somehow it got misrouted, and please accept my apologies: we only have room for Chris's letter this time, but Doris's work will be coming up in Vol. 8! As you know, we switch off between old and new volumes . . .

Dear *OMG!* Staff:

Just a quick note to tell you how much I'm enjoying this series. I must admit, however, I'm a recent convert to the church of Belldandy. My local library started to carry manga and graphic novels a couple years ago and I was finally intrigued enough to take a look. I was aware of *OMG!*'s exsistence before, but figured the series might not be to my taste.

Boy, was I wrong!

This series is great loopy fun, all at once funny and dark and heartwarming. And of course I had to glom onto the OVA and TV series (ADV Films—not Media Blasters—will be releasing the second TV season on DVD, BTW). But I'm really hoping sales continue to be good enough that DH releases the whole manga series. It's kind of interesting comparing the translations between the "Flopped" and "Unflopped" Versions.

And of course, Mr. Kosuke's artwork . . . what can you say about anyone that can draw both intricate machinery AND lovely ladies? Of, course, we all have our favorites amongst the *OMG!* cuties . . . I've enclosed a sketch of mine below.

Keep up the good work!

Chris Smigliano
(For Art's Sake: *COMICS BUYERS GUIDE*)

Well, we've been putting out the English version of *Oh My Goddess!* since 1994 (before some of our readers were born!) and we're now up to Vol. 28, so we have no intention of stopping anytime soon—thanks to everyone's longtime support!

I've been a fan of Megumi Morisato since the moment she first showed up at the end of Vol. 1. Maybe it's because my own sister went to the same college I did (although she's three minutes *older*), and is a mechanically savvy motorcyclist. She has kind of an Indiana Jones perspective on life—that you should know how to do everything, because "what if you had to?" So she learned how to ride a motorcycle, drive a car, fly a plane, ride a horse, etc., just in case she has to make a getaway and one of the above is the only method available.

So naturally I loved the crazed techno-contest between Megumi and Skuld in Vol. 6 of *Oh My Goddess!*, and of course I could relate to Keiichi's conflicted nostalgia at the campus festival in this volume—a side effect of switching off between old and new volumes is being able to look at my own college days both in the present and the past. If you like this aspect of the story, you might want to check out sometime another great 1980s comedy set at an engineering school, *Real Genius*. The dorm scenes were shot at my school, Pomona College—even though the campus itself was much closer to Pomona's pal, Harvey Mudd (I know the film was in fact inspired by Harvey Mudd's arch-rival, Cal Tech, but that's a twenty-minute commute). While there are no goddesses in it, the main female character, Jordan, is _sort of_ like Skuld's mind under Megumi's haircut. Notice the italics and the underlining.

—CGH

:SIGH:
WHY SHOULD THE
GODDESSES
GET ALL THE ATTENTION?

MEGUMI © KOSUKE FUJISHIMA

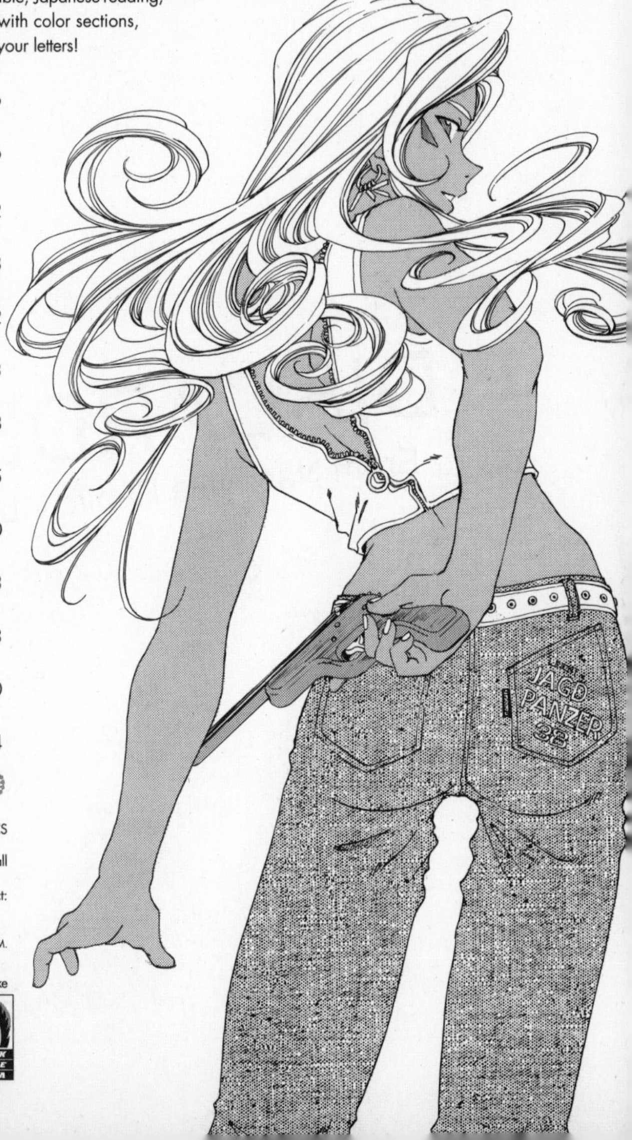
JAGD PANZER 32

STOP! This is the back of the book!

This manga collection is translated into English, but arranged in right-to-left reading format to maintain the artwork's visual orientation as originally drawn and published in Japan. If you've never read comics this way before, take a look at the diagram below to give yourself an idea of how to go about it. Basically, you'll be starting in the upper right-hand corner, and will read each word balloon and panel moving right-to-left. It may take a little getting used to, but you should get the hang of it very quickly. Have fun! If this is the millionth manga you've read this way, never mind. ^_^

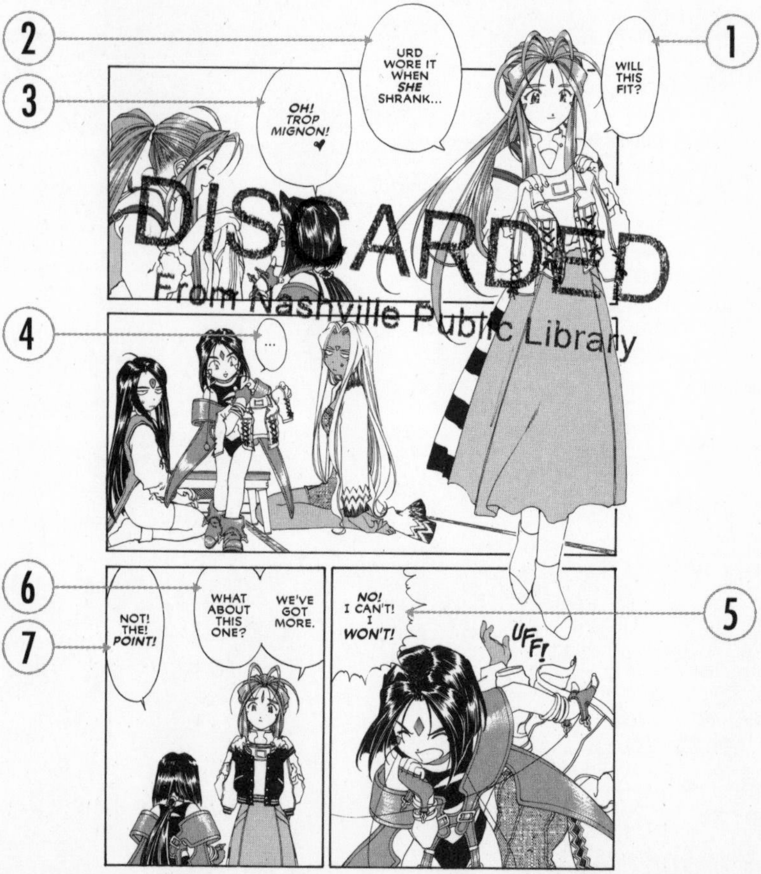
1
WILL THIS FIT?
2
URD WORE IT WHEN *SHE* SHRANK...
3
OH! TROP MIGNON!
4
...
5
NO! I CAN'T! I *WON'T!*
UFF!
6
WE'VE GOT MORE.
WHAT ABOUT THIS ONE?
7
NOT! THE! *POINT!*